HOW TO MAKE IT IN THE

NEW MUSIC
BUSINESS

HOW TO MAKE IT IN THE
NEW MUSIC
BUSINESS

Practical Tips on Building a
Loyal Following and
Making a Living as a Musician

ARI HERSTAND

LIVERIGHT PUBLISHING CORPORATION

A Division of W. W. Norton & Company
Independent Publishers Since 1923
New York • London

For information about permission to reproduce selections from this book, write to Permissions, Liveright Publishing Corporation, a division of W. W. Norton & Company, Inc., 500 Fifth Avenue, New York, NY 10110

For information about special discounts for bulk purchases, please contact W. W. Norton Special Sales at specialsales@wwnorton.com or 800-233-4830

Manufacturing by LSC Communications, North Harrisonburg
Book design by Ellen Cipriano
Production manager: Anna Oler

Library of Congress Cataloging-in-Publication Data

Names: Herstand, Ari, author.
Title: How to make it in the new music business : practical tips on building a loyal following and making a living as a musician / Ari Herstand.
Description: First edition. | New York : Liveright Publishing Corporation, 2016. | Includes bibliographical references and index.
Identifiers: LCCN 2016037591 | ISBN 9781631491504 (hardcover)
Subjects: LCSH: Music—Vocational guidance—United States. | Music trade—Vocational guidance—United States.
Classification: LCC ML3795 .H5 2016 | DDC 780.23—dc23 LC record available at https://lccn.loc.gov/2016037591

Liveright Publishing Corporation
500 Fifth Avenue, New York, N.Y. 10110
www.wwnorton.com

W. W. Norton & Company Ltd.
15 Carlisle Street, London W1D 3BS

1 2 3 4 5 6 7 8 9 0

FOR ROSTER McCABE

CONTENTS

6. PLAYING LIVE   182

FOREWORD

by Derek Sivers

◼

SINCE THE 1980S, I'VE READ EVERY PUBLISHED BOOK ABOUT THE MUSIC business. Every single one. And there have been some good ones. But never before have I seen one book that sums it up so perfectly and helpfully as Ari Herstand's *How to Make It in the New Music Business*. It's so brilliant I feel like doing personal house calls to every musician on earth to make sure they read it.

Now let's clarify a term: The *music* business is different than the *musician* business. The *music* business is covered by *Billboard* magazine, and talks about label executives moving from Warner to EMI, or this year's top-grossing stadium tours by classic rock acts from the 1970s. You don't care about that. The *musician* business is how you make a successful living from your music. That's what you care about.

Even the better music business books are usually written by consultants, executives, lawyers and journalists. Well intentioned, but missing one crucial thing: knowing what it's like to be you—to pour your soul into a song, the terrifying excitement of uploading it for the world to hear, the disgusting discomfort of self-promotion, the devastating disappointment of an indifferent world.

Ah, but Ari gets it. He's you. He's out there promoting his own music right now. He's sharing lessons he learned firsthand. (And lucky for you, he's keeping this book focused on you and your success, not his.)

They say the best teacher is someone who's just learned it themselves, because they still remember what it's like to not know, and how to explain it in a way that gets you from here to there.

I've never met Ari and I've never even heard his music, but I'm a superfan of what he's done on ArisTake.com and now this book. Because I'm a superfan of musicians getting successful, and I think this book is the best in the world right now at helping you do that.

AUTHOR'S NOTE

■

Before you dig in, I need to point out that everything in this book is based on my own experiences or what I've learned from others in the biz. And even though things worked out a certain way for me and others I reference in this book, uh, *results may vary.* Also, I'm a musician, not a lawyer. Please don't use this book as a guide to drafting contracts or navigating legal matters. It's not meant for that. Definitely consult an attorney for all legal issues you may have, and be sure to check out the Some Words of Caution (and Other Stuff You Really Need To Read) on pages 410–13.

Also, without fail, things in the music industry will have changed by the time you're reading this. Companies may get acquired, laws may get passed, revelations may be made.

HOW TO MAKE IT IN THE
NEW MUSIC BUSINESS

■

INTRODUCTION

∎

J ANUARY 15, 2008, WAS THE GREATEST DAY OF MY LIFE. IT WAS THE DAY
  I walked into the Minneapolis City Center Starbucks, shook my
manager's hand, handed him my green apron and made my final triple
tall, nonfat, with whip-caramel macchiato.

It wasn't dramatic. I didn't tell my shift supervisor off or chuck an
iced pomegranate green tea in his face—like I had dreamed of many a
time. There wasn't a big send-off. No parade down 1st Avenue. My manager asked me what I was going to do. I told him that I was a musician
and that I was going to make it.

He thanked me for my work and told me that there would always be
an apron with my name on it if I needed it.

Luckily, I never did. Well, actually, luck had nothing to do with it.

People always ask successful musicians what their lucky break was.
And most don't have an answer. They mention a few instances here and
there that, in retrospect, were turning points or little victories. But very
seldom do you hear, "We were playing the Fine Line and after the show
a bald man in a suit came up to us, handed us a record contract and told
us it was our lucky day."

That is what everyone outside the music industry expects. No one really understands the music business. The songwriting process eludes people. But, even more so, the business confuses the hell out of everyone—musicians included.

I had been fortunate enough to take to the business early on.

I went to the University of Minnesota as a music education and classical trumpet major. Since eighth-grade band class, I thought I wanted to be a high school band director—like Mr. Saltzman (whom I wrote a song about on my first record). But my freshman year of college, that all changed.

I had been in a ska/funk/rock/jam/pop band (we had an identity crisis—more on that later) all four years of high school. I mostly played trumpet and sang backups. All six of us went to different colleges around the country. I was the only one who ended up in Minnesota. The first week of school in my dorm when everyone's door was closed, I planted myself in the floor's lounge with my acoustic guitar and started riffing. Someone walked by, poked her head in and said, "That's cool." Then walked off. (That song turned into one of the first I ever wrote, "Rose Stained Red.")

I wrote a bunch of songs those first few weeks on piano and guitar. I spent more time in the practice space of the music building writing songs than practicing my trumpet.

When a group of friends and I stopped into the European Grind coffee shop on campus where a singer/songwriter happened to be performing, I asked the barista if I could get a gig. He opened up the calendar book and said, "How about October 12? You get all the coffee you can drink."

My roommate (who was also a music major—we lived in the arts dorm), had a superfancy digital camera. He took a photo of me playing guitar, and I printed up a bunch of 8.5 × 11 black-and-white flyers and put them all over the music building and my dorm. My very first concert as a singer/songwriter, at the European Grind was packed (with about 35 people).

My roommate, a cellist, performed the show with me and recorded it on his minidisk recorder. For those of you who have no idea what that is, it was like the Talkboy in *Home Alone 2*, except it ran on a digital minidisk instead of a cassette and was much better quality. These were hot for about twenty-seven months.

Listening back to the show, I realized that I didn't suck too bad. Everyone there seemed to enjoy themselves and the manager of the European Grind asked me back!

A few months later, I found myself in the music section of a Barnes & Noble staring at the bright yellow *All You Need to Know About the Music Business* book by Donald Passman. I bought it and finished it that week.

I had found my calling.

I sat my parents down that spring and told them that I was not going to be a band director and I was not going to finish at the University of Minnesota. I had found a contemporary music industry school in St. Paul and told my parents I was going to transfer there. With credits transferring, I got in and out in three consecutive semesters with an associate degree in music business.

While at the music industry school I worked my a$$ off. I never skipped a class. I was never late (even to the 9 A.M., three-hour music economics class). I went to office hours of all my teachers (they were all musicians or ex-industry heads—not sure if I can call them professors). Contrast that with my music education studies at the University of Minnesota, where I skipped half my classes, rolled into my 8 A.M. (classical) music history lecture well into the Baroque era hung over, and cheated off of my roommate on virtually every test.

When I graduated in August of 2005, I got to work on my first solo album. In December of that year, I released it to 250 people at the Varsity Theater in Minneapolis.

I became a force on the University of Minnesota campus. From sometime around that CD release show to when I left Minneapolis for

L.A. in 2010, I was one of the most popular musicians on campus (and in the Twin Cities). The U had about 40,000 undergraduate students, so it wasn't a bad market to start with. However, the music editor for the *Minnesota Daily* wasn't feeling what I was putting out. He wrote three hate pieces on me in one semester. He despised my presence so much that in the fall of 2008 he listed me in the top three worst bands of Minneapolis (I was #1). Ironically, the top three "best" bands broke up shortly thereafter, and the "worst" three bands all went on to have successful careers. He then wrote a scathing album review of my 2008 release, which garnered some of the most comments of any *Minnesota Daily* article on the website and finally, I made the cover of the December Joke edition next to Lindsay Lohan and the president of the University of Minnesota. My headline? "Surgeons' Attempt to Reattach Local Musician's Balls Fails."

As these articles were pouring out from the desk of a writer who will go unnamed, I was filling the 800-seat Varsity Theater, had just opened for Ben Folds in front of 3,200 people and had begun a massive college tour that paid incredibly well. I had received about thirty other positive reviews that year in papers around the country, but, of course, I can pretty much recite the *Minnesota Daily*'s hate pieces word for word.

Managing my career all on my own from the beginning, booking 100 percent of my noncollege shows and tours (we'll get to college agents in Chapter 9), getting songs placed on multiple TV shows and starting an artist development company where I helped manage another Minneapolis band, I became the go-to person in the Minneapolis music scene for music business advice.

I moved from Minneapolis to L.A. in the summer of 2010. I had done all I could in Minneapolis. The scene was imploding on itself and some of my favorite bands were breaking up. I needed a change. I didn't choose L.A. because of the industry (however, it didn't hurt); I chose it because of the winters.

Many of you are reading this book because you've read some Ari's Take articles. I started Ari's Take for the same reason I wrote this book—to help musicians succeed in the music industry.

Over the course of my career I've had to learn everything the hard way. My education at the music industry school was great. I learned how things used to work in the music business. I got some great history. But I realized very quickly that the old tactics and ways of the biz don't work in today's industry.

We're in a very exciting time in the music industry. It is the best time to be an independent musician. Never before in the history of the modern music industry have independent musicians been able to sustain healthy, long-term careers on their own—without the help of a record label.

Every day, the path to success is being realized on roads not yet paved.

Ingrid Michaelson cracked the *Billboard* Hot 100, has been certified Platinum and consistently performs for thousands a night around the world. She has self-released every digital song/album since day one. Ron Pope also self-releases his music and has hundreds of millions of streams, has sold over 1.5 million downloads and plays sold-out venues around the world. Amanda Palmer broke a Kickstarter record when she made $1.2 million on her campaign and now receives $50K+ a month directly from her fans via Patreon. Chance The Rapper's music has been downloaded over 1 million times. He was #7 on the "Forbes 30 Under 30" 2015 music list. And he made history as the first unsigned artist to play *Saturday Night Live*. Zoë Keating records (and self-releases) her music from her home. Her music has been featured in countless commercials, TV shows, video games and films. She reached #1 on the *Billboard* Classical charts and continues to make a solid living. Peter Hollens built a YouTube empire on his own, amassing over a million subscribers and 150 million-plus views without ever leaving home. For every video he releases, he makes over $8,000 directly from his fans (via Patreon). Clare Means live-streams her street performances and makes thousands a month just from her Periscope followers. Brent Morgan earns over $10,000 a month live-streaming acoustic performances from home on YouNow. Vulfpeck has millions of Spotify plays, performed on *The Late Show with Stephen Colbert*, sells out venues around the country, has hundreds of paying Bandcamp subscribers and in 2016 played main-stage sets at Bonnaroo, Lockn' and Outside Lands music festivals. Gabriel Mann makes six figures a year scoring TV shows, films and commercials, writing theme songs, freelancing as a vocalist, releasing music under his name as well as a few side projects and getting the songs licensed to film, TV and commercials. The Distant Cousins also make six figures annually solely licensing their original music to TV shows, commercials and films. Dane Schmidt, who goes by Jamestown Story, makes around $75K a year from digital royalties and licensing. He has sold over 250,000 songs and 25,000 albums and has had songs placed in over 75 TV shows.

The thing that all of these artists have in common is that they created their own musical career path and refused to follow the traditional method of signing to a major label—surrendering their fate to the powers that be. These artists aren't household names, but they are making it work. And making it work well.

Your uncle Joe will continue to ask you when are you going to try out for the latest singing-contest TV show. Your seatmate on the plane will ask you when they're going to hear you on the radio. Your parents will ask when are you going to grow up and get a "real job." Because they don't understand this new world.

Making it in the music business is not about lucky breaks. It's about hard work. If you want to succeed in music, you have to work harder than everyone else. You have to want it more than everyone else.

If you want to make a living in music, you're going to need to be comfortable doing multiple kinds of jobs that may not fall rigidly in line with your vision (as it is now). When musicians tell me "But I just want to write songs and play music, I don't want to do any of this business stuff," I want to scream *"Yeah, me too!"*

I didn't get good at the business because I love it. I got good at the business side of my music career because I believe in my art so much that I knew if I didn't I wouldn't succeed.

No one is going to handle your business for you. At least not yet. And even when managers, labels, attorneys, agents and sponsors do start knocking, you should know what to expect of them. You should know where they all fit into your business. Never hand off part of your business to someone just because they ask. Hand off part of your career when you have to. When it's more than you can handle. When you know exactly what needs to get done, how it needs to get done, but you just don't have the time (or resources) to do it yourself.

Eventually, you will be at a point where people are pounding down your door begging to work with you. By that point, you will know where you could use some help and what to pass off. But you'll also have a strong handle on how to run your business on your own. You will always be the one in control. You make all the decisions. Never forget that your team works for you. Without you, they have nothing.

But you're a long way from a team.

You have to build up the demand first. The days of the "big break" are pretty much over. A music career is now a slow, progressive upward slope. If you persevere, you will eventually be able to sustain a comfortable life-style, earning your income from doing something you love. If you're looking for quick fame and instant success, you're in the wrong field. There are a lot easier ways to get famous. Go make a sex tape or something.

This book is intended to give you the concrete steps you should take to rise to a level of success where you are making a good living doing what you love. You can get there. It won't be easy, but if you love it enough, and work hard enough, it will happen. I will show you how.

1.

WHY MUSIC?

For Love or Money (or Sex)

It was never about fame back then.
We just thought about what gave us goosebumps.
—QUINCY JONES

You don't do music, unless you have to do music.
—WAYNE SERMON, GUITARIST,
IMAGINE DRAGONS

BEFORE YOU INVEST EVERY LAST PENNY OF YOUR SAVINGS, DESTROY your relationships and hop in a van with four other smelly dudes or dudettes for two months, step back and ask yourself why you want to be a musician. This may seem like a dumb question at first glance. But it's *the* most important one you will ever ask yourself. And it will define the course of your life.

"Because I love music" is not the answer you're looking for. I love Thai food. But I don't want to eat it every day for the rest of my life. A music career, unlike most other careers in the world, requires more than just a passing enjoyment. A music career requires a passion like no other. A drive that will sustain you through the months of eating PB&J and begging your landlord for a break on this month's rent.

After seeing the 2001 Cameron Crowe film *Almost Famous*, I thought a music career was all parties, tour buses, "band-aids" who looked like Kate

Hudson, and sold-out arena shows. Who *wouldn't* want to be a musician if that was the life? The reality is, a music career *can* have these perks, but most of the time it entails working sixteen-hour days, skipping the parties to book a tour or practice your instrument, trekking through blizzards to put up posters for your shows, convincing your friends to pay $10 for an 11:30 P.M., 25-minute set at a dingy bar on a Tuesday, soliciting journalists and bloggers on Twitter, and spending hours following (on the latest social media platform), to get the follow-back. But it will all be worth it when you step out on stage to a packed house for 25 minutes of bliss.

Those who enter music to become famous fail. Not to say that those who have the vision of world domination fail. You need lofty goals and unwavering confidence to succeed in such a difficult field. But fame, in and of itself, will not sustain your drive. Fame should be looked at as an occupational hazard to a music career.

Many guitarists picked up the guitar to impress a guy or girl. I know I did. It worked. I got the girl. But she didn't last. The guitar stuck, though. And I quickly realized that my love of the guitar (and music in general) kept me going long after the thrill of impressing a girl faded.

Hobbyists play the guitar to impress people. Musicians master their instruments to feed their soul.

You must decide early on what kind of artist you want to be. You should please yourself first and always. Don't write music you think people want to hear. Don't play songs you think people want to hear. Yes, it's important to create entertaining shows, but if you bend every which way to attempt to please every single person, you'll forget which way is up and tumble over. Do you want to be in a cover band and play to hordes of drunk people singing along? Then, yes, you do need to play the songs people want to hear. And you could make a decent living doing this. But this book isn't about how to succeed as a cover band. And I presume you have loftier goals than the local cover circuit. To succeed as an original artist you have to pave your own path.

Following musical trends to adjust your production is not the same as writing songs you think people want to hear. If you're true to your art, the fans will come.

The most important thing you should remember is to be authentic. If you're a goofball, be a goofball. If you're an angry introvert, be an angry introvert. The reason fans connect to artists on a deep, spiritual level is because artists bring truth. Artists have a unique way of telling a story that's both relatable and personal. From the beginning of time, artists have looked at the world differently and revealed their compelling visions through their creations. And from the beginning of time, audiences have enjoyed experiencing these special creations.

Before you embark on this crazy journey that is a music career, you must understand that you may not receive much support from your family. Maybe you know that and it's *why* you've chosen this field. Maybe music is your family. Maybe music is the only love in your life. Great. But if you seek your family's approval, you won't get it with music, most likely. Your family will not understand your career. Most of the world doesn't understand the music industry. Everyone you meet will ask you "So are you trying to be a musician?" without actually understanding how truly insulting (albeit innocently naïve) a question that is. There's a great scene in the 2014 film *Whiplash* If you haven't seen it yet, go watch it immediately. It's one of my new favorites. The protagonist, Andrew Neiman, is a nineteen-year-old jazz drummer in the top music school in the country. At the dinner table with his father, aunt, uncle and cousins, his aunt and uncle brag about their sons' success. One is the star football quarterback for his (Division III) university and the other is in the model UN. They ask Andrew, "How's the drumming going," and he tries to explain that he is doing really well, but no one at the table understands what that means. "Will the studio find you a job," his uncle barks. Eventually, Andrew gets fed up defending his career choice and takes jabs at his cousins' seemingly trivial little victories of touchdowns and school records and chides that the

NFL is never going to call his quarterback cousin. His uncle asks, "Got any friends, Andy?" Andrew replies, "No . . . I never really saw the use."

The uncle continues, "Lennon and McCartney, they were school buddies." Andy bites back: "Charlie Parker didn't know anybody until Joe Jones threw a cymbal at his head."

"So that's your idea of success?"

"I think being the greatest musician of the 20th century is anyone's idea of success."

Andrew's father chimes in: "Dying broke, drunk and full of heroin at 34 is not exactly my idea of success."

Andrew protests, "I'd rather die drunk, broke at 34 and have people at a dinner table talk about me than live to be rich and sober at 90 and nobody remember who I was."

Even though Andrew is a jazz drummer, this brilliantly sums up every conversation every musician has with their family at some point in their lives. Even Andrew's father tries to be supportive, but he just can't understand why Andrew wants to pursue a career that's so emotionally taxing, with no clear path to sustained success.

It's one of the first big hurdles we all need to get over. Even though I've been a professional musician for twelve years, my parents still hope (secretly) that I'll become a lawyer or a doctor.

WHAT DOES MAKING IT MEAN?

Making it is survival. If you can survive, you are succeeding.
—BRUCE FLOHR, ARTIST MANAGER/A&R, SWITCHFOOT,
ALLEN STONE, THE BAND PERRY, DAVE MATTHEWS BAND

A lot of people to whom I mentioned the title of this book asked me how I could write a book called *How to Make It in the New Music Business* when I haven't made it. The gall! But, I see their point. I've never reached the level of Super Bowl halftime performance fame that penetrates the world they live in. Maybe I will, maybe I won't. But that doesn't matter. "Making it" is defined differently by everyone. To those outside the industry, "making it" means superstardom. If you want to be a superstar, you need a boatload of money, provided by either a label or an investor. And even then, it's no guarantee. But to make it as a full-time musician just takes lots of hard work. By the time you're finished with this book, you will have a clear idea of how you can make it as a full-time musician. Some of you will go on to be world-conquering superstars, and some of you will make solid livings as regional musicians. Neither is "better."

I love coffee. There's this great boutique coffee and doughnut shop in New Orleans where I have been spending most of my time writing this book. It's not a chain. But the owners are super cool, the employees all seem to enjoy themselves and they seem to be doing solid business. They have been in this same spot for the past three years. But because they're not Dunkin' Donuts, have they not made it? I would say they have.

What about the local bookstore with eight employees that's been around since the seventies and is well respected in the community? Since they're not Amazon, have they not made it?

Or what about the online boutique clothing line that nets $1 million a year? Because they're not in Nordstrom's or Macy's, have they not made it?

For some reason, music seems to be one of the only professions where the sole definition of "making it" is superstardom. If your uncle Joe's coworker hasn't heard of you, then you haven't made it in his eyes. Well, your uncle Joe's coworker hasn't actually heard of hundreds of bands you would probably deem to have made it. It's all relative.

Your goal should be to sustain as a full-time musician. The "big break" you're waiting for will never come—if you just wait for it. If you want to succeed you must put in the work. I know you're saying to yourself right now, "But, Ari, I'm different! I'm better than everyone else. I *am* a superstar and 'they' will find me!"

First, though, you need to define who "they" are? Do you even know? A label? Which label? Specifically. And why that label? Or is it a manager you're waiting for? Will any do?

The thing is, too many musicians are waiting for those with the answers to come a-knockin', without actually knowing why. If the reason you're waiting is because you don't want to put in any work for yourself, then you should just throw in the towel right now. Because even if Capitol Records somehow stumbled on you singing in a bar and said to themselves "This is the next big thing," you would *still* need to put in a hell of a lot of work. But the thing is, Capitol Records doesn't seek out talent in bars anymore. And even if they did, you'd have to virtually sign away your entire life to work with them because you have absolutely no clout. And no negotiating power.

I won't deny that a label, at the right time, can help. But not any label. And not too soon.

I'm going to reveal a startling statistic. Over 98 percent of all acts who sign to a major label will fail. Meaning, 98 out of 100 acts major labels sign this year will not recoup their advance and will be dropped. So even if you somehow get a major record deal, the odds are against you that you will be in the 2 percent. Major labels promise the world to *every* act they sign. And, for the most part, they have good intentions when they sign each act. However, people move in and out of labels all the time. So even if the head of A&R at Columbia Records signs you tomorrow and promises you the full weight of the label, he might be replaced next week, and the new CEO may not give two sh*ts about you and drop you—not without refusing to release your masters (or rights) back to you unless you pay them every penny they had invested in you at the start, of course.

But, "getting discovered" is a fantasy of our parents' generation. It doesn't happen like that anymore. Well, sure, Rihanna was "discovered."

But that's the one in a million. You're better off buying a lottery ticket and funding your career that way. If you actually want a career in music and don't just want to be famous, you have to work for it. Labels typically don't want to sign unknown artists. They're too much work (and money) to develop. Labels mostly want acts that are proven, have a fan base and are making things happen on their own. Of course we can point to the exceptions, but again, they are the exception. Not the rule.

You don't want a record deal. At least not yet. You want to build your career to the point where every label is pounding down your door begging to work with you. And then, at that point, you can decide if you're better off continuing to go at it on your own, or signing.

You have officially "made it" when you're using your creative talents to pay all of your bills. Not when you perform the Super Bowl halftime show.

THE PURPOSE OF THE DAY JOB

If you're a songwriter, you want a job that takes your body
but not your mind, because you want your mind for writing
songs. And if you work in an office, it takes your mind.

—DR. DON CUSIC, PROFESSOR OF MUSIC BUSINESS,
BELMONT UNIVERSITY

I'm going to be asking you "why" a lot in this book because so many people just get caught up in a routine of "how it is" or "how it's supposed to be" that they rarely question why they're actually doing something. And if it's truly the best course of action.

There's not a single musician on the planet that I know of who has never had a "day job." I've had quite a few. Every single musician currently working a day job dreams of the day she can quit. Every time I got a drink sent back for it not being hot enough or too sweet or not sweet enough was another inch closer out the door.

Why do you have the day job you have? The answer should be to make enough money to live on while you're building your music career. It should not be to grow in the company. Or to be able to have money to go clubbing on the weekends. Or to take vacations. Those are the normal person's reasons. We're not normal people!

Every penny you make at your day job (above the cost of living), should be invested in your music career. Do not raise your standard of living because your current day job allows for it—no matter how tempting it is. Continue to drive the beat-up old Jetta. Do not go out to happy hours with your coworkers. Do not go clubbing. As Zig Ziglar said, "The chief cause of failure and unhappiness is trading what you want most for what you want right now." Print out this quote and tape it up in your bedroom.

Treat yourself to these luxuries when you've quit your day job and are bringing in enough money with your music to afford this.

If you raise your standard of living to match the fat paycheck that you're getting from your day job, it will be that much more difficult to strip it back down when you actually quit your day job and have to live extremely conservatively to live on your music income.

You're not going to jump from a day job into a million-dollar record label advance. Get rid of that fantasy.

You're going to quit your day job when you are making enough money with your music to pay your bills and eat.

Do Not Accept the Promotion

I see so many of my musician friends justify a big promotion at work with how much more money they're making that they can now invest in their music. Bull. It never works out that way. They celebrate the promotion by blowing $300 on drinks and a fancy dinner. Which then turns into $300 drinking Fridays and fancy dinner Wednesdays, Thursdays and Saturdays.

If you accept a promotion at work, it means that you are excited to move up in the company. Which you're not. Or, at least, shouldn't be if making it as a musician is your ultimate goal.

Find a job with the flexibility to be able to take off a week to go on a quick regional tour. Find a job that allows you to find someone to cover your shift when you get a last-minute opportunity. Find a job that doesn't make you work five (or six, or seven!) days a week. Find a job that doesn't emotionally, mentally or spiritually drain you, so when you return home from work you don't just want to zombie out in front of the TV.

Yes, try to have a good time at work. It will make you a happier person. But don't get too comfortable there. Because then you'll never quit.

To build a successful music career (like any small business or startup) requires a sh*t ton of time, effort, money and work. Building a music career requires working at it for twelve hours a day. Every single day. Of course, not many humans can actually do that. But that's what it takes. Are you willing to put in the time?

That's why you have to quit your day job as soon as possible. So you can put in the necessary time.

Giving music lessons is a fantastic "day job" because you can ease out of it when your music income starts to bring in more of the total pot of money you need to live. (Or pick up more students when a few months are a bit light.) Driving for Lyft or Uber is also great because you can pick your hours and work more when you need and less when you don't. Playing cover, wedding and corporate gigs is a fantastic way to earn enough to get by. But again, like any day job, don't get too comfortable with this, and make sure it leaves you enough time for performing original shows, writing songs and working on your (original) music business. Cover gigs are a day job. And you should try to get out of them as soon as possible. And like any day job, they can be a trap if you're not careful.

Do not use your degree to get a full-time, corporate job. As happy as it makes your parents, you will be miserable, or worse, content!

One exception to this rule. And I've only seen it done by *the* most disciplined. Set up a one-year plan. Get the highest-paying job you can find. Even if it means working 60 hours a week. Live extremely conservatively. Come home and practice your a$$ off at your instrument. Write as much as you can. Go out and see as much live music as you can (but never buy more than one drink at the venue). And save every cent you get from your cushy paycheck above the cost of living and seeing live music. This is your research year.

Most musicians don't have this amount of discipline because they want everything *now*. But, if you're reading this book, there's a good chance you may be one of the select few who are disciplined enough to succeed with this plan. Because if you do, one year later, you can quit your day job (with enough saved to sustain you for at least 6 months) and you'll be able to rededicate all that time solely to your music career. If you were working 8 hours a day at your day job and 4 hours when you got home practicing, now you can devote 6 hours a day working at your art and 6 hours a day working at the business.

THE BACKUP PLAN

I never had one. If you have a backup plan, you will fall back on it. A music career is just too hard. Do not have a backup plan. If you're currently enrolled in a university getting a degree to make your parents happy for an education that they are paying for, fine. But you make damn sure that this degree is not for you to find a career-job. A one-year, high-paying job as described above? Sure. But if you ever say to yourself "I can always find a job as an architect if this music thing doesn't work out," you will, without fail, in five years find yourself staring at a blueprint.

THE 26-YEAR MARATHON (THE GOALS)

> If you're achieving what you wanted to achieve with
> your musical dreams then you've made it.
>
> — LYNN GROSSMAN, SECRET ROAD,
> INGRID MICHAELSON'S MANAGER

A music career is not a sprint. It's a marathon. So many young musicians think that they will "make it" within the first few years of dropping their first single. I know I did. You need to be realistic about your goals and pursuits. Sure, there is a bit of luck that determines the speed of your success, but there's no luck in determining whether you will succeed. The harder you work, the quicker you will reach your goals.

But what are your goals? Do you even know? "Becoming a rock star" is too ambiguous. What does that mean? Selling out arenas? Hits on the radio? Making a million dollars? These can be some of the metrics you use to define milestones in your career, but you need obtainable, concrete goals that you spend every day working toward. Goals can shift. Mine sure have. But goals help keep you focused at every stage of your career.

Create a word document and title it "My Music Marathon." Then make four sections:

1 Year
5 Years
10 Years
26 Years

Under each section, write down where you see yourself in 1 year, 5 years, 10 years and 26 years. You can have lofty goals, but be realistic. There are many different paths to sustained success, so I can't define your goals for you. If the live show is your bag and you want to build your live game, then your 1-year plan could be to sell out a well-respected club in town and expand into five new cities. Your 5-year plan could be to sell out regional venues and tour nationally twice a year. And the 10-year plan could be to sell out 500-cap venues nationally. And your 26-year plan could include international tours twice a year, being a well respected act in your genre, a collection of records you are extremely proud of, playing with a handful of your idols, and supporting a family on both active (touring) and passive (royalties) income. Very possible.

If you're a studio rat and want to just work the licensing and recording angle, then your 1-year goal could be to secure five clients and one paid placement. Your 5-year goal could be to have monthly placements in film, TV, trailers and commercials while enjoying enough regular studio sessions with clients to pay all of your monthly expenses. Also, quite feasible. Your 10-year plan could be to own a studio. And your 26-year plan could be to own a world-renowned studio that has a waiting list of bands from around the world with multiple producers, engineers and labels booking out regularly.

If humans scare you and you want to create music from your basement, your best bet is to work the Internet. The 1-year goal could be to release monthly songs, garner 100,000 combined plays, 5 collaborations with other artists and 5,000 new followers. Your 5-year goal could be to have over 5 million combined plays, 50,000 total followers and a monthly income of $4,000. Your 10-year goal could easily reach $10,000 monthly, 10 million combined plays and a million followers. And for the 26-year plan, you could run your own production studio developing talent from the ground up.

Or if you're a player, your 1-year plan could be to get fifteen paid freelance gigs. In 5 years you're the go-to musician on your instrument in your local scene, making enough money from just your freelance gigs to live a comfortable life. In 10 years you're the go-to hired gun for touring outfits, and for your 26-year plan you are backing up the stars and one of the most respected players on your instrument.

Once you have your goals laid out, go a step deeper. Get more specific. Is there a venue in town you want to headline? Put it in there. Is there an artist you want to record with? A producer you'd like to work with? A band you'd like to tour with? These examples just scratch the surface. Have fun with this list. If it turns into a mininovel, great! Really put some thought into it and allow it to be a constant work in progress.

Print out this goal sheet and stick it to the wall of your rehearsal space. It's good to glance at every once in a while to keep you on track. Get a highlighter and color the goals you reach. Hopefully, after the first year, section one will be fully colored. Whenever you have updates or slight shifts to your trajectory, make a new goal sheet. Print it out and put it up. Don't just make it a doc on your computer. Hanging this tangible sheet of paper in the physical world gives it life and demands respect.

Have everyone in your band make a goal sheet like this. Then discuss it in a band meeting. Make sure everyone's visions align and make one master Music Marathon sheet for the band. Because if all of you want to be spending the majority of your year on the road except your bassist, who just wants to record, play occasional local shows and raise his family, then you want to address this sooner than later. It may be time to find another bassist. You don't want this to come up a week before you're leaving for your first big tour. Sound absurd? I've seen it happen. "Yo, guys, I don't know about this tour. I mean, we're not going to make any money and I need to be looking out for my family. I really don't think it's a good idea. And I don't want to be away for this long." "Really dude? You couldn't have told us this, like, *a year ago* when we were planning this thing?" Commence epic band fight in which you admit you slept with the mother of his children when they first started dating. Don't let it come to that. For the sake of his children. So have the goals discussion early on.

Your goals and plans can always shift over time. But this will at least give you some focus and direction. Oftentimes, musicians aren't sure where they should be devoting their efforts, but with this goal sheet, you can always turn to it and make sure you're still on track.

HOW TO FORM YOUR BAND

For those of you reading this who are not solo artists and do not yet have a band, there are many great tools these days to help you team up with other like-minded musicians. Having read this book is the most important prerequisite to officially teaming up, obviously. Aside from Craigslist, some platforms you should know about are Fandalism, Gigmor, Grouptones and BandMix. But honestly, the most tried-and-true method of meeting other like-minded musicians is by going to local shows and open mics. You'll start to see the same faces. You'll be able to pick out the musicians. Get to know the other musicians currently performing out.

And, of course, attending a music school is a great way to find a network. Many bands form in college. Some, like Imagine Dragons and American Authors (both formed by Berklee College of Music alumni), become worldwide superstars. Attending a music school throws you into a supportive environment with like-minded individuals. And even after you graduate, the network you built up will always remain. Yes, music school is expensive and yes, it may not be for everyone, but it can be an investment in your career like studio time and new gear.

WHY NO ONE CARES ABOUT YOUR MUSIC

The most frustrating thing is to put out an album that you spent the past two years of your life working on (and sunk way more money than you have into the production) and have it just bounce around your local scene a bit and lose traction before it was ever gained. This is the story of every local band on the planet. Some are putting out truly brilliant records with A-list players and top-notch songwriting. Why does no one seem to care about it when it's so undeniably great? It's because there's no story.

Everyone has a great story, but most just don't realize it yet. People love to be in the know and to be able to educate their friends about their favorite new band's backstory. Radio stations love to be able to give the ten-second explanation of why you stand out. Jimmy Fallon needs a two-line introduction that will get people to stick around. And journalists, especially, need a story to write about.

When was the last time you read a review about a band in your local newspaper (or *Pitchfork*) that discussed the music: the song structure, guitar tones, harmonic and melodic choices, drum tones, the pocket, innovative syncopation, varied time signatures, sonic flourishes, unusual studio techniques that they *heard* in the recording and were not spelled out in the press release? The things that musicians get off to, reviewers and average listeners couldn't give two sh*ts about.

And that, my friends, is the disconnect and the reason publicists and managers exist. These talented folks will help you craft the most interesting story that nonmusicians will actually care to read about.

But for the time being, you are your own publicist and your own manager. You need to find the most interesting storyline for your project and run with it. Everywhere. This should be in your band bio, listed in your press release, told in interviews, written up everywhere about you. It's the "he was discovered while busking on the streets of L.A. and now has chart-topping radio hits" story. Adele's breakup album. Taylor Swift's love life. The White Stripes' brother/sister/husband/wife/ex-husband/ex-wife confusion. Bruno Mars and Meghan Trainor's behind-the-scenes song-writing careers. Bon Iver's northern-woods-of-Wisconsin-cabin recording. Deadmau5's giant, demented mouse head.

You need something that every newspaper reviewer wants to write about. The story that bumps every other album release off the cover. The story every diehard fan tells their friends when showing them your YouTube videos. Some bands decide to go the gimmick route: performing in costume or focusing on their weird instruments. And that's fine. As long as there is a tangible story that people can talk about.

A great song is one thing, but a great song with an amazing backstory is what really sells the project and makes you memorable.

So, what is your story? Everyone has one. Actually, everyone has a million different little stories that have led to where you are right now. Your band bio should not be each member's entire backstory on how they started taking piano lessons at a young age and then you all came together in high school to form "the greatest rock band the world has ever known!" This is so bland it's actually annoying. This doesn't set you apart. Have you overcome personal obstacles? What do you do outside music? Are you an avid reader of fantasy novels? Do you play arena football on the weekends? Is your great-uncle John Coltrane?

Your story must align with your entire project. When people hear your story, see your live show, browse your Instagram, listen to your record, watch your YouTube videos, follow your Snapchat stories, it all lines up. So, home in on this story early on. Sprinkle it throughout your bio and reinforce it (seamlessly) in everything you do. Authentically.

Whether you like it or not, your story is just as important as your music. That cuts deep, I know. I can sense your blood pressure rising. Breathe. In. And. Out. You want to succeed as a musician? You're going to have to accept some of these truths. Musicians used to be able to rely on marketing departments and PR firms to craft their stories and reinforce them through album and tour promo. This is now your job to master.

The Disconnect Between Musician and Blogger

One of the first concerts I ever saw was the Dave Matthews Band at Alpine Valley. I was mesmerized by all the intricate elements they effortlessly incorporated into a jam rock format. In high school, I admit, I became somewhat fanatical. I appreciated (and studied) the astounding musicianship. There are few drummers on the planet who play like Carter or acoustic guitarists who play like Dave. I sang along to LeRoi's sax solos, transcribed Butch's keyboard solos, funked out to Stefan's bass lines and, of course, geeked when Boyd ripped into his screaming fiddle solos that lifted "Tripping Billies" to spiritual heights.

I lived in a Dave bubble in high school, surrounded by my musician buddies who "got it." I went to countless DMB shows alongside 40,000 other Daveheads. So I was quite startled when I got to college and realized that it wasn't actually "cool" to like "Dave." I was chastised by the hipsters of Minneapolis and started seeing DMB top countless Worst Bands Ever lists. But every blog article I read never actually discussed the music. What these bloggers hated were the fans. Not really the music. DMB fans were typically classified as suburban, bro-y frat boys sporting cargo shorts, popped collars and flip-flops packed into SUVs who pound Bud Light. As someone who was never in a frat, didn't own a collared shirt to pop, grew up in the city, drove a run-down old Ford Taurus wagon and drank craft beer, I was always so confused by these takedown articles. Why was my favorite band so universally despised? I started questioning my entire taste in music. But how was it that I could love the Beatles, Bob Dylan, Paul Simon, Miles Davis, Stevie Wonder, Bill Withers, Marvin Gaye, Aretha Franklin, James Taylor, Atmosphere,

Eminem, Ani DiFranco, Death Cab for Cutie, Ben Folds, Béla Fleck, Jeff Buckley, Radiohead and Prince (all acts universally "acceptable" to like by bloggers), but also love DMB (universally hated by these same people)?

I finally got it. (Most) music bloggers don't actually know anything about music. They don't know how to write about music. They only know how to write about the *culture* of music. And a band's culture is defined by who their perceived fans are. These bloggers have never actually been to shows of these bands they claim to hate. They've never studied music. They've never written a song. They exist in a world surrounded by other hipsters who bond over their mutual hatred of popular music('s fans). They claim to "love" music, but they don't. Not like you or I love music. They love the culture of music.

The Dave Matthews Band's perceived image has overshadowed their music. Regardless of whether you care for their music or not, it doesn't matter. All music is subjective. Some people hate Dylan. Some love him. Some hate the Beatles. Some love them. No artist gets a pass. There are plenty of people out there who don't enjoy music the same way you do. Because they're not musicians. You enjoy "great" music. But your definition of "great" is different from theirs. You study music; they study the culture of music.

So, keep this in the back of your mind when crafting press releases, your bio and your entire promotional campaign. Unfortunately, it is *not* (all) about your music. You can't fight this. You must accept it if you have any hope of controlling your own PR and gaining any sort of traction.

DOES AGE MATTER?

The question I get asked frequently by older musicians is "does age matter." There's no simple answer because it all depends on what your goals are. But I'll tell you one thing—age has absolutely no correlation with success (or talent). Uncle Joe will tell you, "If you haven't made it by thirty, give up." Stop listening to Uncle Joe! Joshua Radin *started* his musical career at 30, two years after he picked up the guitar for the first time. Matt Nathanson put out seven albums (and one major-label album) before releasing his chart-topping (indie-label) hit "Come On Get Higher" at 35. Bill Withers released his debut album at 32. Sheryl Crowe released her debut album at 31 (after working as a music teacher, jingle writer and backup vocalist). Daniel Powter's hit "Bad Day" came out when he was 34. Willie Nelson was 40 when *Shotgun Willie* came out. Leonard Cohen was 50 when he released "Hallelujah." 2 Chainz didn't get a #1 album until a month before his 36th birthday. John Ondrasik of Five for Fighting was 35 when their smash hit "Superman (It's Not Easy)" took over the airwaves. Pharrell was 40 when "Happy" took over the world (yes, he was successful prior to "Happy" with the Neptunes and N*E*R*D, but "Happy" is "Happy!"). Andrea Bocelli was 34 when he released his debut album. Rachel Platten was 34 when "Fight Song" reached #1. Butch Vig was 36 when he produced Nirvana's *Nevermind,* and it wasn't until he was 40 that his own band, Garbage, released their debut chart-topping album. Dan Wilson was 37 when his first hit, "Closing Time," was released with his band Semisonic (and he was 46 when he won his first Grammy for cowriting six songs on the Dixie Chicks' Album of the Year *Taking the Long Way*). Debbie Harry was 31 when Blondie released their first album, and not until a few years later did they see worldwide success. Joe Satriani didn't release his first album until he was 30. Christine McVie of Fleetwood Mac was 34 when *Rumours* was released. Michael Fitzpatrick was 40 when Fitz and the Tantrums released their debut album. Thelonious Monk released his best-selling album, *Monk's Dream,* at 46. Louis Armstrong, although a renowned trumpeter-performer for decades, was 64 when his best-selling album *Hello, Dolly!,* was released. Charles Bradley was 63 when he released his debut album. And although a lifelong musician and producer, Seasick

Steve was 67 when he released his first multinational charting (major-label debut) album.

But these are artists you've most likely heard of. And this is when they "made it big." If you take away one thing from this book, it's that you don't need to "make it big" to "make it." Don't let age scare you. There are 16-year-olds writing better songs than I could ever dream of writing. And there are 50-year-olds dusting off their guitar, reconnecting with their soul and deciding to finally pursue a career they can believe in. Age means nothing. If you work hard enough, you *will* make it, regardless of your age.

That being said, life happens. And I'd be lying if I told you it was easy to start a rock career with a spouse and kids at home. Once kids enter the picture, all bets are off. There's this bit in Alex Blumberg's podcast *StartUp* where he jokes with an investor about how parents fool themselves into thinking it's possible to work just as hard at their entrepreneurial pursuits with kids, exclaiming "you just get better at managing your time." They eventually concede that, in fact, parents can't devote as much time to their passions and careers as nonparents.

If a music career is more important to you than a family, you have nothing to worry about. If you're 23, want to start a family by 27 and you just formed a rock band to take over the world, you're going to come to a crossroads very soon. You're going to have to decide whether you want to be an absent parent on the road with your band or at home raising your kids working a 9-to-5. There's a balance, sure, and there are many successful musicians with children. But most of these successful musicians didn't have kids until their music career was coasting a bit and they had enough passive income that they didn't need to spend their entire life on the road.

But again, pull out your goals sheet and ask yourself, "Can this be achieved with a family?" Everyone's situation is different. Maybe your partner has an income to support your family while you devote all of your time (and money) to your musical pursuits. Maybe you just want to play locally and not tour. Maybe you want to be a local hired gun or a pro-ducer-engineer. Maybe you want to be a YouTuber. Maybe you want to live in the college circuit and fly out to one-off gigs every once in a while (more on this in Chapter 9). Not every career in music requires incessant touring. But it's hard to be a successful indie band, singer/songwriter, DJ or pop act and not tour.

It also all depends on what your idea of success is. And no one can define what success is but you. Remember that.

If you're an indie act making five figures staying at home licensing your music to film and television, that's success. Could you make six or seven figures if you toured? Maybe. But you don't have to if you don't want to. There's no right or wrong. You should do what's going to make you the happiest.

Happiness needs to be built into every career decision. There are more important things in life than money. Actually, once you have enough money to support the lifestyle you want, you shouldn't make any decision based solely on money ever again.

2.

THE NEW INDUSTRY

Self-promotion. If you don't want anything to do with it,
stay in your f*&king basement.
—BEN FOLDS

There's so much more to the business than just the money.
—DEREK SIVERS

I have seen the artists change for the better. They have a much
better idea of who they are because they can talk directly to their
audience. They have a much better work ethic because they're
realizing they can create their own business before the manager
or the lawyer or the label comes in. But, the downside is, it's
taking away from what the band used to be able to focus on: The
creativity. All they had to do was write songs, tour and play
live. Now, you're a business. Has it affected the art?
I'm sure it has. How could it not?
—BRUCE FLOHR, RED LIGHT MANAGEMENT

YOU THOUGHT YOU WERE A MUSICIAN

And now, for the most disappointing realization that every modern musician eventually comes to terms with: You will never be able to *just* make music for a living.

The sooner you accept this, the sooner you can get your music career on track.

Sounds simple, but it's astounding how many musicians I meet who think they can succeed by just writing great songs, making great recordings and putting on great shows. Yes, making great music is *of course* important. It's the foundation of the entire operation. Having great music is the baseline. And it's assumed that you have great music before following any other tips in this book. But, it is not (and, actually, has never been) all that musicians have to worry about.

How are you going to play live if you don't know how to book a show? How are you going to get people to those shows if you don't know how to promote? How are you going to grow your fanbase if you don't know how (where, or, *gasp*, why) to put your songs online? How are you going to generate passive revenue if you don't know how to collect all of your royalties? How are you going to get noticed if you don't know how to approach gatekeepers, influencers and tastemakers?

There are way too many musicians who believe that all it takes is to create one great song, throw it up on YouTube or SoundCloud and wait for it to take over the world and get "discovered" by "someone."

Believe me, I wish we lived in a world where the greatest music in the world was instantly and universally recognized, cherished and (financially) rewarded. But, the reality is, that's far from the truth. So! What are you going to do about it? Are you going to live in the majority and do nothing but b*&ch about how 'people are stupid' for liking the music they like (while your music disappears into oblivion), or are you going to work your a$$ off to get your music the recognition it deserves? Your choice.

THE 50/50 SPLIT

You must split your time equally between the music and the business. Early on, of course, most of your time will be spent solely on the music because you don't have a business yet. This period doesn't count. This is the incubation stage. The developmental stage. But once you have decided that music is going to be your business, that's when the 50/50 split comes into play.

When you're writing and recording your album, 80% of your time will be spent on the music. And this is balanced by the period after you release the album, when 80% of your time will be spent on promoting the album (the business).

When you're not working on specific projects, you should be splitting every day (or at least every week) between business and music equally. Maybe Sunday through Tuesday is spent on songwriting, practicing and rehearsing. Then Wednesday through Friday is spent on booking, promotion, social media, networking and research. If you're ever bored as a musician, you aren't doing it right. I haven't been bored since *Friends* was still on the air.

EMBRACE THE HYPHEN

For a long time I made 100% of my income on my original music. I thought that was the singular marker of success: making ALL of my money on music. However, ignoring other revenue streams and creative opportunities denied me personal (and professional) growth. There are few musicians on the planet, big or small, who *only* make money on music. And there's nothing wrong with that. Dr. Dre has Beats. Beyoncé, Rihanna, and Adam Levine have clothing lines. Justin Bieber, Lady Gaga and Taylor Swift have fragrances. Thirty Seconds to Mars frontman Jared Leto is an Academy Award–winning actor.

Musician-actors are not a new thing. And musician-entrepreneurs are becoming more commonplace (if we remove the fact that all musicians are truly entrepreneurs anyway). I'm currently a musician-actor-blogger-consultant-(and now)author. But I was once a musician-barista, a musician-actor-Lyft driver, a musician–sub shop delivery driver. Musician-teacher, musician–camp counselor. "Musician" will always begin your title, but don't be ashamed of your other titles. Embrace them! Initially your titles won't be so glamorous (Musician-Barista), but eventually you'll be able to drop the job titles you don't want and add ones that you do.

The goal is to be making 100% of your income from your creative talents.

WHAT'S RIGHT AND WHAT'S WRONG IN MUSIC

There's one thing I've learned down here in Colombia.
Good and bad are relative concepts.
—STEVE MURPHY FROM *NARCOS*

Forget everything you've ever thought about ownership; right and wrong; good and bad. These are all subjective terms. And we've been brought up to believe that there are absolute truths when it comes to right and wrong. Sure, murder is wrong. That we can all agree on. But is murder for justice, like in the death penalty, also wrong? That is one of the biggest debates in our society today. We could agree that stealing is wrong. But the line that distinguishes stealing from sharing is quite blurry.

If you get stuck in dogmatic ideologies, you can never grow as an artist or businessperson. Allow yourself to evolve in your beliefs. Only when we allow our beliefs to be challenged can we grow. Only when we question the status quo do we realize that what we thought to be absolute truths may, in fact, not be so.

The music industry has evolved tremendously in the last ten years, and every day we are being asked to challenge our beliefs on what constitutes right and wrong. Is file-sharing just like stealing a microwave from an appliance store? Well, no, it's not. But that was the argument by the labels when Napster first popped up over fifteen years ago.

The record labels stood by their perceived absolute truths about what was right and wrong and thought it was a good idea to "defend" their rights by suing music's biggest fans. The Recording Industry Association of America (RIAA), the organization that represents the major labels, sued over 35,000 individuals for illegally downloading music in the mid-2000s. We heard of 12-year-olds being sued for hundreds of thousands of dollars. A recently deceased 83-year-old who hadn't even owned a computer before her passing got sent notices. A grandfather actually died while in litigation, and the RIAA told his family they had sixty days to grieve and then the RIAA would start to depose his children.

Was this right or wrong? Well, at the time, the RIAA clearly thought this was the right course of action. History shows that it was not. Suing grandmas, children, and, in general, music's biggest fans, was in fact wrong. Even if they did actually download music "illegally."

The music industry is not black and white. Just because you have a legal right to stop people from doing something doesn't mean it's smart to try to enforce that right. Like when Taylor Swift sent cease-and-desist letters to moms selling mugs on Etsy that used a T-swift lyric. Sure, Ms.

Swift had trademarked a three-word phrase ("shake it off") and technically had the right to "defend the mark," but is it the smartest move to send cease-and-desist letters threatening to sue fans because they used a song lyric on mugs in an Etsy store? I'm not so certain.

When you make business decisions, don't merely think about how they are going to affect your bottom line this year. Think about how many lifelong fans it will bring you and how these fans will support your bottom line over the course of your entire career. The major record labels' vision became shorter and shorter over the years to the point where if the first song they put out by an artist wasn't a smash-it-out-of-the-park hit, then that artist was typically dropped. Bruce Springsteen's first two albums flopped. But Columbia stuck it out with him because they believed in him as an artist. And because of that belief, allowing him to grow as an artist and entertainer, the third record he delivered was *Born to Run*. How many artists have labels dropped because their first album (or single!) flopped, depriving us of the next Springsteen?

The labels have had it all wrong for sometime now. They have ignored the reason they exist: the fans. They look at fans as numbers on a spreadsheet. The labels have been clinging to the Adeles, Weeknds, Biebers, Swifts, Beyoncés and Rihannas, knowing that if they can just get a couple hits this year, their books will work out and they'll get their Christmas bonuses. Record-label execs turn over these days more than IHOP pancakes. As long as record labels treat fans as one-dimensional customers, they will continue to fail. They have lost touch with what sustains a music career. It's not about the hit of the moment. It's about the connection the fan has with the artist.

Building loyal fans is the most important aspect of a music career. The money will follow.

For every business decision you make for the rest of your career, ask yourself this question: Is this the best decision for my fans?

If you can answer yes every time, then you can never fail.

THE NEW TEAM

Historically, a musician's team was comprised of a personal manager, an entertainment attorney, a booking agent, a record label, a business manager, a publisher and a publicist. And this team hasn't ever been questioned or improved upon. Until now.

Yes, these team members are important when you've reached a level that demands this sort of personnel. But it is no longer enough to just have these members of the team. And what about before you obtain these team members?

The modern music fan demands a constant stream of content to stay engaged: songs, videos, photos, blogs and tweets. It's no longer acceptable to just release content once every three years that a traditional team would help develop, promote and rally behind. Musicians today are expected to put out high-quality content every day.

So how do you do this? By surrounding yourself with talented team members who can help this process—because no one can do it all on their own. Bands have a leg up on solo artists because they can allocate some of these duties among the members. The bands who succeed the quickest are the ones where every member has business duties in addition to their musical duties. That's a lot of duty. I'm 12.

Graphic Designer

Fifteen years ago you could get away with creating one 11 × 17 poster for every local show and one poster per tour. Now, if you're not pumping out multiple square posters on Instagram or rectangle posters on Facebook for every career milestone (local show, tour, TV placement, opening gig, festival slot, radio add, YouTube video, album release and single release), you're neglecting your career. Graphic design artist is now a required position every band must employ. It's no longer a job you should outsource for every design need you have. It's best if someone in your band (or you) learns basic graphic design. You don't need to be a Photoshop pro, but at least become capable enough to touch up photos, resize images, create jpegs and PDFs, add text to images and create good-looking posters. Until your design skills rival the pros, keep your designs simple. The simpler the better. Keep it classy. There's nothing that screams amateur more than a messy-looking poster with five different fonts in 6 different colors, pixelated photos haphazardly sliced together. If you suck at design, hire a professional photographer and just put some text on the photos and crop or resize the image depending on the use.

If you need a brand-identifying design (like an album cover, band logo or t-shirt), then yes, outsource to a professional. 99designs.com and Guru.com are great places to find an inexpensive, yet talented, graphic design artist. They will host a design contest for you: You submit all of the information for the item you need, and how much you're willing to pay, and then dozens of graphic design artists submit designs. You pick the one you like and *boom*, you found the best graphic design artist for your project. Fiverr.com is also a good option for finding inexpensive graphic design artists.

The vertical 11 × 17 poster design is outdated. Unless you're printing physical posters to hang in coffee shops or record stores, why are you designing to these standards? Graphic designers now work mostly in pixels, not inches.

Luckily, there are very simple photo-editing, text-adding and graphic design phone apps you can download to help you create good-looking posters/photos for Instagram. As to not list apps that may be defunct by the time you're reading this, just Google "adding text to photo app" or "beginning graphic design app." Many great ones are free (but they'll add a logo or watermark) and most cost just a few bucks to remove the logo—definitely worth it. Having a text-adding app on your phone is crucial for promoting on the go. Keep an arsenal of promo and live photos saved on your phone, add text and *bam,* you have a good-looking show poster for Instagram, Twitter and Facebook. If you want to get creative and have an eye for design, then go in deep with some design apps.

However, not everything can be done on the phone. It's definitely important to learn basic image editing on your laptop. Photoshop is the industry standard and is what I've been using for years to create all my t-shirt, poster, album and logo designs along with Facebook, Twitter and website cover photos. You need to be able to adjust the size and dimensions of your images without having to contact a graphic design artist every time you need a slight change. So, the person in your band (or you if you don't have a band) with the best design eye should learn a graphic design/photo editing program. Some great ones to look into are Adobe Creative Cloud (which contains Photoshop, Lightroom and Illustrator for a monthly fee), Pixelmator (similar program to Photoshop and currently goes for a small, one-time fee), PaintShop Pro, Affinity Designer and Canva. There are some free photo-editing websites where you can upload your photo, edit in-site, then download it, but it's worth investing a few bucks in a professional program.

Find a program and master it. At the end of the day it doesn't matter what you use as long as you can do what you need with it.

Recording Engineer

It's no longer acceptable to just put out music every three years. Sure, you can still spend time creating an expensive masterpiece in the form of an album every few years, but you also need to be releasing high-quality recordings very often (like once a month). Get Logic or Pro Tools (if your budget is tight you can start with GarageBand—it comes preinstalled on MacBooks), or if you're an electronic artist, Ableton Live, Cubase, Bitwig and FL Studio (formerly Fruity Loops) are all solid options used by the pros. Master your software enough to record demos, rehearsals, live shows and (potentially) "radio-ready" songs and albums. With the onslaught of inexpensive recording programs that have come out over the past fifteen years, there's no excuse to not learn one. You can still hire a producer and engineer and go into "the studio" for your album if you have a budget, but someone on your team needs to be your on-call recording engineer.

These regular releases can be your covers, demos and band rehearsals. Put these on SoundCloud, YouTube, Facebook and Instagram. You can officially release the best songs on iTunes, Spotify, Apple Music and the rest if you want.

And how do you build up a home studio to do this? We'll dig into this in Chapter 3.

Videographer

If you haven't noticed, video is kind of a big deal. People are (unfortunately) way more willing to click a video than a song. Fight this all you want, but if you don't have video, you're missing out on serious engagement. The video you put out doesn't just have to be a high-quality music video. But, every video needs to be high-quality. It's no longer acceptable to record cover songs in front of your MacBook camera and throw them up on YouTube. Sure, in 2007 this was cutting-edge. Not anymore. You're now competing with every YouTuber and label act. Every video you put on YouTube and Facebook needs to be professional-looking. Shot well (with good lighting) on a great camera, edited, with pro sound. It's not as difficult to achieve as it sounds. As with your graphic design program, learn video editing. The top video-editing software available right now is Final Cut Pro and Adobe Premiere; iMovie is pretty good as well (and is free). Choose one and get good at it. It's not hard. Just do it. You don't want to have to outsource this to a pro video editor every time you want to release footage from your latest show or rehearsal.

Smartphone cameras are getting better and better. They're still not as good as DSLR cameras, but they will do for the time being until you can afford to purchase a good camera. When using your phone as a camera, it's all about the lighting. Shooting outside during the day is ideal because there's no better light source than the sun. Experiment with locations. Shade is best (so the sun doesn't wash your face out). You may have heard the term "magic hour," which is sunrise or sunset. Everything looks gorgeous around then.

If you're making Vine, Snapchat, Twitter or Instagram videos, shooting on your phone is standard. If you have an iPhone, you can edit the videos quickly in iMovie (all the biggest Vine stars use it). If you're putting together a longer-form, long-lasting video (like cover video, behind the scenes in studio or music video), you're going to want to spend time editing this on your laptop, using a professional video-editing program.

Sure, as often as you can, work with a professional team and put out high-quality music videos (shot, edited and directed by professionals). But not many indie musicians have the budget to put out expensive videos like that every month. So, get good at video editing on your own (like so many successful YouTubers have) and just start releasing quality content.

Above all, you need to be putting out regular videos, of all types, across multiple platforms. And there's different etiquette for each platform (Snapchat vs. Vine vs. Instagram vs. YouTube vs. Facebook vs. Twitter). We'll get deeper into this in Chapter 11.

Photographer

You need lots of high-quality photos. It's worth it to hire a professional photographer for band promo photos at least once a year. Also, hire a pro to shoot your biggest shows. But you can't just put out promo photos all the time. Instagram demands daily high-quality photos. There are some inexpensive photo-editing apps (for like $3). Edit every photo you post. Notice how the Likes pour in when you post well-edited photos.

Web Developer

If you have a family member who loves you (and your music) and is willing to join your team, keep them close, thank them profusely, shower them with green room beer and get them laid frequently. Hopefully they will stick with you when they're offered jobs paying ten times (or more realistically a hundred times) what you can pay. Because they will be. The most in-demand profession is web/app developer. So, if a band member can get good at web development, that's ideal, but somewhat unrealistic. Unlike video editing or graphic design, web development takes *way* more time to master. At the very least, learn some basic HTML code.

This may be one of the boldest concepts of this entire book, but I'm putting it out there. The musicians who achieve this will zoom past their peers: *Add a creative developer to your team.* First. Before a manager, booking agent, label or anyone else. Offer them an equal cut of your income. Sure, it may be next to nothing now, but if they believe in your music enough, they might be crazy enough to join you on this journey.

You want to be able to track and analyze everything you have online. At the very least, add Google Analytics to your website.

Of course you can quickly and easily create a website with no coding knowledge with Bandzoogle or Squarespace, but going way above and beyond what every other band out there is doing can be extremely beneficial.

Companies like Facebook, Airbnb, Twitter and Dropbox succeeded without spending a penny on traditional marketing. As cool as it is to get a billboard of your band on Sunset Boulevard or hearing fifteen seconds of your song on your favorite radio station (from the ad you bought), some developers have tried to improve their odds. Ryan Holiday, author of *Growth Hacker Marketing* discussed how contractors for Airbnb, through creative engineering, got all of their initial postings listed on Craigslist. He writes, "because Craigslist does not technically allow this, it was a fairly ingenious work-around. As a result, Airbnb—a tiny site— suddenly had free distribution on one of the most popular websites in the world." (Airbnb has since come out strongly against the practice, however, which it claims was carried on without its knowledge.) Holiday, a marketing expert himself, worked with BitTorrent to release a free bundle for one of his clients, musician Alex Day, which resulted in over 2 million downloads, 276,409 page visits, 166,638 iTunes impressions, 52,151 Alex Day website impressions and 5,000 new email sign-ups for Alex's mailing list.

You want to find creative marketing techniques that are trackable. And developers understand how tracking works and can conceive of ideas that typical musicians cannot.

I realize that not every musician can convince a talented engineer to join the team for little to no pay, but it's worth putting in the back of your mind for when you get an investment or start pulling in some decent dough.

For the time being, you can create a great-looking website with Bandzoogle or Squarespace. They charge a low monthly hosting fee and offer tons of good looking templates to choose from with "drag and drop" functionality for adding a music player, show calendar, photos, store, videos, social integration, blog and anything else you need on your website. I've found Bandzoogle and Squarespace offer the easiest way for musicians to create good looking websites with no coding knowledge.

How to Learn All This Stuff

I, like so many other musicians, are completely self-taught at most of this. How did we learn it all? Well, you can learn pretty much anything you need from YouTube tutorials. Or by simple Googling. Working in Final Cut Pro and can't figure out how to slice the video? It's a five-second Google search: "How to slice video in Final Cut Pro." Or want to make an animated GIF in Photoshop? Tons of simple tutorials on YouTube. Or if you learn better in a formal education environment, music industry colleges offer many of these classes. Some even have online courses you can take from anywhere in the world.

TO SIGN OR NOT TO SIGN

There's music and then there's the music business. Make sure
everything is in writing and always protect yourself.
Don't expect others to protect you.
—RYAN PRESS, VICE PRESIDENT, A&R,
WARNER/CHAPPELL MUSIC

Even with the 50/50 split, there isn't enough time in the day for you to cover all of the business duties required to run a full-time music career successfully. Of course you *want* professionals to handle most of the business, but it's not most musicians' realities at first. The most important thing you need to remember is: *Do not hand off your career to someone just because they show some interest.* That's the quickest way to seal your demise. Sure, the right label or manager could help you become a superstar. But the wrong one could make sure you work at Starbucks for the rest of your life. So, choose wisely. If you ever get a contract, get your own lawyer (not one referred by the person giving you the contract—duh) to review it. And, when the time is right, make sure you know the reasons to sign or not to sign with the pros.

MANAGER

Ingrid knows everything going on at all times.
I feel like we are business partners.
—LYNN GROSSMAN, INGRID MICHAELSON'S MANAGER

The manager is the most important person in your operation. Your manager is your teammate. Your partner. Your friend. The two of you (or six, depending on how many are in your band) are in it together. Us versus the world. The manager is the liaison between the artist and everybody else. The manager oversees everything from the recording process to the album release campaign to the tour routing, booking and performing to the social media management to the lead singer's divorce. The manager handles the business, first and foremost. The best managers handle the business with creative finesse. To navigate the constantly evolving musical landscape, managers need truly creative minds. You don't want a manager who is operating the same way this year as she was last year. Every day is new. Every day is different.

The two extremes of artist managers are the Well-Connected Manager and the Best-Friend Manager. Every manager exists somewhere on this spectrum.

The Well-Connected Manager (WCM)

Everyone understands the concept of the Well-Connected Manager. She has multiple clients, usually works at a management company, and one of her phone calls is more effective than 30 emails and calls from a Best-Friend Manager. Well-Connected Managers typically have Day-to-Day Managers who work under them and do just that: manage the day-to-day responsibilities of the band and report back to the Well-Connected Manager.

The Well-Connected Manager gets her band in-studio performances at radio and TV stations. Gets the band a record deal. Obtains a publishing deal. Gets songs placed on TV and in movies. Finds sponsorships and endorsements. Hires the booking agent, accountant and publicist. And obtains write-ups in major blogs, magazines and newspapers (if a publicist isn't involved).

These people have the clout to make these things happen with a phone call.

But what this Well-Connected Manager typically doesn't do is live and breathe the band she's working for (she just has too many clients or is burnt out from all the years of climbing the ladder and busting a$$). That's why a Best-Friend Manager is nice to have. At least at first.

The Best-Friend Manager (BFM)

The Best-Friend Manager starts with zero connections and has to make them all on his own. But, he lives and breathes the band. He and the band work together on a vision and lofty goals. He screams at the top of every rooftop about how his band is going to take over the world and works tirelessly to make it happen.

He's the tour manager when the band is on the road. He imports mailing list names after the show; creates Facebook events; uploads tour photos to Facebook and the website; Snapchats, Tweets, Instagrams and live broadcasts from the band account, runs the merch table (or finds people to do it). Manages the website and works with the graphic designer and web developer to keep the site up to date and truly representative of the band. Writes the press release and bio (or finds a writer to do it). Finds the best distribution company (if a label isn't involved) and distributes the music appropriately. Becomes a master at all of the necessary social media sites (and apps) and trains the band on how to use them. Manages all of the finances (before a business manager is involved). Contacts the street team in every city and arranges flyering, postering and Facebooking in advance of the band's shows. Hires interns to handle all of the above duties that he doesn't have time for. And he is the band's therapist.

But this stuff not only needs to get done, it all has to be up to professional standards. Everything needs to be representative of the band. If the band is unstoppable on stage or has an album that defines a new genre but the website is a WordPress template from 2002 and the Facebook Page has discombobulated information, three different tour calendars, two separate music players, and a tab that's completely nonfunctional, then your band's fan retention is suffering.

Some BFMs see their band to the top and become WCMs. Some get fired and replaced by a WCM when they start to see some success. Some become Day-to-Day Managers or Tour Managers.

WCMs typically make 15%–20% (gross) commission on your entire career. BFMs take what they can get. Which is typically nothing for a while.

If you have a BFM, it's best to just split up everything that's coming in equally with them for the time being. Make your BFM an equal member of the band. If you have 4 members, then your BFM is the 5th member and you split the money equally. If it's just you, it might make sense to give him 30% of the gross income and you keep 70% until you reach a certain threshold. Like, 30% until you make at least $10,000 monthly gross and then the manager's cut drops to 25%. Once you surpass $25,000 a month, the manager's cut drops to 20%. And then once you surpass $100,000 a month, the cut drops to 15%. It may seem counterintuitive to cut the percentage once you're making more. Shouldn't your manager get rewarded for working your income up to this level? Actually, it will still work out to be more money even if it's a smaller percentage: 30% of $8,000 = $2,400; 25% of $20,000 = $5,000; 20% of $50,000 = $10,000; 15% of $150,000 = $22,500.

And managers need to be making more money initially when you're not making much to make it worthwhile for them to work on your project as hard as they are. You get the glory of being on stage every night. They don't. So, show them that you appreciate what they're doing and split your earnings with them. And an occasional "thank you" never hurt anyone.

If you're not bringing in much of anything for any kind of commission to make sense (and you have savings or a day job), you can pay your manager a flat monthly fee until a certain point. Like, $500 a month until you're making $5,000 a month. Then, after $5,000 a month, the 30%, 25%, 20%, 15% model falls into place.

Remember, the manager's commission is typically taken from the gross earnings (all earnings before expenses). There are some expenses that are exempt in some management contracts like label advances, tour support, marketing support and touring expenses.

This sliding scale commission model can work equally for bands and solo artists. Have these possible breakdowns in your arsenal when you're negotiating pay with your potential BFM. There will be much less negotiating with WCMs because they're pretty set in their ways.

Music industry traditionalists will chastise the $500 per month flat and sliding scale models because "that's not how it works." But, you know what, *there are no absolutes in the NEW music industry.* Most BFMs aren't doing it for the money anyway, but if you want them to be able to work on your band as their full-time job, they need to be making enough money to actually live on. No matter how much they love your music, if they can't pay their rent or buy food, they're not going to stick around very long.

I know what you're thinking, "But Ari, we don't have a *BFM or* a WCM? How do we find *either*?"

Finding a manager is about timing, being in the right place at the right time and, really, making it seem like you don't need a manager. No one wants to work with a band that seems to be struggling, but everyone wants to hop on a speeding train. That being said, music is magic. Managers believe this. It's why they chose such an unstable career path. If a manager happens to hear something so special that it moves him on a deep, spiritual level, he may decide to take you on no matter what the stage of your career. Even if this is your first demo on SoundCloud and you don't even have a Facebook Page yet.

But this is rare. Most managers want to see you kicking butt on your own before they will even give you a second glance. They want to know that if they decide to work with you that you will put in the effort needed to maintain a modern music career. Managers know that it's not just about the music. They want bands who will work hard, just like them. So, you should have all of your social media sites up to industry standards. You need high-quality video. You need professional promo photos. You need your live show to be better than bands that are selling out arenas. You need to look like a band ready to take over the world.

Whatever you do, don't sign with a manager who is neither a Best-Friend Manager or a Well-Connected Manager just to have a manager. I meet too many artists who love talking about their "manager." "Oh yeah my *manager* is handling this. My *manager* is handling that." Blah-blah. Unimpressive. I don't care. If your manager really was handling this and that, you wouldn't need to tell me about it and I'd see it. And your manager should never be handling stuff you don't know about. The moment your manager makes deals that you have no idea about is the moment your career becomes their career and you lose all control. Do not wear your ignorance as a badge of honor and proudly exclaim, "Oh I don't know, my manager deals with that." No! You're the boss. You're in charge. You should know everything that goes on. Your manager works for you. Stay in the loop. Stay hands-on.

The Family Manager (FM)

There have been some pretty successful family managers (Joe Jackson for Michael, Joe Simpson for Jessica and Ashley, Sharon Osbourne for Ozzy, Jay Z for Beyoncé, Mac Reynolds for Imagine Dragons (brother of lead singer Dan) and Jonetta Patton for her son Usher. This is definitely an option *if* you have a great relationship with this family member already and they are willing to devote the time and energy it takes to build an indie music career. But, make sure this family member does his homework, learns the industry and will let you move on to a Well-Connected Manager if that's the best move for your career. FMs are essentially BFMs—with more guilt trips.

The Band Member Manager (BMM)

Bands (as opposed to solo artists) have the luxury of splitting up all the required business duties it takes to run a successful indie music career. One member should fill the role of acting manager, until you find someone who will take over this role. This member should be the most organized, levelheaded, personable and friendly member of the group. The BMM will lead band meetings, book most of the initial shows, allocate duties among the rest of the group and do all of the outreach.

I recommend getting a BMM agreement drawn up by an entertainment attorney. Make sure it includes these points:

- BMM will be the acting manager and booking agent until other qualified professionals fill these duties.
- BMM responsibilities include:
  1. scheduling band meetings,
  2. negotiating all deals with talent buyers,
  3. maintaining all outreach via email, phone and social media,
  4. routing tours,
  5. pitching music supervisors,
  6. networking online and off (with music industry professionals, musicians and fans),
  7. keeping up with best music industry practices,

8. allocating necessary business duties to other band members,

9. finding other qualified professionals to assist with these duties.

- Each band member agrees to take on business duties assigned to him/her by BMM and will work at these duties diligently.
- BMM will have the flexibility to make minor decisions on behalf of the band (booking, publicity, social media, etc), but will bring every major decision (hiring/firing of team members, touring prospects, label/agent/management deals) to the band for a vote.
- If the BMM will keep the accounting records on behalf of the band or if this will be assigned to someone else.
- How and when the band gets paid.

Being the acting manager for your project, you're going to have to work out tough negotiations so that they are favorable to your career. To not get stepped on or screwed, you will have to look out for your best interests, but by doing this you will upset people in the process. This is inevitable. This is inherently more difficult for artists to deal with than for cold-hearted business people. It's not how artists are wired. It's a blessing and a curse. To effectively manage your career you need to be strong, but sensitive, smart and ethical. If you're true to yourself, make certain that your decisions and interactions remain honest, and you fill yourself with empathy, you'll be able to shield off the daggers thrown your way.

Band Agreement

Remove any confusion. Create a band agreement. If you can't afford to hire a lawyer, write out guidelines that everyone agrees to. Use the list on the next page as a guide.

1) **Songwriting Credit and Copyright** Coldplay splits every song equally 4 ways no matter who actually wrote the song. The Beatles didn't. How will you split songwriting credit?

2) **Compensation** It's best to split all (non-songwriting) income equally. But make sure you designate what percentage of the net income (after all expenses) you're going to keep in the bank account each month and what percentage you will pay the members. Make a point to revisit this breakdown every six months.

3) **Responsibilities and Expectations** Include that everyone will follow reasonable instructions from the manager or BMM and carry out agreed-upon duties diligently. You should outline some general expectations every member will follow. Show up on time. No vomiting on stage. Those kinds of things.

4) **Termination** If a member quits, (s)he loses all rights to future earnings of any kind (except songwriting royalties paid out by his/her own admin publishing company and PRO—more on what a PRO is in Chapter 13) and this member is void of having to cover any expenses or current debt. If a member is voted out, give the member his/her percentage of the value of all band gear and current cash on hand. If the band breaks up, split up everything equally.

5) **Who Covers Expenses** Initially, you may have family members helping cover expenses. Will they get paid back? If so, how? Will every member cover expenses out of pocket or only from the band bank account?

6) **Band Gear Costs** I recommend every member covers 100% of the expenses for their personal equipment (strings, drum heads, amps, etc.) and every member splits group gear expenses equally (PA, lights, van, trailer).

7) **Power of Authority** You should designate one person who has the authority to sign contracts on behalf of the band (the BMM), but require that nothing can be signed without group consent.

8) **Decision-Making** Every group decision must be voted on by the entire group. If there is an even number, give the manager the tie-breaking vote. Or give the BMM two votes.

9) **Side Projects** Are members allowed to participate in side or solo projects?

10) **Hiring New Members** Bring all new members in by unanimous decision. Make clear that all new members are entitled to all new revenue (including all future royalties of past albums), but not ownership/compensation for songs they didn't write.

11) **Rights to the Name** If (when) the band breaks up or a member leaves, who gets the right to use the band name? You should have a stipulation that if a member leaves (or is voted out), that member loses all rights to the band name.

Manager: To Sign or Not to Sign

If you have been approached by a manager and are wondering if you should sign with her, weigh the options. Make a "Pro" and "Con" sheet and write down all of the qualities, good and bad, this manager brings to the table. Do not sign with a manager just because one asks. Working with the wrong manager could absolutely destroy your career. There are countless stories of managers stealing hundreds of thousands of dollars, intentionally blocking deals, keeping secrets and using the artists to make as much possible money for themselves, while keeping the artists in the poorhouse.

And *always* ask around about this manager. Has he burned bridges? Do his former clients despise him? Google the sh*t out of him. Do not sign until you're certain this is the person for you.

Here are a few general guidelines on whether to sign or not to sign with a manager:

Reasons to Sign

- She has connections you don't.
- You are one of his only clients (if not his only one).
- She loves your music and has been to a bunch of your shows.
- He has been sharing your music relentlessly (without being paid to do it).
- She is a full-time manager.
- He has a plethora of experience in the music industry.
- Her other clients are hot acts of today (not legacy acts).
- He keeps up with the music industry and current trends.
- You respect her.
- You trust him.
- Your career vision and goals align.
- The manager is not you.

Reasons Not to Sign

- She has no more connections than you do.
- He has never seen a show of yours.
- You are one of many clients.
- She acts like she is doing you a favor by working with you.
- He has a day job other than music management.
- You don't trust her.
- She doesn't know the difference between artist and songwriter royalties.
- He doesn't have other clients from whom you can get referrals (or his references don't check out).
- He doesn't know how to hunt down every royalty stream that exists for your digital music.
- She has never booked a tour (or worked with an agent to book one) and has no concept of how club or theater booking works.
- All of his "claims to fame" happened over ten years ago.
- She doesn't understand the intricacies of the music industry.
- He doesn't keep up with what's happening in the music industry.
- Your gut says not to.

Trust Your Manager

Your manager is your teammate and there needs to be trust, otherwise the plays can't be made and the game falls apart. Once you decide to work with a manager, you will have to trust that they are doing what they think is best for your career. They are always looking out for your best interests. They want you to succeed. They want you to win. Remember, the only way they get paid is when you get paid.

Audit Your Manager

But that being said, no matter who your manager is, you must always maintain control of your business. You should know the deals going on. You should know how much you're getting paid for every deal. You should have your own attorney (not one referred by your manager) look over your management contract before signing. And throughout your career, you should be able to take a look at every deal made by your manager if you want to. Don't let your manager manipulate you into giving up control. It's your music and your career. They're just along for the ride. Did your manager say you only made $1,200 on the show last night (even though 400 people came)? Ask to see the performance agreement and settlement sheet from the venue (or from the agent). If your manager ever makes excuses as to why you can't see the contracts or doesn't give you full transparency, it's a serious red flag. Legitimate managers will happily show you any documents concerning your career. Only the shady ones will want to keep stuff from you. Maintain control. Always. And forever. Or find a new manager.

THE BRIDGE
7 Ways to Find a Manager

There are a few concrete steps you can take, when you're ready, to get your music in front of managers.

1) **Chart on Hype Machine** Hype Machine (Hypem.com) is a blog aggregator. They have about 800 music blogs as part of their system. Whenever one of these blogs posts a SoundCloud, YouTube or Bandcamp link to a song, it gets added to Hype Machine's charts. The more blogs that post/write about the song and the more users who "heart" the song, the higher it ranks on the charts. Managers (and labels) review these charts (and read these blogs) daily. More on how to do this in Chapter 15.

2) Reviews In addition to the blogs on Hype Machine, there are still a few publications that will review songs and albums. The biggest are obviously *Billboard*, *Pitchfork* and *Rolling Stone*, but industry publications like *Music Connection* magazine regularly review new and unsigned artist,s and many in the industry subscribe to these magazines. Most sites have specific instructions and guidelines on how to submit.

3) A Lawyer A more traditional way to get in with WCMs is from referrals from respected entertainment attorneys. More on how to find an attorney in a bit.

4) Direct Submission Platforms like Fluence (fluence.io) and Music Xray (musicxray.com) enable you to pay important people to listen to and review your music. Or, if you've done your homework, you can email a manager directly with links to your material. Begin the email to a WCM with compliments about him and express why you think you would be a good fit together; there's a chance the manager may dig in. Remember, you are bringing value to him. Respect his expertise and experience, but understand that you have something he doesn't—amazing music.

5) Showcases Many public radio stations, blogs, magazines and music conferences will hold showcases where they will invite managers out. Be careful, though; there are shady promoters and "talent buyers" who will try to get you to pay to play their "showcases," which are nothing more than regular club shows where you have to buy advance tickets to sell to your friends and fans. Do not take the bait. With legitimate showcases, you have to be invited to play. Many will have a submission process. Most won't pay, but they won't make you pay either. If you have to pay, make absolutely certain you know the names of the people who will be there. "A&R" and "music managers" is not good enough.

6) Public Radio It's nearly impossible to get played on top 40 radio or other Clear Channel–owned stations without a big-time radio promoter. But NPR affiliate stations will regularly play local, indie and unsigned artists. Start with the stations in your town or the closest city to where you live that has a public radio station that plays music. Managers definitely tune in to discover new talent. One of the biggest music-based public radio stations is Los Angeles's KCRW, which gets over 550,000 listeners each week. They play pretty much every kind of music except mainstream pop. Study the music played by each DJ. DJs at KCRW (and most other public radio stations) have the autonomy to play whatever they want. So instead of submitting through the front door, go directly to the DJs who are playing music like yours. Be smart about this and do your research. Some DJs only play 1970s funk/soul, so don't submit your metal band's latest song to them.

7) Business Schools If you're near a business school, target your promotional efforts to these students. Promote your shows on campus and in the business school building. The business students who are interested in music management may come out to your show and offer to manage you.

AGENT

Agents book your shows. They typically do not promote these shows. They will book your tours, but you or your manager will have to work with them on the cities you want to visit. Agents will negotiate what you get paid at these shows. It is in their best interest to get the best possible deal because they only make money when you make money. Agents typically take a 10%–20% commission. Most club/festival agents take 10% and most college booking agencies typically take 15%–20%.

Despite what you may think, however, you don't need an agent to play shows or book tours. We'll get into this more in Chapter 7. Yes, agents are nice to have. As someone who has booked over 500 shows on my own, I can tell you, booking is not fun. It's a means to an end. I've booked many national tours on my own, for myself. It's definitely possible, but, believe me, you want to pass off the booking duties to an agent as soon as you can. Booking is incredibly time-consuming and emotionally taxing.

That being said, unlike managers, no agent is going to want to work with you just because they like your band. They're running a business and need to make money just like everyone else. Sure, they want to like the artists they book, but they're much more willing to take on a band they may not love, but has a proven track record of selling out clubs, over a band they love but hasn't ever played outside their hometown. You're going to have to put in most of the work on your own before any agent will take a look at you.

Once you've reached the level where it makes sense to find an agent, make sure you know who to sign with and why. Always ask the other bands on the agent's roster how their experience has been with the agent. Ask the bands the kinds of deals their agent has gotten for them.

Before you sign, ask the potential agent what their vision is for you. Where do they see you in one year, five years, ten years? Do they book national club tours or do they specialize in the regional pizza pub market? Will they be getting you guarantees or door cuts? What can you expect for income at each show? What kinds of festivals have they booked? What other acts on their roster can they pair you up with? Are they planning to book you on opening or headlining tours? Do they have relationships with reputable promoters or do they primarily work with talent buyers at clubs? Are you willing to play four-hour gigs for $100? Because some agents specialize in this. Do you want to live on the road or only play weekends?

You want to discuss all of these things before deciding to work with the agent.

There are scams out there where "agents" will try to get you to pay them up front to book you shows. If you can't find a legitimate, experienced agent, and really don't want to book your shows yourself, you're better off training and hiring a friend to book your shows and giving them the 10%. Do not pay anyone until you get paid. Playing live is a money-making venture. Of course, if you don't have a fanbase, then you're going to have to work that much harder to get people out to your shows, and it may be worth honing your craft at home and building an online presence before hitting the road. You don't want to lose money on tour. You can avoid this if you're smart about it.

You will typically receive the checks or cash from the club or promoter right after the show. Your agent will send you the agreement in advance of the show, so you can double-check that you receive all of the money you're owed. If there is a dispute, your tour manager should try to work it out on the spot. If he can't, your agent will step in.

Reasons to Sign

- He has connections you don't.
- You can spend time on things other than booking.
- She is a better negotiator than you are.
- He has a roster of artists you respect.
- The agent is not you.

Reasons Not to Sign

- You've never heard of any of the bands on his roster.
- She has a bad reputation from her other bands.
- Your visions don't align.
- You're the smallest band on the roster.
- You're the biggest band on the roster.
- Your gut says not to.

How to Find a Booking Agent

Make a list of 10 bands similar to you whom you'd like to tour with. Research who their booking agents are (check their website or Facebook). You can find contact info from *Music Connection* magazine's excellent list at www.musicconnection.com/industry-contacts. Simply shoot them an email with a link to a live video of yours and your draw in your top five-to-ten cities. If they live in town, invite them to your next show. It's always best, however, to have a mutual friend (or band on their roster) make the initial introduction.

If you're going to be at major festivals like SXSW, CMJ or Coachella, make contact months in advance to start the relationship and then a few weeks before the festival invite them to your slot. If you invite them to a club show, always put them on the list. Sure, they can afford a $10 cover, but it's a gesture that goes a long way.

RECORD LABEL

The major label music industry has completely ruined every aspect of their business. At every step of the way they've had the tools offered to them to create an industry that works, and they've completely blown it. That's why we never had any interest in signing a contract with one of these companies because they're clearly completely clueless.

—WIN BUTLER, ARCADE FIRE

Record contracts are just like slavery.
I would tell every artist not to sign.

—PRINCE

Our function is to make famous.

— AVERY LIPMAN, PRESIDENT, UNIVERSAL
REPUBLIC RECORDS

The bands who form to get a deal are the ones who usually miss.

—BRUCE FLOHR, RED LIGHT MANAGEMENT

You're not going to get a record deal by asking for a record deal.

—MARCUS GRANT, THE COLLECTIVE

The goal of your music career should not be "to get signed." Remember the startling statistic from the introduction? Over 98% of all acts who sign to a major label fail. Success is not marked by getting signed. Sure, getting signed is a stamp of approval from people with money and connections. But, in no way does it mean you're going to be a star. Yes, the right label can help propel you to the next level of your career, but the wrong label can seal your demise.

Many artists these days are succeeding in the new music industry without a label. It's possible. It just takes a lot of hard work.

The biggest asset a label can offer is money. They are your bank. And like a bank, if you don't pay them back, they will take everything you own. No, they aren't going to repossess your car to pay back the advance, but they will refuse to let you release any music you recorded on their dime and will hold onto your masters forever. Most contracts have rerecording clauses that prevent you from rerecording and releasing the songs you wrote while you were under contract with them. Did you spend three years working on your generation-defining masterpiece? Did you sacrifice your relationships, mental health and well-being to create a piece of art that you were certain would be worth it in the end? Your label may not see it this way, decide not to release it, refuse to let you out of your contract, "shelve" the album until you decide to break up. Tough luck. This, unfortunately, is not unique. But we never hear about these stories, because they aren't glamorous and they're from artists you, of course, have never heard of. But some of my favorite artists have gone through just this. It's depressing. And infuriating. Don't let this happen to you.

Major labels historically have disgustingly opaque accounting practices. If you try to audit them, they'll hand you a printed stack of 537,000 pages filled with single lines of download and streaming royalties in 8-point-size font. Play by play. They do this intentionally so no one can even check if their reports are accurate.

It's well reported that the only way the Big 3 major labels—Sony, Universal and Warner—allowed Spotify to launch in the United States was by striking deals incredibly favorable to them, the labels, and completely unfavorable to the artists. The major labels own equity in Spotify and will cash out millions when Spotify launches on the stock market as a publicly traded company (if they haven't already by the time you're reading this). A leaked Lady Gaga/Interscope contract from 2007 showcases how labels were able to screw artists out of streaming royalties altogether. It states, "No royalties or other monies shall be payable to you [Lady Gaga's songwriting company] or Artist in connection with any payments received by Interscope pursuant to any blanket license under which the Licensee is granted access to all or significant portion of Interscope's catalog . . . " Because the label licensed its entire catalog to Spotify, Deezer, Apple Music and other online services, Interscope doesn't have to pay Lady Gaga (or any other artist who signed this standard agreement) the money earned from streams of her music on those platforms.

Labels have always found ways to screw artists out of money. And as long as the labels make the artist famous, the artist doesn't seem to care all that much. And even if they do decide to investigate, they're handed a 40-pound stack of paper. There's absolutely no transparency when it comes to major-label accounting practices.

This is not because the data isn't there. It is. But it's in the labels' best interests to hide this data from their artists. So it's not surprising that so many huge artists and songwriters have jumped ship from their major publishers and labels to Kobalt, which prides itself on transparent accounting. Kobalt boasts that it collects over 900,000 distinct royalty payments for artists and songwriters from around the world, without retaining any ownership. Kobalt's clients, whether they are artists, songwriters, indie publishers or indie labels, are able to log in and track every single payment, every single sale and every single stream from around the world. I haven't used Kobalt personally, but just look at Kobalt's roster. It's the who's who of music.

When labels are courting you, they will make a myriad of attractive promises. They'll basically tell you anything they think you want to hear to get you to sign with them. Unless it's written on paper and signed, don't believe anything they say. Joshua Radin signed with Columbia Records because they promised him they could get him a tour with Bob Dylan. That never happened. Luckily he was able to buy himself out of his contract. Most artists aren't that fortunate. Radin said: "The major record companies are dinosaurs, it's impossible to get anything done with them. When I signed with [Columbia], originally it was to my understanding that I would have full creative control of what I released. And they were by no means dropping me; they just said, 'We want a single on here that's gonna make top 40 radio.' And I said, 'I don't do top 40 radio.' I don't listen to anything that's on top 40 radio. At the end of the day you have to be able to sleep and be able to look yourself in the mirror and say, 'I did what I believed in rather than what some guy in a suit in some office in New York believes in.'" Joshua Radin now has a very successful independent music career, regularly touring the world to sold-out theaters. He self-releases his music.

The major labels are multinational corporate conglomerates that must answer to shareholders. The company doesn't care about you or your music. The company cares about making money. Remember, even though you may love the people at the label today, they could be replaced tomorrow. You're not signing with people; you're signing with a company. A corporation. You're signing a 100-plus–page contract. You better know what every word in that thing means or have a damn good lawyer who can explain it all to you.

Now, there are some damn fine independent labels out there that could be a good fit for you. Indies are constantly changing their terms to be more favorable for artists. Unlike the majors, many indies enter into partnerships with their artists and maintain a level of mutual respect. Some indies have even enlisted Kobalt to handle collection and accounting.

Major labels have gotten so desperate to find new ways to make money, now that sales have been declining for so many years, that striking "360 deals" have become commonplace. These deals mean that the label gets a piece of everything: recorded music, touring revenue, merchandise, sponsorships. Their reasoning is that they helped propel you to stardom and deserve a cut of your entire career—not just revenue generated from your recordings. The problem with this is that the label starts dipping into so many areas of your career that you will be left with nothing for yourself.

Unless you want to become a superstar tomorrow, you should not sign with a major label. Period. There's no need. If you follow the steps in this book, you can maintain a successful, money-making independent music career without the fear of being stripped of everything at the drop of a hat.

So, the lists below will help you evaluate whether to sign with an independent label.

Reasons to Sign

- You respect the other acts on the roster.
- The other acts on the roster are similar to you.
- Your visions align.
- You want to get on the radio and the label has a strong track record.
- The term is short enough that you can get out if you're unhappy.
- You maintain ownership of your masters.
- The label isn't touching your publishing.
- The label is dedicating a lot of money to marketing and promotion.
- The label will get you on tour with other artists on the label.
- The label is offering lots of money up front in the form of an advance to record an album.

Reasons Not to Sign

- You are making a fine living without a label.
- You aren't similar to the other acts on the roster.
- You aren't a fan of the other acts on the roster.
- The label doesn't have a track record of success.
- Your visions don't align.
- The term is longer than three years (or 1 album).
- The label wants to own your publishing.
- The label wants to take a piece of nonrecording revenue (like merchandise, touring, crowdfunding, sponsorships).
- Your gut says not to.

HOW TO GET A RECORD DEAL

When Avery Lipman, president of one of the most successful record labels in the world, Universal Republic, was asked the question "How do you get a record deal," he replied, "Don't try to get signed. Try to become popular first."

Once you have become an unstoppable force, labels will come a-knockin'. If you have built up a substantial fanbase (tens of thousands of fans online and/or are selling out clubs around the country), you can hire a lawyer to shop you around at record labels. Or you can find a list of A&R reps on *Music Connection*'s industry contacts list (musicconnection .com/industry-contacts).

PUBLISHING COMPANY

As with record labels, there are major and independent publishing companies. They operate very differently. Major publishing companies (like major labels) will be able to give you the massive advances in the hundreds of thousands of dollars. But they will, in return, own all your songs. More on what publishing royalties are (and how to get them) in Chapter 13.

If you want to write songs for other artists, a publishing company may be a good fit for you. You can get a massive advance so you don't have to worry about money for a long while and just concentrate on writing music. Some of the biggest songwriters in the world today (you know, the zillions of names on Beyoncé, Rihanna, Adele, Carrie Underwood, Toby Keith and Kenny Chesney songs), get paid a bulk amount up front (around $30,000 or so) by the artist's label to cut the song. Many times, these stars will get 50–100 songs submitted by publishers and the artist/label will choose their 10 favorites for the album. Meghan Trainor, Chris Stapleton, Bruno Mars, Carole King, Luke Bryan, Lady Gaga, Hunter Hayes, and Kacey Musgraves all started just as songwriters with publishing deals and wrote songs for other artists before they broke out as featured artists themselves.

I do not recommend signing a publishing deal if you're working on a career as an artist. We will get into how to collect all of your songwriter royalties in Chapter 13. You don't need a traditional publishing company to do this anymore. Yes, of course, many artists also have publishing deals, but like record labels, major publishing companies are very restrictive and require owning your songs.

Publishing companies also have licensing departments where they will work to get songs placed on TV, film, video games and commercials. There are many stand-alone licensing companies that you can work with who do only this and don't own your songs. This is a much better option in this day and age. More on this in Chapter 14.

Reasons to Sign

- You want to write songs for other artists.
- You spend most days writing songs.
- They are offering a huge amount of money up front in the form of an advance.
- You like cowriting.
- You respect the other songwriters on the roster.
- The publishing company has a proven track record.

Reasons Not to Sign

- You want to own your songs.
- You have a career as an artist.
- You don't care for the songs on the roster.
- They aren't offering you an advance.
- Your gut says not to.

HOW TO GET A PUBLISHING DEAL

The big songwriting hubs are L.A. and Nashville. If you want to be a full-time songwriter, you need to live in one of those two cities. So step number one is relocate. Step number two is go out to songwriter nights around town and cowrite with as many people as you possibly can. You'll have to network your a$$ off. You can't just have voice memos on your iPhone of songs you've written. You have to get fully produced demos that sound like they could be on the radio. So if you don't have the production skills to put this together, you're going to need to find a producer or cowriter who does. Once you have a bunch of great-sounding demos, that's when it's time to shop around for a publishing company. Again, you can submit to A&R reps on Music Xray or Fluence or hire a lawyer to get you in the door at publishing companies. However, the more people you meet and write with in L.A. or Nashville, the better your chances are that one of them will have (or soon get) a publishing deal. Songwriters tend to find each other. There isn't a big division between songwriters with a publishing deal and those without. If you're focused on this singular goal, once you're in Nashville or L.A. (and your songs are undeniable hits), you will get a publishing deal. But your songs have to be hits. Publishing companies aren't looking for art songs. Artists write the art songs. If you want to be an employed songwriter, you have to write hits.

You can also find a very good list of publishers on *Music Connection*'s industry contact list (musicconnection.com/industry-contacts).

PUBLICIST

Want to know something startling? Most publicists charge $500–$4,000 a month. And you aren't guaranteed anything. They could get you on *The Tonight Show* and the cover of *Rolling Stone*, plus 50 blog articles, or . . . nothing. Literally nothing. And they're paid the same either way.

Luckily there are some publicists who have changed this model a bit and cater to indie musicians. Some publicists charge per contact. Like $25 per email sent. This takes a lot of trust that she isn't just blindly sending out press releases but actually writing a personalized email to someone with whom she has a good relationship.

That's really what you're paying for with a publicist: the relationships. Anyone can write a press release or send an email. But will your email get opened? That depends on who the sender is. If the publicist is known and respected, most likely she will get a reply. However, there are tons of publicists out there who charge an arm and a leg and literally just blast out press releases to every "music reviewer" on their master list. Let me tell you a little secret. There's this site called Cision, which is a master database containing contact information of anyone a publicist would ever need to contact. My contact info got included on the site (as a writer for Digital Music News and Ari's Take) and I get, on average, five press releases a day. Rarely are these emails personalized to me (other than a "Hi, Ari," which is a program they have set up within their email that inserts "First Name Here"). I feel bad for the bands these publicists are pitching me. 1) I don't review music, so I shouldn't be getting these press releases, and 2) I know that the publicists probably promised these bands that they had connections, relationships and contacts that they don't. Cision costs about $200 a month to subscribe to. Simply having a subscription to the site shouldn't give you the right to say that you actually have these connections. You want the music booker at *Ellen*? You can find it in thirty seconds in a Cision search.

A publicist can definitely help you come up with your story, image, strategy and schedule. But not every publicist will. That should be part of your initial conversation with your potential publicist. If they don't help you come up with a jaw-dropping story, then you shouldn't be paying them a jaw-dropping price.

The artist vōx (born Sarah Winters), shopped around for publicists to push singles for her new project at blogs. The most reasonable (reputable) publicist she found wanted $3,750 for a ten-week campaign—way out of her price range. So she ended up doing her own outreach to bloggers for new singles she released on SoundCloud. From smart research and lots of tweets and emails, she ended up getting huge blogs like *Pigeons & Planes, Consequence of Sound, Interview* magazine, *Nylon* and *KCRW* to run multiple favorable articles, and she ended up charting on Hype Machine, which turned into managers hitting her up requesting meetings. She had more success working PR on her own than any high-priced publicist could have provided—and saved $4K to boot.

Publicists operate on campaigns. Typically they'll require two to four months depending on the project (single, album, music video, tour, release show, benefit concert). And most publicists charge a monthly or campaign fee. The reason publicists need such a large window is because many reviewers need at least a month in advance of the release to cue up and assign stories. And then after the release date it may take another month or so for all stories to filter in. The publicist will want at least a month of lead time (before contacting press) to get all of the materials together, work on your story and PR campaign. So plan ahead. If your release is August 1, start looking for publicists in April.

Reasons to Sign

- She has great ideas on how to craft your story.
- He has a proven track record getting press for acts similar to yours (in size and genre).
- You can afford her.
- He believes in the success of your project.
- She likes your music.
- You are pushing out something newsworthy like an album, tour, benefit concert or music video.

Reasons Not to Sign

- You don't have a headline-worthy event.
- You can't afford her.
- The publicist seems like he wants to work with you for the paycheck.
- She doesn't have a proven track record.
- He won't refer you to clients he's worked with.
- Her promises seem too good to be true.
- His references don't check out.
- Your gut says not to.

HOW TO FIND A PUBLICIST

See *Music Connection*'s great industry lists with contact info at http://www.musicconnection.com/industry-contacts/.

ATTORNEY

When you're ready, it's worth getting a lawyer who is excited about you to shop you around and open the doors you can't open on your own. But don't spend the money on these pursuits until you're ready. Meaning, if you're drawing only 50 people to your local shows and have very low social media engagement and very few mailing list names, you're not ready. If you're selling out 500-cap local clubs, are killing it in at least one avenue of social media, have a solid email list and are starting to tour, it's worth getting on people's radar. What people? Well, that's what you need to figure out. Refer back to your 1-, 5-, 10-, and 26-year goals sheet. What kinds of people do you need to help you get there? Would a booking agent be most beneficial now? An indie label? A major label (we went over this, but if you like playing the lottery . . .)? A manager?

Once you find a good entertainment lawyer, you can contract her out for specific tasks. Or, if you're interested in getting shopped at a label, an invested attorney might take you on for a percentage of the advance—however, with lower advances these days from labels, this might be a bit harder to come by. And remember, nothing is set in stone. Every attorney will operate differently. The young and hungry lawyers, especially, who are innovating in the new industry, may come up with a creative deal that works for you.

Eventually you'll have an attorney on retainer, but this won't come until you're using her services regularly (and, of course, can afford it). So for the time being you'll use lawyers for specific jobs like negotiating contracts, shopping you around and consultations.

HOW TO FIND AN ATTORNEY

Of course, finding an entertainment lawyer referred by someone you trust is best. First, ask around your scene. If you strike out there, check out *Music Connection*'s annual entertainment attorney guide—they have attorneys broken down by state. You can find a PDF of their annual guide online at musicconnection.com/industry-contacts. This is the best list out there. And the magazine is actually worth subscribing to. Full disclosure, they gave my 2014 album a very positive review and I've written a few articles for them (pro bono). But they ain't paying me for the recommendation.

Another option is to check out the Volunteer Lawyers for the Arts. Many states have active programs, (Google "California Lawyers for the Arts") and you can contact them for free legal services.

Not All Lawyers Are Created Equal

After one of my shows at the Hotel Cafe in Hollywood, a guy in his fifties in a button-up shirt, unbuttoned just enough to admire his ample, greying chest hair, walked into the green room and handed me his card. He was an entertainment attorney. He told me he loved my set and was actually there to see the band after me. He told me that if I needed any help to give him a call. The following week I called him to ask a question about the flood of Music Reports Inc. (MRI) letters I was receiving. He explained to me that they were a rights-licensing and royalty-collections company and they were sending me NOIs (Notices of Intent) for their clients to use my songs on their services. I asked him what kinds of royalties do they collect and what rights do they license and for whom. He said these are primarily mechanical royalties. I asked him, "Oh, like from Spotify and Rdio?" He said, "No, mechanical royalties aren't generated from streaming, only sales." Hold up. From speaking with multiple publishing administrators and the Harry Fox Agency (MRI's competitor), I had learned the contrary. (Rdio was actually a client of MRI at the time of this phone call).

I pressed on, "Uh, I could have sworn streaming generated mechanical royalties."

"No, you're mistaken, they don't."

"OK, thanks for the help." I hung up.

He was flat out wrong. He didn't just give bad advice; he was literally incorrect about music facts. This music attorney didn't know basic music law. Granted, sure, when this conversation took place, streaming was still relatively new (this was early 2014), but still, shouldn't an entertainment attorney with a business card that says as much keep up with this stuff?

So, be careful. Just because they have a law degree doesn't mean they're always right.

Oh, and what the hell are mechanical royalties? We'll get into that in Chapter 13.

WHY EVERYTHING YOU THOUGHT ABOUT STREAMING IS WRONG

People have to see the future. Because free already exists. It's a flawed argument when you say "I don't want my music on any services that offers free" when free already exists. You're ignoring the future. Hurricane Katrina is coming and you're staying in the house right now.

—TROY CARTER, ATOM FACTORY, MANAGER FOR
JOHN LEGEND, MEGHAN TRAINOR

We all heard the stories like "My Song Was Played 168 Million Times and All I Got Was $4,000." Yeah, pretty jaw-dropping headline. Except, what you didn't hear about was that these were songwriter royalties, split among multiple writers. And this was from Pandora, a digital radio ("non-interactive") streaming service (which pays much less than "interactive" streaming services like Spotify or Apple Music). The artist actually made much, much more. We all were told over and over again that streaming was going to kill the music industry. Well actually, we were told first that tape recorders were going to kill the industry (because you could simply record the radio). Then it was burning CDs. Then it was downloads and Napster. Then it was Spotify. The thing is, innovations in technology are inevitable. You could fight progress by refusing to put your music on streaming platforms out of sheer principle (ignoring the fact that streaming now actually collectively brings in more money than CD or digital download sales) or you could work with technology, get creative and find new ways to make money with your music career.

Formats change. Price points change. People didn't like paying $18.99 for a full-length CD when they only wanted one song. So when downloads exploded and broke up the album, labels were furious because they couldn't get people to overpay for an album with one good song and ten filler tracks.

People will sacrifice quality for convenience. And pay for it. It's why cassette tapes were widely adapted when vinyl records sounded better. People could play them on the go in their Walkmans and car stereos. CDs were even more convenient (no more flipping sides or fast forwarding to your favorite track) and became popular despite the fact that audiophiles claimed that CDs (initially) sounded worse than cassettes or records. What stopped Napster? iTunes. Why? Because iTunes was more convenient. More reliable. iTunes downloads' sound quality was well below that of CDs (initially iTunes was 128kbps vs. CDs' 1411kbps). If the choice was between driving to the record store and buying a CD or downloading the song you wanted on Napster, people chose the latter. Not because it was free, but because it was easy. But many times the songs were mislabeled and things were not laid out very clearly. That's why iTunes caught on. It was a cheap and easy alternative to free and inconvenient. But what beat iTunes (and nearly killed piracy once and for all)? Spotify. Even more convenient.

We're never going back to downloads. Just like we're never going back to cassettes or vinyl (or flip phones). Yes, there's been a massive vinyl resurgence over the past few years, but it will never come close to its 1970s peak.

Withholding music from streaming because it doesn't earn as much as downloads is like a farmer refusing to sell eggs because they don't earn as much as the chicken. Sure, it may not make as much money *today*, but it will tomorrow. And the fact of the matter is, people want eggs, they don't want chickens.

Withholding your music from streaming platforms is the worst possible thing you could do to your career. Music fans have put their love of streaming platforms over their love of artists (unfortunately). If your music is not on Spotify and your fans are, they will move on to another artist. They will not go download your album for $10 when they can get nearly every other artist on the planet for $10 a month.

The alternative to streaming is not sales. The alternative to streaming is piracy. When Taylor Swift famously pulled all of her music from Spotify for her 2014 album,*1989,* you know what the #1 album on The Pirate Bay (the largest illegal downloading site at the time) was? You guessed it, *1989.*

Yes, Adele "windowed" her most recent releases, keeping them off of streaming services for a window of time. But you can't model an independent music career off of a major label artist's career. Not to mention that Adele's fans are a very specific (older) demographic of people who are used to paying for music. And Adele (well, her label Columbia) had the team to make sure her music was kept off of YouTube and piracy services. Unless you have a high-tech team with a multinational corporation on your side, you aren't going to prevent people from finding your album online for free if they want it.

And withholding your music from streaming services is extremely shortsighted. Remember, do not make decisions for your music career based on your bottom line (today). What do your fans want? If you alienate them by forcing them to consume music in a way that doesn't make sense to them, they won't stick with you.

Streaming eliminates piracy.

In 2009, 80% of Norway's population under 30 were illegally downloading music. In 2014 (after most of the under-30 population had adopted streaming), only 4% of Norway's under-30 population still used illegal file sharing platforms to get ahold of music. And 75% of Norway's recorded music industry now comes from streaming services. In the United States, over 50% of the recorded music industry now comes from streaming (Spotify launched in the U.S. three years after Norway).

Streaming is great for art. Streaming rewards artists for creating great music that fans want to play over and over. There's much more potential for the long tail. The more someone likes your album, the more she will play it. And you will get paid for every play. Over time, this will earn you *more* money than sales ever did.

We are nearing the end of owning data. It's pretty much already here for most under the age of 30. Who wants to clutter up their hard drives with files if they don't have to? That's why everything is moving to the cloud. Eventually, devices won't need to store any data natively because everything will be accessible at all times within the cloud and connectivity will be uninterrupted and ubiquitous.

There is a generational gap in ideology. Boomers cherish ownership and value things. Millennials embrace sharing and value experiences. Since boomers run the music industry and Millennials run the tech industry, there has been an ongoing battle for clarity.

One thing is for certain, you can't wait around for these two opposing forces to come to an understanding. You must move your career forward and exist in the realities of the day.

FANS AREN'T GOING TO PAY FOR MUSIC ANYMORE—AND THAT'S OK

It's almost a rite of passage every artist goes through in the modern music industry. The moment he accepts that he will not be able to rely on music sales to sustain his career. That people are not buying music like they used to. And never will again.

Just a few years ago it seemed like every artist was passing around articles chastising fans for illegally downloading music. How it hurts the bands. The producers. The session musicians. The labels. The songwriters. And the industry as a whole. We all remember the "illegally downloading music is the same as stealing a microwave from a store" argument. We all bought it. Well, musicians and the industry, that is. Fans? Not so much.

Since 2001, sales of recorded music have continued to drop like an anchor in a sea ruled by pirates. We have to start embracing alternative monetization opportunities and accept that the traditional way that fans support artists is over.

It's time for a new mindset. It's a new era. People *are* valuing artists—but in the way that makes sense to them (not the current industry talking heads and classic rockers screaming the loudest). What's wrong with a 23-year-old who loves a band paying $250 for a PledgeMusic exclusive, $5 per video released on Patreon, $35 a year on Bandcamp to be part of the fan club, an $18 ticket for their concert, a $25 t-shirt and a backstage "experience" for $50, but never download an album or buy a CD? What's wrong with that?

Fans aren't going to pay for recorded music anymore. But that doesn't mean they won't pay you for making music.

The album gets the fan in the door. Gets her hooked. The album is only the introduction. No longer the end game. The album is the gateway. And the album is found online, for free, with a couple clicks.

And major label artists never made much from album sales anyways. They always had to rely on alternative sources of income (like touring and merch) to offset what their labels didn't pay them in royalties. Lyle Lovett admitted that after selling over 4.6 million records he has received $0 in record royalties from his label. But he's had a very successful career. Why are people silent when record companies (legally) steal from artists, but raise hell when fans do it?

> I've never made a dime from a record sale in the history
> of my record deal. I've been very happy with my sales,
> and certainly my audience has been very supportive.
> I make a living going out and playing shows.
> —LYLE LOVETT

So, your options. You can either b*&ch about the "decline of the music industry," exclaim that fans aren't true fans if they don't pay for recorded music, *or* you can get creative, embrace the new technologies that build on the artist-fan relationship, and lead the pack in this beautiful new world full of alternative revenue sources. Your choice.

3.

RECORDING

A musician running software from Native Instruments can recreate, with astonishing fidelity, the sound of a Steinway grand piano played in a Vienna concert hall, or hundreds of different guitar amplifier sounds, or the Mellotron protosynthesizer that the Beatles used on "Strawberry Fields Forever." These sounds could have cost millions to assemble 15 years ago; today, you can have all of them for a few thousand dollars.

—STEVEN JOHNSON, *NEW YORK TIMES*

If you do something different, you excel a little faster.

—RIKI LINDHOME, GARFUNKEL AND OATES

I'M GOING TO START OFF THE RECORDING CHAPTER WITH THE LEAST COOL thing to talk about. You're going to have a knee-jerk reaction. Your blood pressure is going to rise. You're going to want to fight me. Don't say I didn't warn you. But hear me out. It's important.

Before you begin the writing process for the album, and definitely before you start recording, you need to think of what's called in the marketing world Product Market Fit (PMF). Stay with me. Don't let your eyes glaze over. I'm going to explain this as musicianly as possible. What Product Market Fit means is, do you have a product (music) that fits a market (fans). Simple, right? This seems like a no-brainer. And, of course, you probably just rolled your eyes and exclaimed loudly, *"Yes!"* Apologize to your neighbors in the coffee shop.

But, step back for a moment. Before you start the writing-recording process, you should know *exactly* who your fans are and what the purpose of this recording is. Most bands just make albums for themselves without thinking twice about it and wonder why they can't get anyone to listen and share it.

I know you think all you have to do is make "good music" and the fans will find you. But that couldn't be further from the truth. For one thing, "good" is obviously subjective. You probably think half the bands on the charts today are sh*t. But, clearly, others think they're incredible.

So, again, before starting the writing-recording process, make a document entitled "Our Fans." You should have a minimum of 20 points on this list. The more the merrier. It could look something like this:

Our fans('):

1) Are primarily male.
2) Are between the ages of 22 and 35.
3) Listen to KCRW, The Current and World Cafe Live.
4) Listen to podcasts like *WTF, How Did This Get Made?, Startup* and *The Nerdist.*
5) Favorite bands of the past decade include Alabama Shakes, the Black Keys, Cage the Elephant, Jack White, and Dawes.
6) Favorite bands from previous decades include Led Zeppelin, the Ramones, Nirvana and Pearl Jam.
7) Hang out in local coffee shops.
8) Read nonfiction philosophy books.
9) Wear leather coats, black jeans and boots.
10) Attend SXSW, Lollapalooza, FYF, and Governor's Ball music festivals.

11) Eat mostly local, organic foods.

12) Are early adopters of tech.

13) Are college-educated and probably studied philosophy or English.

14) Buy lots of vinyl.

15) Wear trucker hats.

16) Take public transportation whenever possible or own secondhand cars.

17) Shop in thrift stores.

18) Drink at bars like the Fat Dog, BLB, Herkimer and Liquor Lyles.

19) Eat at restaurants like Uptown Diner, Muddy Waters, Jitlada, Hunan Cafe.

20) Live in cities like Silver Lake, Los Feliz, Uptown Minneapolis, Portland, Williamsburg.

21) Favorite TV shows include *True Detective, The Sopranos, Last Week Tonight, The Wire, Better Call Saul.*

22) Favorite movies include *Love and Mercy, Citizen Four,* Wes Anderson movies, Christopher Nolan movies, Quentin Tarantino movies, the *Godfather* movies, *Back to the Future, A Clockwork Orange, Fight Club* and *Casino.*

Now, of course, 100% of your fans will not meet each point. Your fan base is a Venn diagram of interests.

Understanding who the majority of your (prospective) fans are will help you craft your sound, image, merch and overall marketing and promotion.

I know it's hard to hear how calculated you have to be. The labels do this. They know who they're targeting. You're competing with them.

In 2015, in advance of the release of *25,* Nielsen (commissioned by Columbia Records) did a study of who fans of Adele are and they found (unsurprisingly) that more than half of them are women, most of whom are aged 25–44. But they also found, among other things, that most of them:

- Have children.
- Play soccer.
- Shop at Victoria's Secret.
- Drink Aquafina bottled water.
- Drink light beer.

Adele wouldn't release a song expounding the joys of a childless life. And she probably shouldn't bash soccer moms. Unless she wants to alienate 80% of her audience. Sure, this is inherent to who she is, and she probably didn't break out this study before the recording process, like I'm telling you to do, but she has a label to worry about these things. You don't.

To help you figure out what kind of music you want to record and release, what kind of fans you want to gain and what kind of career you want to have, you should think about these things before you lay down a click track.

If you want to get on top 40 radio, you have to understand what top 40 radio sounds like. You have to sound like that. If you want to get your songs placed in commercials, film and TV, you have to know the *sound* of songs that are getting placed the most.

Above all, you need to be thinking about your story. What is going to lead off your press release for this album? Are you getting over a tragedy? Is this album mostly about that? Did your band's van roll off the road on your last tour and you all ended up in the hospital but recovered and made an album about the experience? If you decided to make a full-length album (and not just singles or an EP), why? What is it about? The only reason to make a full-length album in this day and age is if you're making a statement. So what's the statement?

You can always update your story for each album. Or as often as necessary. As often as you evolve. But you always need that story that sets you apart.

The story is public. Your PMF research is private.

The best producers in the world analyze other successful producers' techniques. You need to analyze other successful artists' writing, recording and performing techniques, along with their image, personas and swagger. Every successful artist has a swagger. It's sexy. It's their own. And it's awesome.

All of this, when discussing recording, seems cold, calculated and unnatural. But it doesn't have to be. Of course, you're going to create music "true to yourself." But this could go in a million different directions. The song you heard in the bar last night influenced you whether you want to admit it or not.

So, do your research. Make a playlist of songs that you'll use as inspiration for your upcoming album. What is going to be the *sound* of the album? It will be a combination of all of your influences, of course, but get active with this process. Study what makes these songs great. Is it the guitar tones? The pocket? The hooks? The lyrics? The vocals? The groove? The syncopation? The raw passion? Once you've pinpointed what makes these songs great, then ask why? Why is the pocket so strong? Is it because ?uestlove and Pino Palladino are the rhythm section? Why are the lyrics great? Is it because they tell a story? What kind of story? And how do they tell the story? Is it literal? Metaphorical?

Remember, when reviewers talk about your music, they will talk about your story. They will not discuss these musical elements, because most music reviewers aren't musicians. They aren't going to say "the drummer lays back on the beat, the syncopated horn hits punctuate the Hammond B-3 riffs." The musical elements that you and I get off to, music reviewers don't typically articulate. Of course, these techniques are important. You will perfect these in studio. But, never lose track of what the majority of the listening public will pay attention to: *the story behind the music.* Just getting great players on your album is not a story.

But, don't sacrifice quality because you don't think the majority will notice. Fellow musicians will notice and will or will not work with you based on the sound of your record. Do not make your music for the lowest common denominator. You must create great art first and foremost. Because if your product is not great, then your story doesn't matter.

GETTING INTO THE MUSICAL HEADSPACE

The best art divides an audience. If you put out a record and
half the people who hear it absolutely love it and half the
people who hear it absolutely hate it you've done well.
Because it's pushing that boundary. If everyone thinks
"aw that's pretty good," why bother making it?
—RICK RUBIN

Once you know your PMF and are comfortable with the style of music you're going to make, you need to turn back into the artist. You can't write great songs with your business cap on. You need a clear head and an open heart to write songs that are meaningful to you and will connect with an audience.

Much of this book maintains the basic premise that your music is great. Music, of course, is subjective. A piece of music you absolutely love, others absolutely hate. That's what makes art great. But just because you believe your music is great doesn't make it so.

It takes a lot of failure to make great art. Andy Grammer wrote 100 songs before he wrote his top 10 smash hit "Honey, I'm Good." He said: "The first 50 that I wrote, I'm just being blatantly honest, I was trying to write a hit, and to me, when I listen back to all of them, they sound super sh*tty. They sound like a guy who is really scared and trying to write a hit. So then the next 50 were a process of me finding my way back to my genuine point of view."

And that's what you're trying to find: your genuine point of view. Whether you write pop, folk, soul, electronica, hip-hop, R&B, rock, metal or some hybrid of them all, people will only connect to your music if it's authentic. True to you. Whoever you are. It really doesn't matter what the music sounds like. It can be polished. It can be raw. It can be low-fi, high-fi. It can be recorded in a world-class studio or in your bedroom. It just needs to be honest. Authentic.

INSPIRATION QUESTS

You need to be inspired to create great art. Art cannot be forced. And inspiration doesn't just show up either. Inspiration is always inspired. Wait, what? Yes, you can create inspiration by embarking on Inspiration Quests.

Sitting at home all day every day pressuring yourself to create great art is the worst thing you can do. During your writing process, make sure you have an Inspiration Quest of some sort every day. Go out into the world. Go on a hike. Walk to a coffee shop and journal. Smoke a jay and actively listen to music. Go to the gym. Meditate. Do yoga. Go to a concert. Go to an art gallery. Go see a movie. Watch a TV show (this may seem like procrastination, but my biggest song to date came from watching a *Grey's Anatomy* episode—don't judge). Appreciating other kinds of art will inspire your own art.

Julia Cameron advises in *The Artist's Way* to journal a stream of consciousness every morning to get the creative juices flowing. She calls these "morning pages." This process can definitely help if you're feeling blocked.

Your Inspiration Quests can be anything *but* working on your art or your business. Because most of your life will be consumed by one of these two activities, your Inspiration Quests are a shift in your mind and your heart. Allow yourself to be open to things that have nothing to do with music.

And be careful with these. Home in on only positive IQs. Don't break up with the love of your life to get inspiration for your new album. That's a Destructive Inspiration Quest. It may work in the short term, but you will be miserable for the rest of your life. No matter how great the art you create, your overall happiness is more important. Don't ever lose track of that.

Right now, set the book down, and make a list of 20 Inspiration Quests and make a point to go on at least 3 a week. Keep this list open. It's a living document. Continue to update it with new ideas. And continue to explore. When you're in your writing mode, you may need more IQs, when you're on tour, you may get fewer. On your iCal or Google Cal or whatever synched digital calendar you use, make a new calendar, give it a color and schedule these in. Get an invite to a concert? Make that calendar event your IQ color. It counts. You don't need to go out of your way for every IQ. If you naturally explore outside of your daily routine, fantastic. Going to your day job, however, does not count. Because, let's be honest. How inspiring is that really?

ACTIVE WRITING SESSIONS

Creativity is the ability to take a risk. To put yourself on the line and actually risk ridicule. The creative process often takes place outside of your ego.

—STING

Fear and creativity are conjoined twins. People are so afraid of their fear that they try to kill it. And when they kill it they also kill creativity because creativity is going into the unknown, and the unknown is scary.

—ELIZABETH GILBERT, *EAT, PRAY, LOVE*

> Practice doesn't make you perfect but it does help you stop
> thinking that you have to be.
>
> —GUY RAZ, HOST *TED RADIO HOUR*, NPR

> If you're not prepared to be wrong you'll never
> come at anything original.
>
> —SIR KEN ROBINSON, AUTHOR, TED SPEAKER,
> INTERNATIONAL ADVISOR ON EDUCATION IN THE ARTS

At some point, you need to channel that newfound inspiration into the actual writing. The creation. You can't continue searching until you're struck with the perfect song idea. Just sit down and start a song. If you've gone on Inspiration Quests, the ideas will flow once you're in your studio holding your guitar.

Unfortunately most artists can't spend all of their time creating art. Even major label artists with full teams around them still need to work at the business of their careers in addition to creating their art. Every artist needs to dedicate Active Writing Sessions. Most major label artists still maintain the traditional schedule of creating a full-length album, touring on it for two years and then spend the third year writing the next album. Indie artists don't operate this way. You should be constantly in and out of Active Writing Sessions. When you're not on tour or working on a new album, try to spend at least one day a week actively writing. Not every song you write will be gold, actually most will suck. If Andy Grammer, a chart-topping songwriter, had to write a hundred songs before he landed on the hit single, why do you think you can land on your hit at the first go? So keep writing. And don't worry about writing the best songs ever written, just write *your* best songs. To bring Rick Rubin back into it, he said: "If you're competing only with yourself it's a more realistic place to be. If you say I don't want to write songs unless I can write songs better than the Beatles, it's a hard road. But if you say I want to write a better song tomorrow than the song I wrote yesterday, that's something that can be done."

THE NEW STUDIO

It's no secret that great-sounding records these days are created in home studios. Owl City (Adam Young) was one of the first artists to break mainstream with a self-recorded album (which he recorded in his parents' basement). Sure, his label got world-class mixing engineers to mix the album, but Young recorded nearly everything himself with equipment he purchased on his own before his record deal.

You don't need to invest hundreds of thousands of dollars in your recording like you did twenty years ago. Even Miley Cyrus spent only about $50,000 on her 23-track (self-released, self-funded) album she did with the Flaming Lips. This would have been unthinkable even just ten years ago.

As we touched on in "The New Team" (Chapter 2), it's ideal if you can have your own recording setup in a "light switch" studio (a studio that is always set up and only needs to be turned on). This will enable you to record your rehearsals, demos, new song ideas and (potentially) official releases quick and easily.

The more you record, the better you will get at it. The more producers and engineers you work with, the more knowledge you will gain. Maybe someone in your band studied recording engineering and production in school. Maybe you're studying this right now. Fantastic! Build your own light switch studio and get to work. But also, take every opportunity you can to attend other studio sessions with producers and engineers who are more experienced than you. You will always learn something. Never get comfortable (or arrogant) with your recording techniques. There is always something to be learned. There is always room for improvement.

If you're like me and don't want to devote the time, money, energy and effort into building your own studio, then build up relationships with people in your scene who will work with you, regularly, on the cheap. Of course, pay them as much as you can afford, but when you're getting started, you won't be able to afford the best. Many up-and-coming producers and engineers are willing to work on the cheap (or for trades) to build their résumé. Start with your local scene.

However, if you're in a small community and there are literally no talented producers and engineers to work with, check out SoundBetter.com, AirGigs.com and Fiverr.com. These are online marketplaces of professionals offering their services remotely. You can record your album on your own and find an L.A.-based Grammy winner on SoundBetter to mix it. That's what the Tanzanian-based musician Geeva did. Need a violinist, drummer or singer for your project? These platforms have a plethora of them with full résumés and recordings. They will record their parts in their studios and email you the full WAV files.

If you decide to build your studio from scratch, you can learn everything you need to know about recording from YouTube.

HOW YOU CAN GET ANYONE IN THE WORLD TO WORK ON YOUR ALBUM

The most important thing you need to know going into the recording process is this: It doesn't matter *who* works on it, it matters *what* the finished product sounds like.

So many bands get approached by "big time" producers with their long lists of big-time credits who explain they will give you the privilege to work with them—for a fee, of course. An *enormous* fee, at that. Lucky you.

Don't take the bait.

You can get virtually anyone to work on your project and record in virtually any studio in the world if you can pay for it. And don't be fooled by these for-hire producers' credits. Fact-check them on AllMusic.com. If they're approaching you as a producer, but they were only a drum tech on one of their "big time" album credits, it's definitely not a good indication of their expertise. Where you record and with whom does not guarantee stardom. It doesn't even necessarily give you a leg up.

WHO DO I NEED TO GET TO DO THIS THING? HOW MUCH SHOULD I PAY THEM? WHAT ARE THE STEPS?

If this is your first recording or 500th, there are simple steps you can take to make sure you create the absolute best-sounding album for a very low cost.

Preproduction

This is an incredibly important aspect of your recording process. Maybe even the most important step. Working out as much as you possibly can before you step into the studio (on the clock) will save you a tremendous amount of money. You want to rehearse the studio version of your songs to the point where you could play them in your sleep. Get the arrangements locked in. There should be no debate about how to get out of the bridge when you're tracking. Have your guitar or keyboard player and singer record scratch tracks to the click (of the exact BPM you will use for the song). Write the tempo BPMs down for every song, so when the engineer opens the first song on day one, all you have to do is tell him "this song is called 'Maybe' and the BPM is 132." Don't waste time figuring out tempos in the studio. You should figure out what program the studio is using (Pro Tools, Logic) and if you can, record the scratch tracks in that program so all the engineer has to do is dump in those tracks. You'll most likely do much of the preproduction with your producer before hitting the studio.

PRODUCER

This is the most important person for your project. When you're seeking out producers, the first check you need to make is the gut check. Don't hire a producer before having an informal meeting, lunch, jam, whatever. This person will be with you every step of the way. You guys need to get along. You need trust. You need to know that she *gets* your project, your songs, your band. Figure out what her favorite albums are. Listen to some past records she's produced. Some producers will even offer to track one test song with you from start to finish for free. If you're on the fence about this producer, take her up on it—even if it's just in her home studio. It's worth it to get a feel for how she works and to see how well you vibe. You don't want to step into a $700-a-day studio and start fighting with this producer. Not only will it mess up the overall vibe, you'll waste a ton of money.

"Producer" is a broad term. Rick Rubin, one of the most successful (and versatile) producers of all time, was asked by Tim Ferriss on his #1-ranked business podcast, "What do producers do?" Rubin responded "I honestly don't know. I can tell you what I do." That's the thing, every producer operates differently.

There are a thousand different producers out there, but most fall into one of four categories.

The Beat-Maker

The beat-making producer typically creates and mixes an entire electronic instrumental production on her computer and has the top line artist (the singer or rapper) come in when the track is completely finished. Some of these beat-makers sell these "beats" online. There are many marketplaces where you can purchase fully produced tracks from these beat-making producers. Most offer various price points based on the use. If you want the track exclusively (meaning, no one else can use it), it costs much more. Some will offer "tracked out" downloads, which contain every track in the mix so you can alter the mix if so desired. Want to mute the bass on verse two? You need the "tracked out" version to do this. Some restrict the number of downloads you can sell. Some beat-makers want to retain the rights, but will "lease" the beat to you to use commercially. And some will require credit to be given. Many producers embed self-managed audio stores like myFlashStore.net, Sound-Click, RocBattle, PMPWorldwide and TunePort directly to their website to sell their beats. You can Google "buy beats" and find a bunch of marketplaces selling instrumental productions ranging in price from about $15 to a few thousand dollars.

But, be careful. Make sure the beats you're buying are 100% original. Any samples used either need to be Loops from within a recording program (all professional recording programs like Logic allow you to use their royalty-free Loops and samples), or recorded by the producer. Unless you get explicit permission (in writing) to use a recording (sample) from the owner (label or artist), you can't use it. Not 6 seconds of it. Not 2 seconds of it. Not 4 bars. These are all myths. Good rule of thumb: *If you didn't record it, you must get permission to use it.*

The Guru

The guru-producer is the guide. She has a network of diverse musicians and chooses the right ones for the project. She may not be a gearhead or know the shortcuts in Pro Tools, but works with her go-to engineers. She has relationships at the best studios in town at every price point. She is there every step of the way and manages every step of the process from preproduction through final mastering.

The Songwriter

The songwriter-producer cares less about creating a "sound" and more about getting the best possible song. This producer primarily works in the folk world. She has her go-to engineers who know all the technical aspects of the recording process. She doesn't typically take many production risks (you're not going to create the next Kid A with a songwriter-producer), but she does what's best for the song.

The All-In Producer

Today, the all-in producer is the most common producer out there. He typically has a home studio and will do the tracking, mixing and mastering himself. He knows how to create beats if need be and has a strong command over sound-mimicking software like Native Instruments and Alicia's Keys. He is a multi-instrumentalist and can play every instrument for a basic production (or create the necessary sounds via his MIDI programs). He helps craft the sound and direction of the project and respects the power of the song (not just the beat). He is a part of the process from start to finish and works very quickly.

The thing that all producers have in common is they are idea people. They understand what it takes to craft a production to make it sound a certain way. Many producers, like Max Martin and Dr. Luke, have distinct "sounds." Everything they touch is stamped with their trademark sound. Others, like Rick Rubin, aren't defined by genre or instrumentation.

Every producer's main goal, no matter which category he falls into, is to bring out the artist's best. Whether he is creating the entire production "in the box" (completely on the computer) or working with a 10-piece rock band, gospel choir and symphonic orchestra, the producer is there for the artist.

The producer is the architect. The artist is the homeowner.

How Much Do Producers Cost?

Of course, like everything, there is a range. Some will work on an hourly, daily or all-in basis. Their rate depends on their skill level and experience. Many "all-in" producers in L.A. charge about $50 an hour or $300 for a 10-hour day. If you're a more established artist and have a track record of heavy sales/streams or high-paying synch placements, you can negotiate a percentage of revenue. Like, $300 up front, all-in for a single, plus 20% of all revenue over $10,000. The $10,000 bench mark is so you don't have to pay out $2 checks every four months if the song doesn't make much money. But if it makes $10,000, you pay your producer from dollar one. So, if he's making 20%, he gets $2,000 for $10,000 gross song revenue. Often times, the song won't sell much but gets placed in a commercial for $200,000. (Yes, this happens to indie artists all the time. More on this in Chapter 14.)

How to Find a Producer

As I stated a couple pages back, you can get virtually anyone to work on your record if you pay them. Start by gathering up your favorite all-time records (of the last twenty years, as earlier guys may be out of the game . . . or dead). Also gather up your favorite local records. Get a full credits list for all these records. You're mainly looking for the producer, since all other people will be worked out with you and your producer (you don't want to lock anyone else in before you lock in your producer). You can find most credits on Allmusic.com. For the local records you may actually need to Facebook the artist and ask. They'll be flattered.

Once you have this list of producers, track down contact info (a Google search should be sufficient or the *Music Connection* list has many contacts [musicconnection.com/industry-contacts]) and send one a pitch email. Start with your first choices and work down the list. You should have one great-sounding demo of your best new song (don't send a crappy board feed from a live concert). Spend a couple hundred bucks to record a demo if you need to. Open the email with *specific* praise for her past projects. Ask her if she would be willing to work with you and what her rates are for a 10-song album (or whatever). Again, this will start the conversation. If she says "$10,000 is my rate for 10 songs, and I have hookups at studios and engineers to get us good deals on the rest," don't be afraid to write back and tell her your exact recording budget and ask if she can be flexible. No sweat off your back if you give her $15,000 to handle everything (studio, players, engineers) or give her $10,000 and you pay the rest directly.

Producers will pitch you their ideal rate for an indie record. Don't be scared off by the high price tag. If they pitch you $20,000 but you only have $15,000 budgeted for the entire record, feel free to write back and see if they will work with you for $10,000. Don't worry about insulting them. If they don't have any projects right now, they will consider your counteroffer. But remember, always have a meeting with them first before you agree to anything. Ask if they would consider tracking a test song.

THE RECORDING STUDIO

As with the producer, it doesn't matter how successful the previous projects that were recorded in this studio are; it matters that you like the sound of the albums. Sure, it's a fun tidbit to include in the album's press release, but at the end of the day all that matters is what your album sounds like. I recommend getting a studio with a great-sounding live room to record drums at a minimum if you're creating a big rock or pop sound. You don't need a state-of-the-art studio to track vocals. You need a good vocal mic and an isolation booth. That's it. But you do need a good-sounding live room to get good-sounding drums. The vibe of the studio is also very important, as are the house engineers, who will have the first hands on your project. While your drummer is tracking, you're going to be hanging out in the control room for hours on end. You want to make sure this room is comfortable. It should be bursting with energy to encourage inspiration, but also should be calming enough when you need some relaxation (or have a lounge that you can retreat to).

The ways studios get bands to block out multiple days, if not weeks, for their sessions are by offering top-notch gear, a vibey space and great amenities (coffee, fridge, Pac-Man, pool tables, couches, Nintendo). If you want to experiment with amps, drums, pianos, Rhodes, organs and guitars, then it may be worth it to find a studio with a plethora of these choices.

Get the mic and outboard gear list (most studios will have all of this info on their website) and do some research. Discuss with your producer what gear and mics are best for your project.

The studio's console is also a selling feature. Neve consoles populate some of the most well-known studios in the world, like Abbey Road, Electric Lady, Capitol, The Terrarium and Ocean Way. The Neve 8028 was the console that Dave Grohl went through such trouble purchasing and transporting to his home studio from the old Sound City studios where Nirvana recorded *Nevermind*. Because of Pro Tools and Logic, most sessions aren't actually mixed through the consoles anymore, but it's nice to run as many of the instruments through the console for warmth and vibe. It was fun to say most of the instruments on my album were run through the same console that John Lennon's "Imagine" was run through. But don't spend additional money to stay in that studio just for the console—99.99% of your listening audience will not be able to hear these nuances.

If your producer has a decent home studio with a few excellent mics and great outboard gear, and you're comfortable with all of the gear your band has, then all you need to do is spend a couple days in an expensive studio to track drums, then you can move to your producer's home studio to track everything else. Your vocals are going to sound nearly identical run through a U47 at your producer's home as they would in the big studio.

ENGINEER

This is the guy who runs Pro Tools/Logic and other digital audio workstations (DAW) at the studio. He sets up all the mics (after discussion with the producer). Some engineers will tune the drums. A good engineer will have the session open and ready (BPMs plugged in along with the scratch tracks) and have the room set up with all the mics you'll need for that day, before you arrive. He'll know the ins and outs of the studio (how to blow into the Mario cartridge to get it to work), the trick to get the pizza oven to not burn, to make the best cup of coffee and which amps need just the right tap on the left corner to get the sound you need. Some producers always work with the same engineers. On big sessions there will be the producer (who usually won't set up any mics or touch Pro Tools), her favorite engineer to run Pro Tools and set up mics, the studio's house engineer (to be the project engineer's assistant), studio interns to make coffee and wash dishes, and various drum/guitar techs. Small sessions will have just a producer (who covers everything above and more— except dishes: that will then be the drummer's job, clearly).

Mixing Engineer

Do not overlook the importance of your mixing engineer. Great mixing engineers can take a pile of sh*t and turn it into top 40 gold. You know the saying "You can't polish a turd"? Well, great mixing engineers actually can. Getting the right mixing engineer is almost more important than the producer, engineer and studio.

Mastering Engineer

My last solo record was mastered by Bernie Grundman and before that there was Scott Hull and before that Greg Calbi. These are big names. And they cost a lot. I didn't hire them to master my records because they've won Grammys (they have) or because they have countless platinum records on their walls (they do). I honestly couldn't care less about that. I hired them to master my records because they are the best at what they do.

In the world of mastering, there are only a handful of greats out there. And mastering is incredibly important, even though it's one of the most elusive parts of the recording process. But mastering can dictate the overall vibe and feel of a record. So it's important.

Mastering is the final step of the process. It gives it the sparkle that truly brings the track to life. Mastering brings out the highs and the lows and typically makes the entire track louder. Different genres demand different degrees of loudness. You won't master a jazz record the same way you'd master a pop record. Pop is typically mastered as loud as you can possibly get. In mastering, typically the louder you get, the more compressed the track. It's a trade-off. And only the truly exceptional mastering engineers with years of experience can keep a track open and big and bring up the volume without distortion or noticeable compression. If you get the chance to listen to unmastered final mixes and final masters (done by a professional) I highly recommend this. If nothing more, to train your ears.

Make sure you leave a budget for mastering. Heavyweights charge $2–4K per album (for indie projects) or $200–$400 a track. Some mas-

tering engineers offer deals at slow times of the year. It may be worth calling them and asking if they do and when. Some will give you discounts
depending on your situation. They'll send you a rate, but you can start the
conversation from there. Some will budge, some won't. You don't need
the best in the world, but get someone great. Some mixing engineers can
also master. But, many swear by the rule that the person who mixes the
track should not master it. Fresh set of ears. That sort of thing.

Similarly, listen to the records they have mastered and see if it's appropriate for your project. For instance, Greg Calbi's coworker (down the
hall at Sterling Sound) Ted Jensen is also one of the greats; however, he
masters in a complete opposite style from Calbi. Calbi's records feel like
a lavender massage; Jensen's feel like a knockout punch to the face. It's all
what you're going for.

What About Mastering Programs?

The most popular instant mastering platform on the market is currently
Landr.com. You can basically upload your final mixes to their site, hit a
button, and Landr's algorithm will master your track in minutes. You
can master your entire album for about $40 (a fraction of what the pros
charge). Does it get the job done? Will it replace high-priced mastering
engineers? Well, it's an option. If you're on a tight budget, it's definitely
worth exploring. Landr was initially built for DJs creating electronic
music regularly. It wasn't built for bands creating full-length albums
every couple years. That's why they started with a monthly price versus a
per-track price. So, naturally, it will work better for electronic artists than
for bands.

As producer, DJ, mastering engineer (and blogger) Brian Hazard put
it: "The algorithm will get better over time, but it can never replace a professional mastering engineer, because it lacks musical understanding.

"It can't know whether occasional high frequency bursts are vocal sibilants that demand de-essing, or cymbal crashes. It can't tell if the excess energy at 200 Hz is the characteristic warmth of a rich fretless bass, or vocal mud that needs to be cut. It doesn't even know what genre your track is in. One size fits all.

"Most importantly, it can't tell you to go back and fix your mix!

"When I hear a problem best addressed in the mix, I ask the client for changes. That applies to everything from excessive sub bass to thin guitar tone to ultrasonic synth spikes to questionable vocal intonation. Maybe it's coincidence, but my clients' mixes tend to get better with every release."

Having a great album can bring you to the next level of your career. But once you have the album mastered, your work has only just begun.

THE HOME STUDIO

If you're interested in building up a home studio, great! It's actually not as hard as it seems. But it will take a lot of time and some money. You'll either need to invest in a recording school and work alongside knowledge-able instructors to help guide your process, or spend hundreds of hours on blogs, YouTube tutorials and in your home studio working out the kinks and learning how to make it work.

4.

THE RELEASE

OH, HOW THE TIMES HAVE CHANGED. TRADITIONALLY, LABELS WOULD release a full-length album once every three years for an artist. The album was preceded by the lead single and an accompanying music video. And once the album was out, every few months a new single would be pushed at radio.

Most major labels still operate this way—despite the changing times. You should not approach your release the same way major labels do. For one, you don't have the bank account they do. NPR revealed that Def Jam spent over $1 million to create, market and release just one Rihanna song. You can't compete with that.

But what you have that the labels don't is an ability to try and fail. Quickly. You can change course if something's not working without worrying that you're going to hurt a record exec's ego. You can come up with creative promotional strategies that have never been tried before without running it up the chain of command.

THE POWER OF VIDEO

Have you noticed how Facebook has become mostly videos? Remember when it was just status updates?

Unfortunately, most people are much more willing to watch a video than listen to a song. You can't just release a recording anymore. A video should accompany every song. Every time.

I know I just turned your world completely upside down.

YouTubers figured this out early on.

You don't need to make a $10,000 music video for every song (or even one music video that costs that much), but you must create a video for each song. Whether it's a lyric video, performance video or music video (or all three), you need a video for every song. Artists (and labels) missed this boat early on. In the early days of YouTube, traditional artists only put up official music videos. But fans made lyric videos. Sometimes, these fan-made lyric videos became more popular than the artist's official music video—especially if the lyric video predated the artist-uploaded music video. Bruno Mars's "When I Was Your Man" fan-made lyric video got over 100,000,000 views. Talk about missed revenue. Had WMG (Bruno Mars's label) uploaded this video first and monetized it, they would have made much more money on the ad revenue than monetizing it after the fact on the fan's channel.

So, if you'd like to control your video presence (and make the greatest amount of money), be first. Be consistent. Be active.

HOW TO CREATE A GREAT-LOOKING MUSIC VIDEO ON A TINY BUDGET

Most of the time if you do a video, unless it's a Kanye West video
or something, it doesn't have a real shoot. You scrape together a
little bit of money and go out and do something.
—BEN FOLDS

It's hard to look good on camera. And it has nothing to do with your looks. The act of lip synching (and acting on cue) is incredibly unnatural.

But then again, so is performing onstage in front of a bunch of people. It takes practice to get good at. Whether you're creating a $200,000 music video with a cast and crew of 150 union members or a $100 music video shot by your roommate with a cast and crew of your girlfriend, brother and mom, there are some key components that every video needs in order to meet today's professional standards.

You don't need a ton of money these days to make a great-looking video. All you need is a great concept, people who know what they're doing, a little bit of gear and lots of time.

The Concept

An inexpensive creative concept will perform better than a high-priced paint-by-numbers video every time. So get creative. Obviously, if you're making a video for an intimate piano ballad, you aren't going to go skydiving for it. The concept, as creative as it may be, should match the song's vibe, energy and feel. The purpose of a music video is to enhance the song. Not detract from it. A supercreative video (that perfectly complements the song) is how you go viral. And it doesn't need to be expensive. OK Go were the first to prove this with their "Here It Goes Again" video back in 2006. The video, which got over 50 million views, helped propel the single to the *Billboard* Hot 100 charts. The video cost very little. It was shot with a single, stationary camera and had no cuts. No edits. The band did a choreographed dance on six treadmills. It matched the tone of the song (and band) perfectly. Gotye exploded because of his creative, body-paint, stop-motion video for "Somebody That I Used To Know." Sia's near one-take video for "Chandelier" featured an uber-creepy, wildly talented and supercaptivating dancing 11-year-old girl. Kina Grannis spent over a year making her jelly-bean–themed stop-motion video for "In Your Arms." The

Black Keys' "Lonely Boy" video is a single-take shot of a boisterous dancing businessman. Oren Lavie's "Her Morning Elegance" video is a single-angle shot of a bed while the sleeping protagonist gracefully explores pillow adventures through fantastical wonderlands all by the magic of stop-motion photography.

These videos were all created on a relatively low budget. But this takes convincing very talented people to work hours upon hours for free or very little. So, getting the right crew is crucial.

To help generate inspiration and focus your creative direction, make a list of music videos you love that don't look too expensive.

The Crew

Hollywood has special titles for every single person who works on a film set from Best Boy and Grip to 2nd AD and PA. Two minutes of network television could take 6 hours and 100 people to create. Your music video doesn't need fancy titles or craft services to be great. You need a dedicated crew of passionate people who all believe in the success of the video. For most of your early videos, you will wear most of the hats, but you'll need at least a few people to help out. You should learn as much as you can, though, so you can be as independent as possible.

Producer

Whether you're working on a multimillion-dollar film or a $100 music video, the producer is one of the most important people for the success of the project. The producer is the project manager. She finds and hires the entire crew, finds all locations and tracks down all necessary equipment. A producer who has tons of connections can get all sorts of deals. If she really believes in your project, she can call in all of her favors.

Director

The director is the brain. The leader. The idea person. He has the vision. The director will work with you on putting together the concept. He will, uh, direct everyone on set and has a solid understanding of everyone's role and the equipment necessary to achieve the goal of the video. He is a part of the project from concept to final editing. If he doesn't do the shooting, editing and coloring himself, he works alongside these individuals to attain his vision.

DP

DP means director of photography. This is the person who runs the camera. For low-budget shoots, it will most likely be the director or a fellow bandmate. For higher-budget shoots, a DP is hired specifically for her expertise and ability to realize the director's vision. Professional DPs know how to operate the most complicated (and expensive) cameras in the world and know what it takes to realize nearly any concept.

PA

PA means production assistant. These are your friends who have volunteered to help you throughout the shoot. They do everything and anything you need from positioning lights (when there are no lighting crew members), to running the playback, to making coffee, to running to Home Depot for an extension cable, to washing the windows you're shooting through.

Work with Students

Bring a film student on board to help with something. Call it an internship. Film students have access to state-of-the-art equipment for free.

Regardless of their confidence level, most film students aren't experienced enough to create a video up to the professional standards you require on their own. But if you have one very experienced filmmaker to lead the operation, the film student can help with equipment and location needs (and more PAs), while getting great experience and building his résumé. Most film students would jump at the opportunity to work on a band's music video—no matter how low-budget it is.

The Performance

If you're going to sing in the video, you should practice re-creating the vocals from the recording to a T. Learn every breath and every inflection. If the visual vocals don't match up to the recorded vocals, it will be jarring to the audience. Sure, everyone knows this isn't a live performance, but make it look as close to one as possible. You should actually sing the part when you're shooting the video. People can tell if you're faking it. Actually sing. This goes for every instrument. The drummer should learn the part verbatim and play it like he's onstage in front of 10,000 screaming fans. The guitar player should plug into an amp, if possible, and similarly rock out like her tubes are reverberating through Madison Square Garden. Practice the performance before you get on set. Each band member should practice his performance on his own. If you're a live band and perform often, this will come much more naturally. It will feel unnatural to perform for the camera (and not a packed room of fans). Here's where the acting comes in. Each member should film and critique himself before shoot day. Rehearse your performance, on your own, until it looks like how you think it should. If your performance looks dumb to you during your rehearsal, it will look dumb during the actual shoot (and to everyone when the video comes out). An expensive camera, lighting package and editor cannot save a sh*tty performance.

Camera

Jack Conte made some pretty darn good-looking videos with his iPhone (in 2013!) which have gotten millions of views. So it's possible. But I recommend either investing in a $1,000 DSLR camera (a Canon 80D is a fine option for now) and a couple great lenses or hiring a DP with a DSLR camera to shoot you. Freelance DPs typically range in price from $100 to $500 for the day. Most will have their own camera, but some superprofessional DPs will only work on high-end cameras like a Red ($50,000) or Alexa ($100,000). In L.A., it's quite simple to rent these high-end cameras. If you have insurance, you can get a Red for about $500 a day or an Alexa for about $1,000 a day. But you don't want to just rent the camera if you don't know how to use it. These high-end cameras should only be handled by professional DPs.

Lighting

It doesn't matter whether you're shooting on an iPhone or an Alexa, if your lighting is sh*t, your video will look like sh*t. Plain and simple. At the very least, buy, rent or borrow a sufficient lighting package. If you're just shooting a simple, YouTuber-style solo performance video at home, a $150 softbox lighting kit from Amazon will do the job. Get the brightest lights available. And make sure the kit is for video (not just still photography). You can head down to a camera shop and ask them for recommendations. There are some great YouTube tutorials on simple video lighting techniques. If you're creating a multilocation, indoor, narrative music video, you'll most likely need to rent a lighting package. So be aware of this when coming up with your concept. Your DP will be able to instruct you on what she requires. But be careful, DPs aren't managing your budget. Make sure to reign them in. If they say they absolutely need a $1,500 lighting package, they may actually be able to (grudgingly) do it for a $500 lighting package. These are rental prices. You'll also need people who know how to set up and operate these expensive rented lights (so they don't explode on you—yes, this can happen if you don't handle them properly).

Shooting outdoors is the easiest way to avoid increasing lighting costs. The sun is the best lighting package on the planet. And it's free! All you'll need is a bounce (reflector disc) to help guide the light. These are $10 from Amazon.

Playback

This is one of the most forgotten-about elements of music video shoots. And it's the most important. Make sure you have an extremely loud sound system. And if you're shooting outside or in multiple locations, it needs to be portable. This is easier said than done. A little Bluetooth Jambox may not be loud enough—even if it is just you and your acoustic guitar. If your full band is performing, you may need a full sound system to get the playback loud enough. You'll want one PA on playback duty for the entire duration of the shoot. There will be lots of starts and stops.

Editing

You should learn basic video editing. This will save you tons of money down the line. It seems daunting to learn at first, but as someone who has taught himself Final Cut Pro (by watching YouTube tutorials), I can tell you firsthand, it can be done. And it's not as painful as you'd expect. It can actually be quite fun once you get good at it. You will be putting out lots of video content over the course of your career, and you don't want to have to rely on editors. Once you can afford to outsource the editing, then by all means, do it. But until then, it's much easier to just learn by doing. I never took a course or spent time practicing. I learned by editing a Christmas video of mine that had to get done.

For your official music videos, it will be worth hiring a professional editor if you can afford it. But for all other videos, you can edit yourself.

Coloring

What separates the amateurs from the professionals is color correction. There are people out there whose sole job is color correction. It's the final step of the workflow. Make sure every single one of your music videos gets color corrected. There are color correction plugins and presets you can purchase that when used effectively can give your video a Marvel comic look or *The Notebook* look. Sure, the camera is important, but color correction is what really gives it the "look." And if you don't color-correct, it will look like a home video shot by your mom. I've seen too many of these. Please, for your sake, color correct.

You Pick Two

No, this is not Panera's lunch special, this is the Iron Triangle of project management. And it applies to virtually every project from albums to videos to app creation. Everyone wants their project to be good, cheap and fast. But you can only pick two. Want something good and fast? It will cost a lot. Want something cheap and good? It ain't going to be fast. Want something fast and cheap? The quality will most likely be crap.

This Euler diagram will help illustrate this.

You Pick Two project triangle.

WHAT ALBUM CYCLE?

Remember the first time you heard *The Dark Side of the Moon*? I do. And believe it or not, I was completely sober. I was in tenth-grade English class and, for some reason, our teacher cued up *The Wizard of Oz*, more specifically the second lion roar, with the DSOTM CD. And the class watched in awe as the visuals from this 1939 film seemed to match up perfectly with this 1973 musical masterpiece.

The Pink Floyd album is a true piece of art. Start to finish. It was conceived as such. There are no breaks in the music and, it's said, the five tracks on each side reflect various stages of human life. Pink Floyd created an album. They did not throw their ten best songs together to release a full-length LP. They worked within the limitations of the format for which they were creating (a vinyl LP). And created a true piece of art.

Did you know that *The Dark Side of the Moon*'s run time is only 43:00? Know why? It's because a vinyl record can only hold about 22 minutes of music a side before the quality gets drastically reduced. Had records been able to hold 35 minutes of music per side, *The Dark Side of the Moon* could have been a completely different album.

It's funny that artists are still putting about ten songs together and releasing them as an album. There are a few reasons for this:

1) Most of today's artists grew up admiring full-length albums. Albums (not singles) are why most of us fell in love with music and chose to make it our profession. So artists want to create full-length albums—just like their influences.
2) Even though CDs are on their way out (and vinyl has made a serious comeback), the format still sells. It's my top-selling merch item at shows. And over 100 million CDs sell globally a year. So, we

can't run away from the format completely—however, we are walking away, briskly.

3) Labels still want to release full-length albums because they can maximize their marketing efforts around one campaign (versus a bunch of smaller, single campaigns).

But there are no time constraints with the digital model. You could have a 1,000-minute album if you wanted. Hell, many people open an artist's profile on their favorite streaming service and just hit Shuffle anyway, in effect giving them an infinite playlist of their favorite artist. An infinite album.

SHOULD YOU RELEASE A SINGLE, AN EP OR AN ALBUM?

If you're going to make an album, there better be a reason for me to give a sh*t.
—BRUCE FLOHR, RED LIGHT MANAGEMENT

Despite what you see from the major labels still utilizing an antiquated release strategy, you should not be releasing an album every three years. You need to be consistently releasing music.

Unless you have a *Dark Side of the Moon* statement to make, you don't need to create an album. Spend your resources on creating a great song and a great video and get it out. Fans expect music so much more regularly now than they did ten years ago. If you don't continue the engagement and continue to feed them musically, they will move on.

Yes, artists still tour on albums. For one, it gives reviewers something fresh to talk about and the old guard still understands "album campaigns." But there's no need to create a full-length album unless you truly have a statement to make. So don't stress yourself out about building the funds for a full-length album.

How often should you be releasing music? That depends on a lot of factors. If you make electronic music in your bedroom and primarily use SoundCloud to distribute it, then you should be releasing a new song every month. If you're a full band and require a studio for every recording, you should still release a new song every month, but maybe a studio recording just every three months. You can release live versions, demos, covers and acoustic versions (on less formal platforms like SoundCloud, Bandcamp and YouTube) in between the official studio releases.

Many YouTubers release a song a week. Sure, many of these are covers, but the most successful YouTubers make every single release sound super-pro. They have their writing, arranging, recording, filming and release workflow down to a science.

Eventually, you will too.

ARE SALES DEAD?

Overall album sales have been steadily declining since 2000. Digital sales have surpassed physical sales. And streaming revenue has overtaken digital (and physical). The numbers would tell you that sales are dying. And for the under-25 demographic, they are virtually dead.

So, you have to understand who your audience is. What is the age breakdown? What is your niche? Country artists sell way more CDs than downloads. As do blues artists. But pop and hip-hop, by a large margin, are dominated by downloads and streams over CDs. And indie rock fans love vinyl. You have to know who your audience is and who you are targeting. If your fans still want CDs, make CDs. If your fans want vinyl, make vinyl. If your fans don't care about albums, don't make albums.

Above all, your fans want to support you. So make attractive ways for *all* of your fans to do this. Some will want to do it in the form of a CD purchase. Some will back your crowdfunding. Some will subscribe to you on Bandcamp or Patreon. Some will send you a check.

Some fans don't buy physical albums and don't download music and exclusively listen to music on Spotify, YouTube or Apple Music, but still want to support you. So allow them to stream your music and give them opportunities to pay you in other ways. We'll get into more ways to do this all throughout the book.

If you really believe that your fans do still buy CDs, then I encourage you to check out the Music Marketing Manifesto to set up a sales funnel and really focus on that for your release.

DIGITAL DISTRIBUTION: HOW TO GET YOUR MUSIC ON ITUNES, SPOTIFY, APPLE MUSIC, AMAZON AND EVERYWHERE ELSE

CD Baby, TuneCore, DistroKid, Symphonic, ONErpm, Ditto, Reverb-Nation, MondoTunes, or . . .

The major on-demand music consumption platforms of the world like iTunes, Apple Music, Google Play, Spotify, Tidal, Deezer, Amazon, Rhapsody, all require receiving their music from authorized distributors. Before CD Baby cracked this open in 2004, you had to be signed to a label that worked with a distributor to get your music into iTunes and the bunch. But over the past ten years, the field has been flooded with digital distribution companies accessible by millions of unsigned musicians looking to get their music out to the world. I keep an updated comparison on Ari's Take.

Things to look out for when researching which digital distribution company to use:

- **Cost**

  Do they charge you up-front fees? Yearly recurring fees? Fees per release?

- **Commission**

  What percentage of the royalties does the company take?

- **Speed**

  Some will get your music to outlets within days (or hours), others take weeks.

- **Number of Outlets**

  Most companies distribute to nearly all the most popular retailers; some just pick a few to work with.

- **Opt Out of Stores**

  If you get a U.K.-only record deal, you want to be able to omit the U.K. region when you distribute to the rest of the world.

- **Adding Stores**

  Do they charge you to add new stores when they become available or do they add your music automatically?

- **Custom Label Name**

  If you have a record label you're working under, make sure you can use the name when you distribute.

- **ISRC and UPC Codes**

  ISRC codes are assigned per song. UPC is assigned per album. Some companies charge for these, some give them to you for free.

- **Payment Frequency**

  Weekly, monthly, quarterly, immediately?

- **Payment Threshold**

  $10? $100? How much do you need to make before they pay you?

- **YouTube Monetization**

  Good to keep this under one roof.

- **Flexible Admin Publishing Options**

  Good to keep this under one roof if you wrote your songs. More about this in Chapter 13.

- **Beatport and Pandora**

  Both platforms curate their music. Some distributors will distribute your music for approval, others require you to submit your music for approval directly to the platform.

- **Obtaining a License for Cover Songs**

  If you distribute a cover song, you need to obtain and pay for a mechanical license. You don't need permission, but you still need the license. Some distributors will do this for you (for a fee); others require you to obtain it on your own.

Self-Managed Download Stores

There are self-managed music stores like Bandcamp, Bandzoogle, Loudr and TunePort where you can upload your music and sell it directly to your fans. These self-managed download stores take significantly smaller commissions than the big online stores and don't require a digital distribution company (some of whom also take commissions).

THE BRIDGE
26 Things to Do Before You Release Your Song or Album

1) Market Research How do you know if you suck or not? You're biased. So is your mom and your boyfriend. Your friends aren't going to tell you if they hate your music. They will come to your shows to support you. To make sure your music is ready for prime time, you need some unbiased opinions. You can submit to industry experts, influencers and curators on Fluence (Fluence.io). Fluence allows you to pay people who are difficult to reach to listen to your song or watch your video. Most 'curators' (as they're called on the platform) charge a few dollars a minute. If you're asking for feedback, prepare for it to be brutally honest. I'm a curator on Fluence and I typically write five-to-ten-paragraph critiques of songs submitted to me. Eighty percent of the stuff I receive is not very good; 15% is decent, but not great; and 5% is so great that I have to share it (if it's released) and help the artist make connections.

But Fluence can get quite pricey. To hit the general public, you can use Audiokite. You basically pay about $20 to get 100 people to listen and rate your song. This is a great way to help decide which demos should make the album or which master should be your single. Use my affiliate code AK-ARISTAKE for 30% off your report. You can filter by genre (so folk lovers aren't rating your heavy metal song).

ReverbNation has a similar program called Crowd Review and TuneCore has Fan Reviews. SoundOut also has a very similar standalone product worth checking out. Then there's Music Xray which specializes in submitting your music to gatekeepers (for a fee), but also offers Diagnostics. For $10, five "Music Industry Professionals" will rate your song on five criteria: Composition, Production, Arrangement, Performance and Hit Potential.

Use one of these platforms to test out your song before it's released.

2) **Register Your Publishing** There are a ton of royalties out there. Kobalt estimates there are 900,000 distinct royalty payments for a single recording. So, to make sure you grab as many of those as possible, you have to register your music in all the appropriate places and sign up with an admin publishing company. We'll get into this more in Chapter 13.

3) **Register Every Song with a PRO** In America, the 3 main PROs (Performing Rights Organizations) are ASCAP, BMI and SESAC. In Canada the sole PRO is SOCAN. Most admin publishing companies will register your songs with the PRO of your choosing so you don't have to worry about taking this step once you sign up for an admin pub company.

4) **Register with SoundExchange** SoundExchange is how you get paid for Pandora and SiriusXM (and all other digital radio) plays. Make sure to register an account and submit your catalog.

5) **Get on AllMusic.com and Discogs** AllMusic is the most inclusive credits database in existence. Discogs is a close second. Why Spotify or Apple hasn't integrated this info into their system is beyond me. Your music should be registered on AllMusic.com and Discogs so people can find out who played the violin on track 3 and who cowrote track 7, because most people won't ever see your physical liner notes. To get registered on AllMusic, you go to http://www.allmusic

.com/product-submissions and follow the instructions. For Discogs, you can submit the info directly through the site (Discogs.com).

6) **Register the Copyrights** You can currently register all of your songs at once for $55 with the U.S. Copyright Office. You can do everything at Copyright.gov. Just be extra careful with this, because if you file the applications incorrectly and you later have to file a lawsuit against someone, the court may say that your registration is invalid. The safest bet is to hire an entertainment or copyright attorney to do this for you so you don't screw it up!

7) **Register for YouTube and SoundCloud Revenue** You are going to be putting all of your music up on YouTube, so you want to collect all of those royalties. Pick a YouTube and SoundCloud collections company such as Repost Network, Audiam, InDMusic, or AdRev. Or, better yet, your distribution company will be able to collect these royalties for you. CD Baby, DistroKid and TuneCore (among others) have this as an opt-in add-on. I recommend just keeping everything under one roof and having your distribution company collect these royalties for you. (Many of them actually outsource to the aforementioned third-party YouTube/SoundCloud collections companies anyway)

8) **Pick Your Distribution Company** To get your song in iTunes, Apple Music, Spotify, Amazon, Deezer, Google Play and 80-plus other stores and streaming services worldwide, you need a distribution company. The top digital distribution companies (for indie artists) in the world are currently CD Baby, DistroKid and TuneCore. I keep an updated comparison on a bunch of these companies at http://aristake.com/?post=92. If you want to go one step deeper, you can start a record label and apply to work with a bigger distribution company like INgrooves, The Orchard or Believe Digital. These distributors work only with labels, but they can offer more personal attention and benefits than the open-to-everyone distributors can.

9) **Get a Licensing Company** If you're interested in getting your music in TV shows, commercials, movies, video games and trailers, you'll want to get a licensing company. More on this in Chapter 14.

10) **Create the Folder of Assets** More on what this is in a couple pages.

11) **Get New Photos** You should build up a network of photographers in your city. You can never have enough high-quality photos. Every release is a new beginning. It's a time to update and enhance your image. To rebrand if necessary. Photos give your audience the first impression of the music. People will judge your project based on the artwork and photography before they choose to listen to the music. So your photos should have the same vibe and energy of your release. Make sure your photographer listens to the new music. And make sure

the photos you release alongside the new music make sense. You need to wear an outfit conducive to the new sound. John Mayer moved to Montana to write his albums *Born and Raised* and *Paradise Valley*. The photos were taken in Montana and were indicative of his new direction. Your new album needs a story. And those photos need to match the story. Pick your top 10 (edited) photos and include them in your Folder of Assets. Pick your top 3 and use these for all initial press and promo. You can roll out the other 7 in time with new videos, singles, tours and shows.

12) **Write a New Bio**

13) **Write a New Press Release** This is different from your bio and doesn't need to be posted anywhere online. You will send this directly to media outlets. We'll get more into how to write these in Chapter 15.

14) **Make a List of Blogs to Contact** More on this in Chapter 15.

15) **Create the Videos**

16) **Create a Bandcamp Page** Bandcamp is the #1 independent music store. It is self-managed by you. You don't need to use a distributor to get on Bandcamp. You can go to Bandcamp.com and sign up for free. You can offer "name your price" downloads. A fan once paid me $200 for my album (set at $5 minimum). Bandcamp now offers subscriptions and a physical merch store as well.

17) **Create (or Rebrand) Your Website** A new album demands a new website. It's a good idea to rebrand your website every couple years regardless if you have a new album or not. Bandzoogle and Squarespace are website builders that require no design or coding knowledge. They have beautiful templates to choose from and are very simple to use.

18) **Create (or Rebrand) Your Social Sites** Now that you have new photos, album cover and bio, use these assets to rebrand all your social sites. You are bringing an entirely new package to the world. Make it shiny, sparkly and tasty. And put a bow on it!

19) **Get a Mailing List** If you don't have a mailing list yet, start one. This is the most important fan engagement tool you have. A McKinsey & Company study recently concluded that email marketing is forty times more effective than Facebook and Twitter combined. MailChimp, FanBridge, iContact, Constant Contact, Benchmark and SendinBlue are some of best and most widely used email list services.

20) **Submit to Pandora** Pandora is the #1 internet radio station in the United States. You can submit at http://submit.pandora.com.

21) **Create New Merch** A new album or tour demands new merch. Get creative with your merch offerings. More on this later.

22) **Dropbox and Box.com** Music supervisors want a quick and easy way to listen or download your music. Most prefer Box.com or Dropbox links because they can

stream your song in the browser or download it if they want to use it. Get all of your songs, metadata tagged mp3s and wavs, full versions and instrumentals, up on Box.com or Dropbox. Click the Share button and grab the link for every song. Put that in a text document in your Folder of Assets.

23) **SoundCloud Profile** You'll want to get all of your music up on SoundCloud. Not only is it an active community, like YouTube, it is the easiest way to send someone a streamable song. You can also put a SoundCloud playlist on your website and embed players around the Web.

24) **SmartURL.it Links** SmartURL is one of the best link-tracking services out right now. Like Bitly, smartURL will let you know how many people clicked your link, but will also give you much more detailed analytics, like location, device used, referring domains and other stats. You can also decide to point users to different destinations based on their device. Like a "download" link could send iPhone users to iTunes and Droid users to Google Play or Amazon. *Boom!* SmartURL was initially one of the only ways to post iTunes links that actually send people to iTunes (and not Apple Music). Create smartURL links for every link you save.

25) **Register Your Trademark** For your band name and your logo.

26) **Form a Corporate Entity (like an LLC)** It gives you some legal protection and enables you to open a band account (and get paid).

THE FOLDER OF ASSETS

On your laptop, create a folder on your desktop. Title it the name of the new album. Inside the folder will be all of the assets you will need to access frequently. The folder should include:

- Text doc of all lyrics.
- Wavs of every song (including instrumentals).
- 320kbps (metadata tagged) mp3s of every song (including instrumentals). More on why/how to metadata tag in Chapter 14.
- High-res album cover (at least 3000 pixels x 3000 pixels).
- High-res album cover without text (to use for posters).

- Stems (for remixes). These are isolated vocals, drums, bass, guitar tracks.
- Print-ready promo photos (300dpi, no larger than 10mb in size).
- Web versions of promo photos (74dpi, around 1mb in size).
- Merch designs.
- Album press release.
- Text doc with album credits (break these down by song).
- Short and long bios.
- Promotional materials like poster, flyer and advertising designs.
- Demos.
- Music videos.
- Behind the-scenes videos.
- Text doc containing login information to all your sites and links you will need to reference frequently (Dropbox, Box.com, SoundCloud, Spotify, Bandcamp, PledgeMusic, iTunes, etc.).

HOW TO WRITE YOUR BAND BIO

Your bio is your story. It is the single most important piece of your release—next to the music, of course. It should reveal why people should care about you. What sets you apart? Why are you unique? And more specifically, what is the album's story? Go back and reference "Why No One Cares About Your Music" in Chapter 1. With this in mind, you can craft your bio. Many outlets will copy and paste your bio for their needs. Make sure you have three bios, a long one, a short one (1 or 2 paragraphs, definitely under 500 words) and an elevator pitch. Make sure every bio includes pronunciation of the name. Your bio should be written in the third person.

Your long bio can be structured like this:

Quote

Start the bio off with a quote from a band member or press outlet or a lyric from one of your songs. Something that will set the tone and is completely indicative of what your project is about.

Hook

The hook is your story. What makes you unique. Sets you apart from everyone else. Open with this. It doesn't need to be more than one or two paragraphs.

Accolades

Move right into discussing your accolades. Once your hook intrigues your readers, your accolades showcase that you are an artist on the rise, worth paying attention to.

Newest Project

This is where you talk about your latest project. Most of the time it's the newest album. But you can also discuss music videos, tours or anything else that you're currently working on.

The Boring Stuff: Backstory, Influences, Song Meanings

This section is primarily for your die-hard fans who want as much possible information about you and for journalists doing their research. You don't need every band members' birthplace, but include interesting, pertinent information about how members met, how the band was formed and career highlights. You can also include some of your influences, back stories on songs on the record or any other interesting info.

Your short bio should just have your hook, accolades and newest project. You don't need any of the backstory.

THE ELEVATOR PITCH

Your elevator pitch doesn't need to be posted anywhere or sent out; it's just for you to verbally describe your band quickly and easily when people ask. You'd be surprised at how many musicians have a very difficult time talking about their own music. Pick two or three artists people say you sound like and use that. "David Bowie meets Bob Dylan." "If Janis Joplin got into a bar fight with Sly and the Family Stone." "If Bill Withers married Katy Perry." "It's Taylor Swift for grown-ups." "Marvin Gaye meets Paul Simon in New Orleans." "Imagine Dragons flew into The Fray while riding Train." We'll stop there. And obviously reference well-known artists. It's no use comparing yourself to an artist they haven't heard of. By doing this, it gives them a frame of reference. You may think your sound is unlike any which came before and that you shouldn't be pigeonholed by referencing one or two artists or genres, but believe me, you will drastically help your (potential) audience by giving them a frame of reference.

THE RULE OF 7

There's this old adage in the marketing world called "the Rule of 7." Basically, it states that a prospect needs to hear an advertiser's message 7 times before the prospect will take action to purchase. What this means for you, is that your fans need to be hit at least 7 times with whatever you're selling (album, song, music video, tickets, crowdfunding campaign) before they will even think of taking action. You may feel like it's overkill, most artists do, but it's science. And it's why marketing departments still employ these tactics. Just think about it, the first time you see a photo to an article on Facebook you typically ignore it if the topic doesn't immediately interest you. But if you see a bunch of your friends post the same article, you almost certainly click to read it.

Leading up to the release, there are tactics you can take to make sure your target audience gets hit at least 7 times and is certain to take notice.

THE ALBUM RELEASE TIMELINE

To me, the way PledgeMusic puts out
music is what the future of the release
of an album looks like.
—BENJI RODGERS, CEO AND FOUNDER,
PLEDGEMUSIC

If you're planning to release a full-length album or EP, you can loosely follow this release timeline as a guide.

8 Months Before the Release

■ **Launch the Preorder or Crowdfunding Campaign**
The album cycle has totally changed. It no longer begins the day your first single is released, it now begins eight months prior. Before you step into the studio, set up a crowdfunding/preorder campaign to, sure, raise the funds necessary to record and promote your new album, but also to invite your fans to be a part

of the process. They will happily pay you for it. These are your hard-core fans who will be on the front lines helping you spread the word about your album when it's released. We'll discuss more fully how best to approach these campaigns in Chapter 12.

5 Months Before

- **Order the Vinyl**

  By this point, your album should be mastered. If you're ordering vinyl, start no later than 5 months out contacting the plant to make sure they will be able to turn your order around by your release date. Because vinyl has seen a massive resurgence over the past few years, vinyl pressing plants cannot keep up with the demand. So turnaround times are frustratingly long. And because of the nature of vinyl, a lot can go wrong, so leave time for all of this. Fortunately, because of the rise in vinyl popularity, more and more plants are popping up these days and rates are dropping.

- **Album Artwork**

  Make sure your album cover art is finished 5 months before the release. If you're hiring a graphic design artist for this, You Pick Two (good, cheap, fast) applies. The only exception, as I mentioned earlier, is if you find royalty-free images (but remember that those images don't come with the same legal protections as images that you license from, let's say, iStock) or images that are controlled by a Creative Commons license that specifically allows commercial use. Any fonts in image editing programs like Photoshop are fine to use. Other fonts that you download may have restrictions, so be sure to check the legalities of the font you're using.

All vinyl plants will send you art templates to design the artwork from. Make sure your graphic designer creates the art to their specs.

■ **Liner Notes**

Obviously, if you're creating vinyl, you need all of the packaging completed before sending it in. AllMusic.com will also require this info.

■ **Promo Photos**

You'll also want to get new promo photos done to potentially include on the album cover and within the booklet. If you're not including any promo photos within your vinyl packaging, then don't worry about this until 3 months out. But, it's nice to include at least one shot of the artist within the packaging. And yes, it should be a new photo, to capture what you look like now (not two years ago). People want to know what the artists looked like at the time of the creation and release of this album. The music is a snapshot of where you are in your life at the time of the recording, and the accompanying photographs should be the same.

■ **Route the Tour**

We'll get into how to do this in Chapter 8, but you'll definitely want to start about 5 months in advance to plan the tour supporting the new album.

■ **Record Release Show Holds**

If you do it right, this show will sell out. This will be a hometown celebration of all your hard work. You'll want to do this on a Friday or Saturday, and venues book these prime slots out well in advance. Make sure you get a least a few holds 5 months out.

3 Months Before

- **Pick the Lead Singles**

  This is where Audiokite, Fluence and Music Xray can come in. Do the market research to figure out which are your strongest songs. The answers may surprise you. You can also invite your crowdfunding backers into this process to help you decide. They are your biggest fans and are looking out for your best interests. Hold a listening party (in person or live-broadcasted) and ask your fans to rate each song from 1 to 5. If they aren't there in person, you can set up an online survey via Survey-Monkey for digital attendees. Ask your fans to associate words and feelings to each song. You can make a list for them and ask them to circle (or check box on SurveyMonkey) all the feelings they felt for each song: Calm, Mellow, Thoughtful, Relaxed, Loving, Sad, Happy, Joyful, Excited, Bored, Angry, Inspired, Intense, Party and Horny. Oh, why not? Ask them to circle whether they are male or female and their age range (under 18, 19–22, 23–34, 35–44, 45–54, 55–64, 65+). Ask them what artists they think you sound like. This will help with your Elevator Pitch.

- **Pick Your CD Replication or Duplication Company**

  If you're going to make a CD and want to get it professionally replicated, start early. You don't need the 5-month lead-in like you do for vinyl, but you can definitely save some money if you give it at least a month turnaround. Remember, you'll most likely need to fulfill your preorder/crowd funding packages and get them shipped out to arrive before release date. Disc Makers, Oasis and CD Baby (all owned by the same company) pretty much own the commercial CD replication space. However, there are many other quality replication companies out there to look into (I use Noiseland out of Minneapolis) which may be cheaper and save you shipping costs if you order locally. If you just need a small run of CDs, you'll need to go with duplication. Replication is the commercial industry standard. The replication process actually presses the information to the CD (most companies won't replicate CDs for orders less than 1,000). Duplication is burning CD-Rs. Yes, just like you did back in the day from your Gateway.

■ **Create the Videos**

From your market research you will be able to decide which songs you should create music videos for.

■ **AllMusic**

It takes a while for AllMusic to process all of their info. To make sure they get your credit info up in time for your release, get your package to them sooner rather than later.

■ **Start the Record Release Show Promo**

Now that you have triple confirmation from the vinyl and CD plants that the shipments will arrive at least a month before the release show, lock in the date and start the promo campaign. We'll discuss exactly how to do this in Chapter 7. You will sell a lot of merch at this release show. Prepare yourself.

2 Months Before

■ **Hit Up Local Press for Your Release Show**
Press outlets, especially those in print, plan far in advance. Start on this early. More on this in Chapter 15.

■ **Set Up the Preorder**
If you didn't run a PledgeMusic campaign, it's time to setup the preorder. Don't just set up a digital iTunes/Bandcamp preorder; include packages like you did for your crowdfunding campaign.

■ **Pick Your Distribution Company**
Reference my updated comparison on Ari's Take (http://bit.ly/distribution-comparison) to figure out which digital distributor is best for you. Many companies can get your music to stores within hours or days, but some require weeks. And once in a while Apple randomly selects a release to quality-check, and it can delay your release by up to 16 days. Best to get on this quickly.

It's worth noting that some companies, namely CD Baby, INgrooves and Symphonic Distribution, also offer physical distribution and fulfillment. If you have a significant national (or international) fanbase and think you could move some serious product, hit up your distribution company and see what the possibilities are.

The Month Before

■ **Launch the New Website**
This is when you begin to let the world know about the upcoming album and release show. Sites like Bandzoogle and Squarespace make it easy to create a website and reskin it (change the design)

at will without having to beg your web developer to just update the header image one more time. More on this in Chapter 11.

■ **Release the First Single**
Release the first single (distribute it via your digital distributor and get it on SoundCloud and Bandcamp) along with the accompanying music video. Upload the video to Facebook and embed the YouTube video on your website and submit to blogs for review. What blogs should you hit up and how to do this? We'll dig deep into this in Chapter 15.

■ **Send Out All Crowdfunding Packages**

■ **Launch the Preorder**

■ **Listening Party**
Use platforms like Periscope, YouTube Live, or Google Hangouts to hold a digital listening party for your new album. You'll get the first reactions from fans in real time. Or, even better, host a local listening party in your living room and live-stream it out to people around the world.

■ **Release the Album Sampler Video on YouTube**
YouTubers (What is a "YouTuber"? We'll dig in in Chapter 11) initially led this front, and the industry followed suit (as it has gone with much of the digital landscape). Just search on YouTube "album sampler" to see how artists are making their samplers these days. Album samplers are just one long video with clips of every song. Some just display a photo of the artist with the track listing (with each track title annotated to enable the desktop user to jump around songs on the sampler video)

and others have video clips that match up with each song with Next/Previous or Skip buttons (similarly powered by YouTube's annotations).

■ **Run Contests**

To help promote the new music video, release show and tour, rally the troops and start running creative contests all the way up until release day. You should target your fans everywhere they are. Send an email out to your list to let your biggest fans know how they can get involved and help promote the album.

Here are some ideas on how you can use the social sites to run contests:

1. **Snapchat**   If your fans are living on Snapchat, run contests on Snapchat. Maybe ask everyone to post a video in their Story saying "I just got tickets to White Light Riot's record release show!" And then have them send you the Snap as well. Pick a couple winners who will win merch packages at the show. And for the fans outside your city, do the same for the upcoming tour.

2. **Instagram**   Have them post a photo of them holding tickets to your show. Start a hashtag like #newalbumtitle and encourage your fans to post photos of themselves doing something that relates to the album (or single) title. Then pick one for a special merch package to be sent to them in the mail (who doesn't love getting presents?) or given at the release show. Rachel Platten started a movement with her song "Fight Song," encouraging her fans to post photos of themselves holding up their arm making a muscle and then posting in the description what obstacles they have overcome with the tag #fightsong. A year after the song's release, the movement was still going strong.

3. **Facebook**   Even though Facebook isn't quite as cool as it was five years ago, it's still an incredibly powerful platform—especially if your fans are over 25. Unlike Instagram and Snapchat, you can post links. Ask your fans to share your new music video (which you uploaded directly to Facebook) with the link to purchase tickets to the release show, or preorder the new album. Then have them write "Mission Accomplished" on your Musician Page. Pick one for a special merch package.

4. **Twitter**   Ask your fans to post their favorite lyrics from the lead single with the hashtag #newalbumtitle.

5. **Tumblr**   If your fans exist on Tumblr, ask them to post the new music video or lyric meme (that you create) alongside the link to preorder the new album. Make sure they include the hashtag so you can find them and reward the winner.

6. **SoundCloud**   If your fans exist on SoundCloud, ask them to repost (and comment on) your song.

7. **YouTube**   Ask all your fans to comment on your new music video and/or album sampler.

8. **Street Team**   Rally up the street team and start hitting your town with posters and flyers for the release show. Hit the coffee shops, record stores, college campuses and anywhere else your fans hang out. If the venue's into it, make coupons for drink discounts and include them on your physical postcard flyers (4×6). Give a small stack to each street team member. Put a number on each flyer and run an internal street team contest where whoever turns in the most drink coupon flyers at the bar gets a cash prize. This will really up the ante for your team. Of course, your street team gets free tickets to the show. You can do this in every city of your tour.

9. **Send Out an Email Blast**   Lead off with the story of the album creation process. Be vulnerable. Be open. Be authen-

tic. Don't just say, "This is the best album we've ever made." That's boring. Everyone says that. Why did you make an album? Use the hook from the press release (we'll get more into this in Chapter 15) and welcome your fans back to you. Or introduce them to the new you. Include a link to the pre-order site and focus on that. Open and close with the preorder link. Make it so they can't miss it. But also include the contests you're running and invite your fans to find you on the various social sites to participate. Gather more people for your street team. Give away your first single to your email list for free. Embed the music video in the blast. Link to your album sampler to whet their appetites. Invite them to your listening party. And invite them to check out the new website.

Yes, this seems like a lot and like you may overwhelm your list, but this is the beginning of a longer email campaign. This is to engage your biggest hard-core fans.

Two Weeks Before

- **Send Out an Email Blast with a Timed Discount**
  Yes, you sent a blast two weeks prior, but in this one, just include the preorder link (twice—beginning and end). It's good to give them a reason to preorder right now. Try a limited-time, free-shipping or discount offer, such as:

  Subject: " 72 hours left for free shipping"

  Body: Grab any *preorder package* (link it) in the next 72 hours and get free shipping. There are limited items left available for preorder and this will expire in 71 hours, 59 . . . 58 minutes.
  Get it now (link)

Marketing experts will tell you that adding a "limited time offer" and "limited availability" pushes people to take action and gives them a reason to do so RIGHT NOW.

The Week Before

■ **Release the Second Single**

I know you're thinking, "Already?! Ari, we just released our first single. This seems too soon." Trust me, it's not. We live in an on-demand, ADD society. People lose interest quickly. All the blogs that were going to write about your first single have already written about it. Time to follow it up. If your first single didn't get the massive virality you were hoping it would get, don't fret. You, of course, can still promote it for months to come (now, along with this second single).

■ **Upload to SoundCloud**

Upload all your songs to SoundCloud and create an album playlist. Set it to "Secret" until release day.

■ **Upload to Bandcamp**

Create the new album on Bandcamp, but keep it private until release day.

■ **Create a YouTube Album Playlist**

Upload all the videos that you have completed to YouTube, make the album playlist and schedule them to go public on release day. Remember, you need a video for every song, either a music video, lyric video or performance video.

■ **Send Out an Email Blast**

Yes, send another one. Push the preorder once again (twice—open and close), but this time, also include the behind-the-scenes video as a private link and explain that those on your list are getting a special sneak peek.

The Day Before

■ **Create the Email Blast**

Now this is the big one. Launch day! Make sure it includes links to everything you're releasing. Prioritize Bandcamp and let your fans know they can "name their price" or subscribe to you (more on this in Chapter 12). Explain that 85% of the money from Bandcamp goes directly to you. Believe it or not, the fans who didn't back your crowdfunding or preorder your album may be happy to drop $50 on just a digital download of your album to support you.

■ **Triple-Check All Your Links**

Go through your Folder of Assets and make sure all the links are updated and correct. Remember to add all the new smartURL links for YouTube, Bandcamp, SoundCloud, Spotify, iTunes and everywhere else.

■ **Change the Preorder**

Make sure your preorder switches over to purchase links.

■ **Update Merch**

Make sure your new merch, photos and bio are all up to date and will be synched everywhere to all platforms.

Release Day

It's here! All of your hard work and planning will pay off when you play to the sold-out club at your release show, start trending on Hype Machine, get added to popular Spotify playlists and take the whole project on the road. There are still a few things left to do to continue the momentum and have your album explode into the world.

- **Release the YouTube Official Album Playlist**
- **Release the Behind-the-Scenes Video**
- **Publish the Bandcamp Album**
- **Publish the SoundCloud Playlist**
- **Publish Everything to Your Website**
  Good idea to keep an updated press page of all the press you receive.
- **Send the Email Blast**
- **Live-Stream the Release Show (via Facebook Live or Periscope)**

The Week Of

- **More Contests**
  Run some more creative contests to keep the buzz going strong. Have you come up with creative contests or release campaigns you've run that you want to let me know about (and potentially share with the Ari's Take community?) Shoot me an email about it (ari@aristake.com).

- **Seek Out Playlists**
  If you or anyone you know has connections at any of the streaming or playlisting companies, match every song on your album

to a popular playlist. If you have no connections, don't fret; many times these playlist creators read music blogs and they monitor new releases. Many times artists get included on hot playlists and don't even know it until they see their play counts skyrocket.

Every Month After Release

■ **Release a New Video**
Try to release a new video at least once a month following the release. It can be new music videos, lyric videos, performance videos, live videos or vlogs. But make sure they are extremely high-quality. No sense in making your album sound pro if your video looks like dung.

■ **New Single = New Blog Outreach**
Every new music video you release, push to the blogs who have been responding well to you.

This Campaign Is Carved in Play-Doh

Even though you just finished reading my very specific formula of how you can release your album, you should only use this as a guideline. Every project is different, and the beauty of managing an indie music career is, you have the freedom and flexibility to call your own shots and experiment. The indie albums that do the best are the ones that are not only undeniably great, but have creative release campaigns around them.

A FEW CREATIVE CAMPAIGNS TO GET YOUR JUICES FLOWING

■ **Vulfpeck—*Sleepify***
In 2014, after it was revealed that Spotify was paying about $.005 a play, the indie funk band from Michigan, Vulfpeck, released a 10-track album of 31- and 32-second "songs" exclusively on Spotify. Except each song was completely silent. Spotify counts a play as at least 30 seconds. The band encouraged their fans to stream the album on repeat on Spotify while they slept explaining that they would fund their upcoming *Sleepify* tour (and make every show free) with royalties from this experiment. The band ended up making over $20,000 before Spotify took down the album, claiming it was against their terms of service. The press (and music community) went nuts over this stunt and this niche funk band from Michigan got on everyone's radar, so when their follow-up record (containing actual audible music) was announced in 2015, they not only raised over $55,000 from 1,673 backers on Kickstarter, the album exploded out of the gate with hundreds of thousands of first-week plays (on Spotify, of course) and an appearance on *The Late Show* with Stephen Colbert. All this, with no label and no management, from a brilliant stunt.

■ **Ali Spagnola—*Power Hour* Drinking Game Album**
Ali Spagnola made her name while a student at Carnegie Mellon University with her *Power Hour* drinking game concert. She wrote 60 original drinking songs, each 1 minute long and created an interactive drinking game where every time she changed songs the crowd took a shot of beer. The concert series got so

popular around Pittsburgh that national media started talking about it and she gained a massive following online. Ali designed, developed and manufactured a plastic shot glass necklace that comes with a removable USB drive with *The Power Hour Album* (which she also self-released online). Ali raised $40,234 from 1,486 people on Indiegogo to fund the *Power Hour* tour and determine which cities to visit. Ali now has over 2 million Twitter followers and popular Vine and YouTube channels.

The *Power Hour* Shot Glass USB was designed and created by Ali Spagnola. The USB contains Spagnola's *Power Hour* Album of 60 1-minute drinking songs used during her famed *Power Hour* concerts. (Ali Spagnola)

■ **Allen Stone—Evolution of An Artist**

Leading up to the release of his 2015 album *Radius*, Allen Stone returned to his hometown of Seattle, to play a week-long string of shows celebrating the city that had supported him from the beginning. On Monday, he played the first venue he ever performed at in the city. On Tuesday, the second venue he ever played in town. And so on. The week culminated with a Saturday night performance at the 2,800 seated Paramount Theater.

Tickets for all the shows went on sale the same week and every show sold out. It created a massive buzz around the release of the album.

■ **Counting Crows—*Somewhere Under Wonderland* 3D Sidewalk Chalk Art**

In 2014, in advance of Counting Crows' new album, they commissioned a 3D sidewalk chalk artist to create drawings inspired by the album in cities across America. On the morning of each city's drawing, the band posted clues on Facebook where the artist was going to be. The first people to show up and use the given password were awarded with free concert tickets or deluxe CD sets of the new album.

Counting Crows *Somewhere Under Wonderland* 3D sidewalk chalk art in Berkley, California. (Chris Carlson / Red Light Management www.chriscarlsonart.com)

■ **Oh Wonder—Monthly Releases**

The London electropop duo Oh Wonder wrote, recorded and released one song a month for a year. Each song reached #1 on the blog aggregator Hype Machine, and they were the second most blogged-about band in 2015, with streaming figures (mostly on SoundCloud and Spotify) surpassing 100 million plays worldwide. They officially released their debut album (the 12 monthly songs plus 3 more) a year after the project began, to critical acclaim, selling out venues all over the world.

■ **Foo Fighters—*Sonic Highways***
Dave Grohl and the Foo Fighters visited eight cities to record their new record. Grohl interviewed musical legends of each city and visited iconic studios and music venues to fully take in the musical history and vibe of the city. Grohl then wrote a song in each city and the band recorded it (with the respective city's musical guests). The whole thing was filmed and released as a 2014 HBO miniseries entitled *Sonic Highways*. Each episode covered a different city. The album, of the same name, was released alongside the miniseries.

■ **Justin Bieber—Lyft Campaign**
For the release of the Bieb's 2015 album *Purpose*, he teamed up with Lyft to allow riders to select "Bieber Mode" in the Lyft app. Five dollars was added to the cost of the ride, and after the ride finished, the rider got an email to download the album along with a $5 credit for their next ride. *Purpose* broke a Spotify Week 1 streaming record with 205 million global streams.

■ **Transviolet—Anonymous Cassette Tape Packages**
In the summer of 2015, teenagers around the United States started receiving manilla bubble-wrapped packages with no return address. Each package contained a single cassette tape. On the cassette tape were the handwritten words "Just Press Play." When the tape was put into a cassette player, Transvio-

let's debut single "Girls Your Age" played. Also handwritten on the packaging of the cassette: "Don't have a cassette player??? Visual Shazam the other side." What was on the other side? Nothing. Just whiteness. But, sure enough, when you opened the Shazam camera and scanned the blank back of the cassette insert, the artist's Shazam profile appeared where you could play the song. Fans took to the band's Facebook Page proclaiming things like "Got the tape in the mail today. I'm already in love. No freaking clue how you got my address, but A+ marketing. Hopefully all will be revealed soon so it will be less creepy . . . " The song got over a million plays on Spotify and 200K+ plays on SoundCloud within weeks of the tapes going out with virtually no other promotion other than a few blog articles. But word of mouth spread and even celebrities started getting in on the hype, with Katy Perry and Harry Styles tweeting about it.

■ **Beck—*Song Reader* Sheet Music Album**
In December of 2012, Beck released his new album. Except this time there was no audio, only sheet music. He released 108 pages of sheet music for 20 new songs (and 100 pages of art). His musical fans learned the songs and uploaded their versions to YouTube and SoundCloud. In 2014, Beck released an actual (audio) record of *Song Reader*.

■ **Wu-Tang Clan—One Copy Art Piece**
Some artists boycotted streaming. Others boycotted iTunes. And Wu-Tang Clan boycotted streaming, downloads, CDs and every other format. In 2014, they released their 31-song new album as a singular, double-LP package. The album toured art galleries and fans could hear the album in a museum setting

before the band auctioned it off to the highest bidder. Talk about contemporary art!

■ **Daft Punk—*Random Access Memories***
This album includes one of the biggest hits of the past decade, "Get Lucky," but the promotion around the album focused more on the Daft Punk brand and the multitude of collaborators on the record than just on the lead single. They rolled out a collection of cryptic 15-second TV commercials during *SNL*, huge billboards in cities around the country, an album trailer unveiled at Coachella, and a Vine unveiling of the album cover.

■ **Nine Inch Nails—*Year Zero* Real Life Video Game**
In 2007, Nine Inch Nails ran a worldwide marketing campaign that included a cryptic YouTube video that you had to pause to decode, USB flash drives in bathrooms of venues the band played, and secret messages on t-shirts sold at the shows that when Googled brought up even more confusion, with a webmaster email to contact that returned an autoresponse giving away a bit more of the puzzle. It was a real life video game that Nine Inch Nails fans had to come together from around the globe via the Wikipedia page to complete. It all culminated with NIN's album *Year Zero*.

"The eighteen-to-thirty-five-year-old demo has grown up in a marketing-saturated environment and has developed a sophisticated set of tools for avoiding the vast majority of marketing messages," Jordan Weisman, the marketing director in charge of the project said. "As a rule of thumb, the bigger the neon sign, the faster they'll run the other way. So the premise here was, instead of shouting, go the opposite way and whisper."

5.

BUILDING A FANBASE
ONE FAN AT A TIME

You need to confidently exclude people and proudly say what you're not. By doing so, you'll win the hearts of the people you want.
—DEREK SIVERS, *ANYTHING YOU WANT*

The music fan is more passionate about music than ever before. But they're not immersed in it. They're sampling. Everything is a charcuterie plate as opposed to "give me the steak and the potatoes and I'm diving in."
—BRUCE FLOHR, ARTIST MANAGER

THE NEW FAN

The "rock star mystique" is all but dead. Before, the closest a fan could get to their favorite musician was by waiting at the stage door after the show hoping their idol would stop by for a few autographs and a photo. But many didn't. Many self-righteous rockers bolted from the venue to the tour bus in their shades without so much as a wave to their fans who waited for two hours in the rain to meet them. Now, a fan can literally get inside their favorite artist's pants (pocket, via a tweet to their phone) without having to wear a low-cut shirt. Oh, how far we've come.

Not only has social media broken down the barriers of access; it has created a new reality where it's virtually impossible for artists to hide their true colors—for better or worse. Fans have always been attracted to authenticity, but now one can more quickly and easily weed out the impostors from the true artists. You can't fake it and make it in the new era.

Similarly, the new music fan has a completely different set of expectations. If a fan tweets a band with just a few thousand followers and doesn't get a response or even just a heart, that fan feels snubbed. Obviously, artists with millions of followers won't be able to respond to every tweet (and it's not expected), but for up-and-coming bands, early engagement can be the difference between cultivating hard-core evangelists who talk about your band every chance they get and fair-weather fans who casually turn on your Pandora station from time to time.

Some artists these days, however, go a bit too far and overly engage with people who are not fans and who would rather not be spoken to by an artist they don't care about. There's a way to be respectful of your fans, to embrace the new reality while still maintaining your privacy.

A perfect example of how you can engage with a fan in an authentic, noncreepy way is offered by Brittany Howard, lead singer and guitarist of Alabama Shakes. It all started when a 24-year-old fan from Louisville Instagrammed a short video of herself playing half of the opening riff to "Future People," stating "Doing my best." She tagged Howard (@ blackfootwhitefoot). Howard posted a response video on Instagram with a close-up on the neck of her guitar and finished the complicated lick for the fan, with "Here's the rest," and tagged the fan.

Every artist at any level can learn from this. You don't need to be a superstar to give back. Even if you have ten fans, make one of their days. Word will spread. But again, you don't need to be the creepy, over-engaged Facebook responder. Sure, Like comments, respond occasionally, Retweet, Instaheart, but there's a difference between giving back and giving up your life.

Younger artists are much better at creating an authentic social media presence and knowing how to engage just the right amount to maintain a bit of mystique but also not insult their fan. Ashley Nicolette Frangipane (or as you know her, Halsey), is considered an overnight sensation by the music industry. She sold out her first tour ever (of 500–1,000-cap rooms) in 30 seconds with zero radio play, no album and no label. But she had been cultivating a loyal fan base for over six years. When she was 14 in 2008, she had 14,000 Myspace friends and at 18 she had 16,000 YouTube subscribers. She built her following online. Whereas most artists try to get the viral video, viral photo, viral tweet, viral anything, Halsey worked on fostering a deep relationship with her followers. By staying open, vulnerable and intimate, her fans became loyalists. Halsey wasn't pushing or promoting anything. She was simply existing in a reality understood solely by those on the inside. So, when she had a piece of real content (her first song/music video "Ghost") to share, her fans were finally able to engage with something other than just a photo or a tweet. The track exploded online. Halsey told the *New York Times* about her first meeting with Capitol Records. She said, "I remember walking into Capitol Records, sitting down with the executives and having them say, 'Look at what you did while none of us were paying attention.' That was one of the proudest moments of my entire life. I put all the groundwork in myself, and they let me do my thing, because it's working."

Engagement > Followers

Followers, plays and Likes can be bought. Everybody knows it. And you look foolish if your YouTube video has 200,000 views with only 7 comments and 12 likes. Those views were clearly purchased from a bot. There's no point in spending money to puff up your numbers for vanity's sake. Advertising for real human followers is one thing, paying for bots to Like your page or watch your video is another.

Bots don't come to shows. Bots don't back your crowdfunding. Bots don't buy merch. Bots don't help you become a full-time musician.

Startup guru and angel investor Sean Ellis states that "focusing on customer acquisition over awareness takes discipline . . . At a certain scale, awareness/brand building makes sense. But for the first year or two it's a total waste of money."

Plays mean nothing if you have no way to connect with those listeners and follow up with them. That's why I completely tune out artists who tell me they got 100,000 plays on their most recent song. OK, but how many of those listeners signed up to your email list, bought a ticket to your show, Liked your Facebook Page or supported you in any way financially?

THE PYRAMID OF INVESTMENT AND THE PYRAMID OF ENGAGEMENT

Every fan exists on a Pyramid of Investment. The fans who stream your music but never spend any money on you directly are at the bottom of the pyramid. Those who buy your music are one level up. Those who come to your shows are a level higher. Those who buy your merch are a level above that. Those who back your crowdfunding campaigns are another level up. The fan club members are yet another tier higher. And the fans who buy the high-priced, VIP experiences are at the top of the pyramid. You should give every fan, of every level, ways to support you financially.

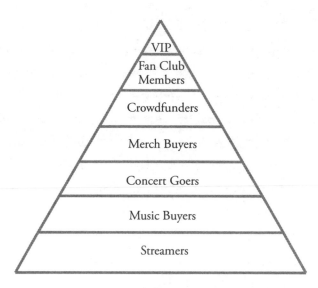

Pyramid of Investment.

But "investment" isn't just financial. Fans invest in artists with their time as well. The Pyramid of Engagement is nearly as important. Because the more engaged a fan is, the more she will be willing to purchase.

The fans who gave your Facebook Page a Like three years ago and haven't seen a post from you since are at the bottom of this pyramid. Those who follow you on Instagram, Twitter, Snapchat and everywhere else you may exist online are one level higher. The fans who actively Like, comment, rate, retweet, vote and heart are a level higher. The fans who are on your email list are a level above that. The fans who are not only on your list, but open and read everything you send, are a level higher. And at the very top are the fans on your street team engaging with every piece of content you put out and are constantly telling everyone they know about you. You know, like your mom.

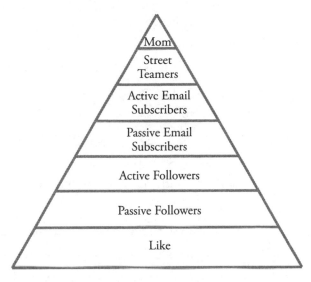

Pyramid of Engagement.

GET RICH IN YOUR NICHE

Own your niche. If you are an acoustic folk artist, get to know all the folk artists, listening rooms, labels and managers in your scene. Start there. Play the spots. Hang out at the spots when you're not playing. Cowrite with other folk artists. Find one to mentor you. Eventually, if you're good, word will spread. And then you expand to neighboring scenes.

But go deeper. Are you an acoustic folk artist who writes protest songs that appeal to college-age activists? Target that demo. But go deeper. Are you a blues artist? How about a blues artist from the south who only plays standards written before 1960? Target traditional folk lovers from the south. Embrace what makes your project unique. But go deeper. Are you a metal band? What kind of metal band? Metal-pop? Metal-core? Emo-metal? Are you a pop artist? Are you also Christian? Start with the Christian community. You don't need to label yourself a Christian artist, but target that community. Build your base of loyalists and let it spread from there.

You're not just a folk artist, blues artist, metal artist, pop artist, jazz artist, soul artist, singer/songwriter. Go as deep as you can with your niche to help you find your audience. The more that sets you apart and makes you unique, the easier it will be to target a demographic, a scene, a niche.

Once you've conquered your local scene, expand to neighboring scenes. The reason I say scenes and not towns is because not every town may have a scene in your niche. So do the research.

You can, of course, simultaneously network online. The electro-dream-pop artist vōx actually started with the SoundCloud electro community. She lived in L.A., and because it's such a massive town and she wasn't interested in performing live initially, she started online. She's not an extrovert who goes to shows and makes connections with everyone in the room. That's not her strength. But she's a master at the Internet. Through her ninja SoundClouding, she teamed up with DJs from around the globe to remix her songs and post (or repost) to their followers. Some of these DJs had hundreds of thousands of followers, so word spread quickly. Since vōx was an avid reader of electro and hip-hop blogs, she knew exactly who to send her songs (and remixes) to. She trended on Hype Machine, got tens of thousands of SoundCloud plays (hundreds of thousands on some remixes) and her inbox flooded with managers and labels seeking to rep her.

YouTube is also a scene in and of itself. And there are fans of You-Tubers. The one thing most of these YouTubers have in common is they all, pretty much, appeal to a younger demographic (mostly teens). There are now YouTube conferences around the world (VidCon in Anaheim has over 20,000 attendees) where fans can come to meet their favorite YouTubers—because very few of them ever tour. Most YouTubers live in L.A. and collaborate with other YouTubers. Their scene is YouTube. And it works for them.

But, of course, the YouTube scene didn't exist ten years ago. Maybe there's another online community popping up that you feel connected to that you want to develop.

So, home in on your sound, your scene and your niche. And start there. And you want to surround yourself with like-minded individuals. They will influence you more than you know. If everyone around you is kicking ass, working toward their dreams, you will be inspired to do the same. If everyone around is quitting music, starting families and settling into 9-to-5s, you will feel the pressure to do the same.

Your immediate community is so important. Which brings us to:

ARE YOU IN THE RIGHT CITY FOR YOUR MUSIC?

Of course, in the digital age, you can theoretically get your music out from anywhere in the world. But developing a music career where literally every other person in town is in a different field of work is unbelievably difficult. Of course, you can start as "the guy" or "the gal" in town who plays music and initially gets hired for any event where they want some music. And it may work for a little while, but eventually you will most likely go stir crazy and yearn to get out. You don't have to go far either. Move to the nearest big(gish) city where there is a music scene. And more specifically, a scene of like-minded artists in your genre. And go from there.

Don't underestimate the importance of a physical community.

LOS ANGELES, NEW YORK OR NASHVILLE?

New York feels like it's all about "making it." L.A. feels like it's all about making things.

—JULIA PRICE, L.A.-BASED (FORMERLY NYC)
SINGER/SONGWRITER

Wonder why so many acts break out of L.A., New York and Nashville? It's because the industry exists in those places. And so many other like-minded musicians live there, constantly inspiring each other, collaborating and trading tips and tricks. If you live in one of the cities, you are constantly rubbing shoulders with the movers and shakers of the industry. They hang out at the same music venues, go to the same coffee shops, grocery stores and dog parks. You may get introduced to someone at a show and then see them the very next day at the gym and make a deeper connection. They may need a singer/guitarist/cowriter/producer/fill-in-the-blank and think of you first for the job because you're top of mind. Everyone knows someone in the industry, and even if a person is not in it, if they like your music, they may pass it along to their industry friend. Friends like helping friends out. And people trust their friends.

You don't need to be in these cities to "make it," of course, but it can definitely help to be there. That being said, each town has its own strengths and weaknesses, and you should not move to any of these cities before you're ready and understand why you're moving.

Before even considering moving to any city, make sure you visit and spend a good amount of time there exploring. And make sure you do your research about the city you're thinking of moving to.

Future of Music Coalition released an extensive report in 2013 which surveyed over 5,300 musicians from all 50 states (and outside the U.S.). Eleven percent of the respondents lived in Los Angeles, New York or Nashville. The study found that Los Angeles–based artists grossed an average of $78,545 per year from music, Nashville artists grossed an average of $54,263 per year and New York artists grossed an average of $47,568 per year. These were the top-grossing cities on the list (Chicago was 4th). But, once adjusted for cost of living, the numbers were $59,958 (L.A.), $60,292 (Nashville) and $21,235 (New York). And yes, it's way cheaper to live in Nashville than L.A. or New York—hence the increased adjusted income. Also worth noting, of the respondents in the three cities, over half make 100% of their income from music. More specifically, 66.3% of respondents in Nashville, 55.7% in L.A. and 51.2% in New York. Chicago ranked pretty high on the list with 46.4% of respondents earning 100% of their income from music with an average gross income of $31,755 ($27,856 adjusted for cost of living).

LOS ANGELES

I moved to L.A. mainly to get away from the Minnesota winters. The fact that the industry is here was a bonus. The beauty of L.A. (unlike most other music communities around the world) is that it is incredibly diverse. There isn't a "music scene" per se; there is a singer/songwriter scene, a hip-hop scene, an indie-rock scene. There are hard-rock, pop, EDM and jazz scenes. And every scene has artists fifty-deep. And many of the scenes have subscenes, like the under-30 singer/songwriter scene. The '80s-rockers scene. And so on.

It seems virtually everyone I know in L.A. is a creative of some sort. Musician, actor, screenwriter, director, filmmaker, YouTube personality or Viner. L.A. is a creative town. Even the agents, managers and those who work in the industry in other capacities are mostly creative. You have to be when you work in a creative industry. So, in L.A. you are constantly vibing off of the creative energies around.

But Los Angeles is not a town of hippie-dippy artists (well, Venice still is). It is a town of creatives who want to make a living with their art. The artists in L.A. are smart, driven, passionate and hardworking. No matter what field you're in, if you're in L.A. you have to *hustle your a$$ off.* You can't sit around, work a day job and hope to be discovered just because you're here. Everyone in L.A. who makes it does so because of their hard work. There is very little luck that goes into it.

The Three-Year Test

No matter what field of work you're in, if you can make it three years in L.A., you can make it in L.A. Making it in L.A. is defined the same as making it in the music business: survival. I've seen many people come, live in the city for a bit, realize it's not for them and take off. Within three years. Because it's a town of hustlers, nontraditional career paths and instability, you do what you have to do to get by and make a living. And pretty much everyone I know in L.A. does a million different little jobs to make up the whole pot of money they need to live in the City of Angels. Because, let me tell you, it's a wonderful place to live if you can make it. Yes, it's expensive (but not as expensive as New York). But what L.A has that New York doesn't is the constant sunshine. Nearly every day of the year it is gorgeous out. Seventy-five degrees and sunny. Sure, there's some smog. But it ain't Beijing. And there's traffic. But now that the subway system is expanding, hopefully more people will take it and reduce the traffic and smog. L.A. gets a bad rap because of the plastic people and the traffic. But you don't have to surround yourself with the plastics. Yes, of course they exist. But they mostly exist in Beverly Hills. You know how often I go to Beverly Hills? Only when I stumble onto the other side of the city lines after leaving the Troubadour. And if you place yourself in a part of town where other, like-minded artists are, you won't have to drive much.

If you're thinking of moving, talk to a few musician friends and start there. Unlike New York, everything is extremely spread out. So if you live in Santa Monica and your bestie lives in Silver Lake, plan on seeing her twice a year and grabbing coffee over Skype.

Here's how I describe the various neighborhoods.

West Hollywood

I'm starting with WeHo because it's where I've lived for six-plus years. It has a special place in my heart. If you walk down Laurel Avenue, look down and you'll see "Ari and Amy 2013" carved into the sidewalk. WeHo is the gay capital of the country. It has been for decades. It's a great neighborhood—clean, comfortable and hopping. Aside from the Santa Monica Boulevard strip, where all the gay bars are (with men pole-dancing in thongs), there are plenty of lower-key restaurants, cafes, bars, restaurants and, of course, music venues. The Troubadour is in WeHo. As are the Sunset Strip clubs. If you pick the right location, you can be in walking distance of Trader Joe's, cafes, bars, restaurants and a gym. (You soon realize once you settle in town, everyone goes to the gym—often. Everyone. It rubs off. You will lose weight and you will become healthier.)

To be honest, I rarely drive, despite the city's reputation. West Hollywood is very centrally located—equidistant from the beach and the Eastside (25–45 minutes, depending on time of day). But it's far from the highways and the airport.

Hollywood

Don't confuse West Hollywood and Hollywood. Separate cities. Separate mayors. And completely different kinds of people and energies. Whereas West Hollywood is clean, comfortable and pleasant, Hollywood is rough, brash and flooded with tourists. Turn the wrong way at night, and you'll get solicited by women in short skirts and high heels. All the bumping dance clubs with DJs are mostly in Hollywood. Bottle service galore, with promoters who literally scour the city all day to find hot girls to stuff into their clubs and entertain the high rollers. But, that being said, there are a few really excellent music venues (and comedy clubs) in Hollywood, which is why I go there so often. Hollywood is significantly cheaper to live in than West Hollywood, so it may be a suitable option initially if you're looking to save money. Get some pepper spray though.

Downtown

Ten years ago downtown was a ghost town at night with tweakers roaming the streets. Nobody went down there. But today is different. It's the hottest up-and-coming neighborhood in town. Condos, apartment complexes, lofts, restaurants, bars, photography and recording studios, and music venues are popping up left and right. Many artists are renting lofts and setting up shop. Downtown definitely has much more of a New York feel than the rest of L.A.

The downside is, downtown is pretty far away from everywhere else. It's a solid 25 minutes from West Hollywood, without traffic. But there's always traffic. However, the subway will take you from downtown to Hollywood in no time at all.

Silverlake, Los Feliz, Echo Park (the Eastside)

Hipsterville. Local, organic, fair trade coffee shops, independent bookstores, tattoo shops, and pot shops (well, there are pot shops everywhere in L.A.). Mustaches and suspenders galore. Irony upon irony upon satire. It's the Williamsburg of L.A. Most young indie-rock musicians start on the Eastside. So the community of young rockers is strongest here. Lots of living room and basement concerts.

Koreatown

Not much here except the 1,800 capacity Wiltern Theater, a ton of amazing Korean BBQ restaurants and lots of Latino and Korean families.

Well, there are lots of Latino families everywhere—it is L.A. It's definitely more affordable to live in Koreatown, but you're pretty far removed from the rest of the city—except Downtown, which is right next door.

South Central

You've heard the songs, right? Not much has changed. Think metal detectors and barbed wire fences around the high schools. You don't want to go there.

Santa Monica, Venice and Neighboring Beach Towns (the Westside)

Two words: beach air. Whenever I go to Santa Monica, I stop and take a deep breath and sigh. Fresh. Call me a hippie, but there's a heightened consciousness in Santa Monica. It's the hub of yoga and meditation in L.A. Many of the TED speakers who live in L.A. live in Santa Monica or Venice. Venice borders Santa Monica and there is still the Venice hippie/surfer/artist culture on the beach and boardwalk. Not many music venues on the Westside though. However, Silicon Beach is here with Snapchat at it's center. As is YouTube Space.

Pico-Robertson

There are more Jews per capita here than anywhere else in the world, save Israel. If someone says they live in the Pico-Robertson neighborhood, they basically mean the one square mile surrounding the intersection of Pico and Robertson. It's where you'll find kosher markets, kosher delis and kosher Chinese restaurants (yes, they exist). The Mint is the closest music venue and Moshav Band hosts its annual Hanukkah party there. It's always sold out and oftentimes Matisyahu makes a guest appearance.

South Bay

This includes Manhattan Beach, Redondo Beach, Hermosa Beach and other nearby cities. It's very far removed from everything L.A. So much so that most don't really consider it L.A. It's a hike to get there and back. Most only go there to visit friends when their arms are twisted. However, the popular 280-capacity music venue Saint Rocke is there. But, again, the South Bay is so far away that many touring acts play L.A. one night and Saint Rocke the next. No one drives from L.A. to South Bay (or vice versa) for a small show. Hollywood Bowl? Sure. Viper Room or Saint Rocke? Fuhggetaboutit!

The Other Side of the Hill

"L.A." is generally considered everything from the ocean (Santa Monica, Venice) to downtown. The northern border is generally defined by the Hollywood Hills. Most people who move to L.A. populate L.A. proper. When you think of all the beautiful people of Los Angeles (and no, people aren't exaggerating), they mean south of the Hollywood Hills. But once they settle down and start a family, many move to the Valley (over "the hill") to raise kids. However, with rising rents south of the hills, many musicians are jumping over to Sherman Oaks, Studio City, North Hollywood and Burbank to get situated. It's much more affordable and really, not that far from Hollywood and West Hollywood—without traffic, of course.

Culver City

Tech companies and movie studios heavily populate Culver City. No one I know lives there, though.

Miracle Mile

Yeah, L.A. has a lot of neighborhoods and cities. The most confusing part about it is some are actual cities with separate mayors and city councils and others are technically part of the city of Los Angeles. I still haven't figured out which are which. I went to vote for mayor of Los Angeles only to find out that he wasn't on my ballot for West Hollywood. Miracle Mile is familyville. No one I know who doesn't have kids (or dogs) lives there. It's mostly houses and businesses.

Live Near Your Work, Play Where You Play

Above all, the determining factor of where you live should be proximity to work. If you get a day job before you move, live near it. The key to happiness in L.A. is avoiding traffic as much as you can. That being said, if you do end up living on the Westside, you will never want to make it to Eastside or Hollywood venues. So be cautious of that. When you get to town, you need to be out most nights networking at venues around town. I recommend not getting a day job before you move and just find something near where you live once you settle in.

How to Make the Quick Bucks

If you're a touring artist and move to Los Angeles, you obviously aren't going to want to get an inflexible day job that will prevent you from hitting the road every few months. So you have to get scrappy on how to make rent money. Many musicians (actors, screenwriters, etc.) drive for Lyft, Uber or food delivery services like Postmates. You can sign on when you need to make some money and sign off when you have a gig, rehearsal or anything else.

Some musicians work catering/event staff jobs. There are a bunch of catering companies and they typically pay between $15 and $25 an hour. Some of the best current companies to look into are Food by Lene, Joan's on Third and Chinois on Main. Catering companies come and go. The best way to find reputable event staffing companies is to ask other musicians, actors, writers and other freelancers you meet once you get to L.A. It's hard to gauge from online searches which catering companies are worth it. You'll work a lot of celebrity events. Your first few gigs you may get a bit star-struck.

Many musicians teach lessons as well. But be careful not to take on so many students that you don't have any time for your own music. When you get to town, ask other music teachers about best practices for acquiring new students: hint, target the rich family neighborhoods. Price yourself high. You're a professional! You can get away with $100/hour easily in L.A.

If you're a player, you can freelance; however, it's incredibly competitive since there are so many available players. Singer/songwriters, music directors and band leaders typically only hire musicians their friends refer. And if a current player can't make a gig, the buyer will ask the player for a referral. So meet other players on your instrument. If you have a decent cover repertoire, you can get on GigMasters and GigSalad to get hired for private events. More on these later.

Keep Your Problems to Yourself

When you first move to Los Angeles, if you don't already have serious passive income (like royalties), you're going to quickly realize how tough it is to get by financially. It is for everyone initially, so you'd think everyone would empathize. You'd be wrong. Needy people are unattractive. People like to surround themselves with winners, and complaining to your new friend that you have no money or how tough it is to make it in L.A. is a complete turnoff. It's tough for everyone. You're not special. Sure, pick people's brains on how the town works. People are happy to share their knowledge (if it works with their schedule), but no complaining. Stay positive. You can commiserate with other struggling artists if they bring it up first, but when you're meeting "important" people, this is not a topic of conversation to get into. I learned that the hard way. Many initial connections of mine became far less available when I casually revealed in conversation how tough it was for me to make money in L.A. as a musician. I stopped making that mistake very quickly.

Building It Live in L.A.

You are not going to get a manager, agent or label to come see you just because you're playing a hot club in L.A. You need something happening online first. Or you need someone they trust and respect (like a manager, lawyer or musician) to get them there. Your email will go straight to the trash. Your box of cookies you send to their office will get eaten, but without any indication of whom the box was from.

Believe me, I've tried it all.

Pitching yourself to important people in L.A. rarely works. You have to remember there are bands buzzing a hell of a lot more than you are, playing nearly every night of the week. Personally, I could go out every single night in L.A. to a show of someone I know who is performing. The city is unbelievably saturated with musicians. So, don't expect to get anyone out to your show if you have nothing happening online.

That being said, because of the saturation, most people (musicians and nonmusicians, in the industry and not) are constantly barraged with a slew of invites from their biannual Facebook friends who only send a message when they have a show (guilty!).

In other cities, you have many more friends who are not involved in the music industry and who actually enjoy going out to see live music.

The Clubs

■ **The Sunset Strip**

> To get in a van and drive out (to L.A.) to play the Viper Room
> so that I show up is a waste of time and money. I ain't going.
> So many people spend time on the sh*t that doesn't matter.
> —BRUCE FLOHR, RED LIGHT MANAGEMENT

Once you get to know Los Angeles, it's a lot less scary and daunting than it seems. Everyone knows of the Sunset Strip. Legendary clubs like the Whisky a Go Go, the Roxy, the Viper Room, the Rainbow Room, still exist. The House of Blues just shut down at its long standing location on the Strip. The Troubadour technically isn't on the Strip, but it's nearby and just as legendary.

Most of these clubs work with infamous, pay-to-play promoters (more on this practice in Chapter 7). These clubs primarily host hip-hop acts, rock and pop bands, the kind of music that made the Strip famous in the '70s, '80s and '90s. The only difference is, back in the day the Strip actually developed talent and helped artists get known, paid and signed. Now, the Strip has all but become a museum. A relic of a time since passed. Young bands from around the country shell out hundreds of dollars for the opportunity to (pay to) play these interactive museums.

Let me make this crystal clear. Break out your highlighter. Type this out and post it in big letters on the side of your rehearsal space: YOU WILL NOT GET DISCOVERED PLAYING ON THE SUNSET STRIP.

Or any club in L.A. Live discovery rarely happens anymore. Promoters and venue bookers used to care about quality. They used to be respected gatekeepers. And if you got a coveted spot playing their club, people cared. Now, it seems that all venues and promoters care about is getting paid. Whether it's from the band's pocket or the fans'. There are definitely some exceptions, but not really on the Sunset Strip.

■ **Eastside Clubs**

This is where indie rock and electronic music live. Even though I'm not really cool enough to live on the Eastside, the clubs there are some of my favorite spots to see music. Venues like the Echo (and big sister Echoplex), the Satellite and the Bootleg have some of the best live sound and highest-quality talent in town. The Bootleg is probably the most versatile of the three, with two (soon to be three) rooms varying in size, and hosts Americana, funk, soul, pop electronic, indie rock and everything in between, whereas Echoplex is the biggest (700 cap) and also hosts a range of talent including electronic and hip-hop. Many young artists, especially indie-rock bands, start with the Eastside clubs and develop in that scene, playing everywhere and anywhere to just get known in the scene, and then start spreading their shows out to actually build a fanbase.

■ **Singer/Songwriter Spots**

My area of expertise. The L.A. staples are Genghis Cohen and the Hotel Cafe. Sadly, the singer/songwriter incubator Room 5 closed down in early 2016, but the curators of the room now run the second (smaller) room at the Hotel Cafe. The Hotel Cafe has been a launching pad for acts like Katy Perry, Sara Bareilles, Joshua Radin, Meiko, and Ingrid Michaelson. It's been my home ever since I got to town. To be clear, the Hotel Cafe is neither a hotel nor a cafe. But it is a spot where John Mayer, Ed Sheeran, the Roots, John Legend, Chris Martin and other superstar musicians will randomly show up and play an unannounced set. People love going to the Hotel Cafe. Nearly every act booked at the Hotel Cafe is handpicked by the owner, Marko. There's no pay-to-play and nights are actually curated by Marko. Bar Lubitsch, the Bootleg and Open Space are also popular spots for singer/songwriters. Songwriter nights have started popping up around town as well, with many taking place in the Valley.

■ **Downtown**

Lots of hip venues are popping up seemingly everyday downtown. The Edison has been a classy stable for a few years, but it's definitely worth exploring some other spots—including the many secret loft shows and gallery parties.

■ **Hip-Hop Spots**

Aside from the Sunset Strip clubs which also book hip-hop, the Echoplex also hosts hip-hop regularly. Low End Theory at the Airliner has been rated by the *L.A. Weekly* as "one of the most influential hip-hop and electronica music nights in North America."

■ **Jazz Clubs**

The Blue Whale, the Baked Potato, Catalina and Vibrato lead the Los Angeles jazz front. There's definitely a mix of local and touring talent, and the best part is, people go to listen to the music. At the Blue Whale, with a packed house, I had to whisper to the bartender to put in my drink order. Whisper!

■ **Residencies**

There are many spots around town like hotels and lounges that hire singer/songwriters and DJs to provide their clientele entertainment for two to four hours or so. These spots typically pay a guarantee. Unlike the cover grind, oftentimes originals are welcomed and encouraged. Having a hip artist (not a bland cover act) is a point of pride in L.A.

Don't Move to L.A. Before You Are Ready

This is important, so break out that highlighter again and pay attention. *Do not move to L.A. until you are ready.* How do you know if you're ready? Well, if you haven't played more than just a handful of shows, and want to be a live act, you're not ready. If you haven't established something in your hometown, you're not ready. Just because you have a good voice is no reason to move to L.A. People there hustle their a$$ off to make it as a musician. It's not a place to "see how it goes" or figure yourself out. Because, unlike your hometown, L.A. is very unforgiving. And unbelievably competitive. If you get someone, anyone, in L.A. to come to your show and make them pay $10 to watch you suck, they will never come again. Ever. You may think you're great because your mother tells you how amazing you are. But unless you look, sound and perform like the next big thing, no one is going to care. I can't tell you how many local artists' shows in L.A. I've been to that are godawful. L.A. has some of the best talent in the world, but it also has some of the worst.

The only exception is if you're young. Like under 20. People are much more forgiving of youth. Not only will you be relegated to the few 18+/all ages spots in town, you will play many more makeshift, DIY, pop-up venues early on. The Eastside scene has a lot more youth and a lot more "local" clubs. So start there if you're young and need the experience.

So, if you're thinking of moving to L.A., wait until you're great and are ready to make that leap.

NEW YORK CITY

Not many things are inaccessible here; the only thing
holding you back in New York is really yourself.
—A. SARR, DJ/PRODUCER, NEW YORK CITY

You shouldn't come here when you're totally green. You should
have an idea of what you're doing or New York will eat you alive.
—CHAMPIAN FULTON, JAZZ SINGER/PIANIST/BAND LEADER,
NEW YORK CITY

When we started out, there were more musicians and artists
that banded together. We all played on each other's records,
in bands, rocked shows together on a regular basis, recorded
together, helped on the business and marketing tips. We basically
fostered ourselves—the more people, the merrier. Today it's super
different. Kinda lonely. Feels like everybody is out for themselves
and nobody else. Rent is expensive as f**k. Studios are closing.
Artists are moving further from Manhattan every day. It's hard to
make music in NYC and be successful enough financially to keep
it moving 100%. You have to hustle really hard to make ends
meet and that's time consuming—leaving less time
available to hang in the scene.
—TERMINATOR DAVE, DRUMMER, SHINOBI NINJA

New York City constantly has people coming from other places
to make it here. And it's constantly spitting out those who can't
take the spin cycle anymore. Basically its like being trapped on
Gilligan's Island and you need to shoot as many flares up as
bright and as far as possible so you can get rescued.
—DUKE SIMS, SHINOBI NINJA, LIFELONG NEW YORKER

New York City is my favorite city in the world. Don't get me wrong, I love L.A. and the sunshine, but nothing beats the energy of New York. Life moves fast in the Big Apple. The people are always on the go and move a million miles a minute. It's a true melting pot of cultures, backgrounds, races, religions and ethnicities. You can walk four blocks and hear six different languages. If you walk four blocks in L.A., it's because you couldn't find parking any closer. I love the walking culture of NYC. My iPhone told me that on my last weeklong trip to New York I walked an average of five miles a day. I'm lucky if I walk five miles a week in L.A. Actually, unlucky. Again, that means my parking luck was off.

I create better art in New York. I'm more inspired there. I can walk outside and the inspiration starts flowing. I don't have to seek it out—it finds me. When I walk outside in L.A., I just smile because it's so darn gorgeous out. It's more difficult to create great art when you're happy all the time.

Because there are so many band leaders in New York (and theater groups), you can make a decent living as a freelancer. There's always someone looking for a hired gun. But, as in L.A., it takes a serious hustle.

In the United States, the borough of Manhattan is the most expensive place to live. The average rent for a one bedroom apartment is a cool $3,100 a month. And now Brooklyn, as a whole, is pretty darn expensive as well, with average one-bedrooms costing around $2,700 a month. So, if you're just moving to New York, Queens may be your best bet to start out and until you figure out how to make a living. Queens averages about $2,000 a month for a one-bedroom. Of course the further away you get from Manhattan, the cheaper it gets.

Just getting started in New York, you'll most definitely need a few roommates and a big savings account.

Like L.A., you want to find your scene. New York is such a massive city, with so many artists and musicians, that it's best to start with your genre of music and the clubs where its hosted.

The Clubs

■ **Jazz**

Few cities in the world have the reputation that New York has for jazz. And for good reason. Of course there are strong traditions in many American cities, like Chicago, Kansas City and New Orleans, but New York's jazz scene remains one of the best. New York jazz musicians may tour, they may move, but they always seem to return home. Clubs like the Blue Note, Birdland, Smoke, Iridium, the Village Vanguard, Smalls and Zinc are New York institutions, while fabulous dives like Fat Cat, Barbès and 55 Bar are hopping most nights of the week as well.

■ **Singer/Songwriter**

The New York counterpart to the Hotel Cafe is Rockwood Music Hall. Most singer/songwriters in New York make this their home, and for good reason. Initially, just a tiny, 70-cap (that's generous) room, Rockwood has now expanded into three music venues (in the same building): Rockwood 1, 2 and 3. Most shows are free and on Saturdays (in Rockwood 1) music starts at 3 P.M. This is a great spot to go and hang out if you're a singer/songwriter. You'll meet fellow singer/songwriters and build up your community. Rockwood 1 and 3 are much more intimate spots (caps at 70 and 64 respectively), whereas Rockwood 2 typically has bands and has a sizable cap of 300. Other spots in town frequented by singer/songwriters are the legendary Bitter End, the Living Room (in its new Brooklyn location), the Mercury Lounge and Pianos. The Sidewalk Cafe, Pete's Candy Store and Caffe Vivaldi (my very first NYC show was here) are great spots to start out with—and pop in for the open mics. The New York Songwriters Circle has been hosting songwriter rounds (more on what these are in the Nashville section) since 1991 and have showcased artists like Norah Jones, Lana Del Rey, Vanessa Carlton, and Gavin DeGraw over the years.

■ **Indie-Rock and Other Bands**

The indie-rock tradition is still going strong in NYC. Clubs like the Mercury Lounge, Bowery Ballroom, Gramercy Theatre, Cake Shop, Arlene's Grocery, Pianos, Webster Hall and Santos Party House are all solid spots to find some of the best up-and-coming indie talent out there. While Baby's All Right, Palisades, Silent Barn, Secret Project Robot, Shea Stadium, Living Gallery, Death by Audio and the Stone are hot DIY spots for more punk and experimental projects.

■ **Hip-Hop/R&B/Soul**

Aside from the bigger rooms that host a range of genres, such as Bowery Ballroom, Webster Hall, Brooklyn Bowl, Baby's All Right and SOB's, more intimate spots like the Flat, Shrine, B.B. King's, Pianos, Santos Party House, Nuyorican Poets Cafe, Village Underground and DROM have hip-hop, R&B and soul nights, but most feature all kinds of music. It's also worth checking out the rich poetry scene New York has to offer and get started there as well.

■ **Residencies**

As in L.A., many artists get weekly residencies at hotels or lounges that pay a guarantee. Oftentimes this is a two-to-three-hour gig. DJs and producers as well as singer/songwriters are seeing most of these residency opportunities. Pay is typically $100–$500 a night. Don't do them for "exposure."

NASHVILLE

So many people get record deals in Nashville
and they don't ever get an album.

—LUKE BRYAN

Imagine you're an insurance salesperson working in an office.
You don't make money by trying to sell insurance to people in
the office. You gotta get out of the office to make the sale. So,
Nashville is our "office." It's a great place to learn, network,
be inspired, party, listen to music, but you gotta
get out of town to make money.

—JEB HART, NASHVILLE-BASED TOURING MUSICIAN

If you're a country singer/songwriter, Nashville is where you need to be. Plain and simple. Music City, as it's known, is a songwriter's town. And not just country songwriting. But country music is the city's heritage—almost as much as Hot Chicken.

Nashville, despite what you may think, is a relatively small town. And it definitely has that feel to it. The people are polite and have that famous southern hospitality. It's not spread out like L.A. or built up (literally) like New York. The people are much more laid back. And unlike in L.A. and New York, pretty much everyone you meet works in the music industry.

Like Austin's 6th Street during SXSW, the bars on Broadway have live music (mostly country) from 11 A.M. until 2 A.M., 7 days a week. During the daytime, you can find songwriter rounds with a mix of up-and-comers and, believe it or not, hit songwriters, at many of the hot spots, like Tootsie's, but come nightfall, nearly every club turns the party on with mostly country cover bands rocking the strip. Honky-tonk, bluegrass, country-pop, bro-country-rock, all of it is showcased at different clubs up and down Broadway. The street is packed with mostly tourists, but country-loving locals are often scoping out the talent as well. If you're a player looking to break in, this is where you want to be hanging. Every country-rock band knows 75–100 country staples. If you're a guitarist, bassist, fiddle player or drummer, learn these tunes and you will find work. If you're the best on your instrument, word will spread and your work will improve. If you're the best on your instrument and you're a great hang, you will work often and be well compensated. But, of course, it takes time. But it takes less time the harder you hustle and the more you network.

Believe it or not, most bands and songwriters aren't getting paid much (if anything) to play the clubs on Broadway, but they can make a decent amount in tips. Some get cuts of the bar for the time they're performing. None of the clubs have a cover and most are packed every night. Learning to work the room (and get the most amount of tips) is an art in itself that is mastered by working Broadway musicians.

Songwriter Rounds

The songwriter round is an honored tradition in Nashville. Despite what the name suggests, most songwriter rounds don't actually take place 'in the round' (except at the Bluebird Cafe). Two to five songwriters typically sit in a line on stage and each trade off playing a song. This goes round and round (hence the name) for hours. Occasionally you can find a songwriter round in L.A. or New York, but those in Nashville happen multiple times a day, every day, at various venues around town. Songwriter rounds are not open mics. The rounds are booked with top-notch talent, of, you guessed it, songwriters playing mostly their original songs. Many songwriters who participate in the rounds aren't aspiring to be artists. Most of them are seeking a publishing deal (or already have one and are testing out their new material). It seems like many more writers in Nashville get publishing deals than do those in L.A. or New York (just by the sheer number of great writers in town), but most initial deals may just be for a single song, or 18. A typical initial writer's pub deal in Nashville is what's known as the 18-18-18: 18 songs, for 18 months, for $18,000 (or less). Which isn't much of a commitment on the part of a big publishing company. Publishing deals these days (in Nashville, L.A. and NYC) with a major publishing company can pay hundreds of thousands of dollars up front. This, like a record deal, is not a paycheck; it's a loan that is paid back in royalties. The platinum-selling, country act Cam turned down her first publishing deal offer. She told *Billboard* magazine, "The next time I show someone my music, they're not going to underestimate or undervalue me." She was right.

Many songwriter clubs have 6:00 and 9:00 shows. If you're new to town, start hanging out at the 6:00 shows. This is where your community is. The 9:00 crowd is made up of established Nashvillians. Most people's initial community is made up of other newbies. Nashville is all about the community, from the get-go.

Open Mics

Open mics, unlike rounds, are open to anyone who wants to sign up. Like most places around the country, you arrive early (or call in) and put your name on the list. There are many popular open mics that happen multiple times a week around Nashville at venues like the Commodore Grille at the Holiday Inn Nashville-Vanderbilt, the Bluebird Cafe, the Listening Room and Douglas Corner Cafe.

PROs and NSAI

The PROs (ASCAP, BMI and SESAC; more on these in Chapter 13), along with the Nashville Songwriters Association International, are extremely helpful resources for getting your songs critiqued and passed along. Get in touch with your PRO when you move to town (once you have a batch of killer songs) and join the NSAI.

Breaking In

Before you move to Nashville, make sure you visit at least once to get a feel for the town. One of the best times to go is during the Tin Pan South Songwriters Festival in the spring. I also highly recommend getting Liam Sullivan's book *Making the Scene: Nashville: How to Live, Network, and Succeed in Music City*. He gives great tips on venues to check out, neighborhoods to live in, restaurants and bars to frequent and even where to buy a mattress. He also interviews some big players in town about their tips on how to break into Nashville.

Above all, Nashville is a networking town. Even more so than L.A. or New York. The most important thing to do in Nashville is get out and meet other songwriters. You also want to play everywhere and anywhere all the time. This gives you a chance to showcase your songs in front of other writers, make tips and, more important, make connections.

And unlike in L.A., publishers do actually frequent open mics and songwriter rounds to scout out talent. You most likely won't get signed off of a single performance at an open mic, but you may get a meeting.

Nashville is all about the community. You can't bust into town and carry yourself like you're the greatest thing since Garth Brooks. That may work in L.A., but in Nashville, people top to bottom, left to right, appreciate humility. Yes, your songs have to be top-notch, but above all, people want to work with those they like. If you're a d**k, you won't get anywhere. Be humble, be gracious, be kind and be awesome.

The Demo

Many songwriters seeking publishing deals (or even artists seeking major record deals) first cut demos. What's the difference between demos and albums? Demos aren't released, but merely pressed on CDs and put up as private links online. They are meant to pitch publishers to get your songs bought and recut by a current star. Every songwriter signed to a publishing deal, in any city, records demos, but typically these are funded by the publishing company. Because there are so many unsigned songwriters in Nashville, many demos are made on spec and the demo recording business is strong. You can find an engineer, producer and studio to track your demo for about $500, start to finish. But you'll also have to hire your players. The demos, many times, sound good enough to be on the radio, but they're meant to shop, not publicly sell. That being said, many songwriters do sell (or just give away) their demos at their gigs. And a business card is always included. You don't build a local following in Nashville like you do in other cities in the country. It's a totally different scene.

However, many noncountry musicians and songwriters live in Nashville. Many L.A. singer/songwriters have migrated to Nashville. East Nashville, like East L.A, is the hipster part of town and is becoming rapidly populated with musicians of all sorts. There are rock clubs where local bands do build followings (like they would in other towns), and there are growing rock and hip-hop scenes outside of the city's country music epicenter.

HOW TO FIND WHO YOUR FANS ARE

Remember when you made an "Our Fans" list back in Chapter 3? Now it's time to actually figure out where they exist. Geographically, demographically and internetgraphically (yeah, I know, that's not a word).

First, make a list of artists who you sound like. Or at least, artists whose fans will get into your music. The best way to find out where (and how many) of them exist is on Facebook. Since, virtually everyone on the planet is on Facebook, this will give you a pretty clear idea.

If you've never run a Facebook ad before, it's a great platform to search very specific demographics. Facebook, as we all know, can get creepily specific. You can create a (fake) ad without actually paying anything to run it. Select the city you want to target, age range if you want, and then in the Interest field type in your similar artists. Facebook will tell you how many people in that city meet the criteria. So, if I want to see if anyone in Minneapolis between the ages of 21 and 35 like Alabama Shakes, Facebook tells me that about 3,000 people do. However, only 2,100 people do in Phoenix and "fewer than 1,000 people" do in Cleveland. This tactic can help route your tours and focus your promotional campaigns.

THE FOLLOW-BACK

A good way to grab high-quality followers online is through the follow-back method. First, in your Instagram and Twitter profiles, put in the description "for fans of Alabama Shakes, Gary Clark Jr. and Jack White" or "we sound like . . . " or even just something witty that you think would appeal to the fanbase you're targeting. Then link your best YouTube video, SoundCloud or Spotify song. And link (or pin to the top of your profile) a place where they can join your crowdfunding/subscription campaign or sign your email list (incentivize that—more on that in a minute). Now, go to these bands' Twitter and Instagram profiles and start following all of their followers. Each service limits you to about 1,000 follows a day, so do this every day (or have your interns do this). There are apps like Unfollow for Twitter, Followers+ for Instagram and Crowdfire for both that enable you to unfollow accounts who don't follow you back and can automate this process a bit. Give people at least a few days to follow you back before you unfollow them. The reason you want to unfollow people who don't follow you is so your ratio looks good. It's not cool to have 1,000 followers and be following 8,000. It is cool though the other way around. People judge you based on your Followers/Following ratio.

Think this is tacky? Well, it works. Lost In A Name was down to the wire on their PledgeMusic campaign and was only at about 75% of their goal after exhausting their fanbase, friends and relatives. They had only a few days left and were running out of options. The follow-back tactic pushed them across the finish line.

IS RADIO STILL IMPORTANT?

To get a song on the radio is expensive. If you just have radio
leading the charge and you swing and miss,
you just bet $200,000.
—BRUCE FLOHR, RED LIGHT MANAGEMENT

Radio is still how superstars are born. But commercial radio no longer breaks acts like they used to. Radio gets to the party last—only after the act is proven and getting serious traction across other mediums like Spotify and YouTube. Commercial radio rarely takes chances anymore. And they really only play major-label acts. And even if the act is indie (as in the cases of Macklemore and Ingrid Michaelson), they use a major distributor with a powerful radio promotions arm. It's a complete waste of time for you to hire an expensive radio promoter. Even if you get a $200,000 investment, this is not a good use of your money. I've seen very talented acts blow this kind of money attempting to break pop radio. Lay the groundwork. Build the fans. Grow loyal followers. Get some traction online first. If you're not getting serious YouTube, Spotify or SoundCloud numbers, radio will completely ignore you. That being said, the only reason radio played indie acts like Ingrid Michaelson and Macklemore was because they had serious traction already. Ingrid had her hit single "The Way I Am" not only in a popular Old Navy commercial, but it was featured in *Grey's Anatomy* (in 2007 this was a big deal) and she got on the front page of the *Wall Street Journal* for it. Not to mention the millions of plays on MySpace (remember that) she was receiving. Using that ammunition, the radio promoters at Sony RED Distribution (whom Ingrid used for physical distribution) were able to go to AC and AAA radio stations and pitch it confidently. Same with Macklemore & Ryan Lewis's "Thrift Shop." They already had a massive YouTube following when "Thrift Shop" was released and the video went viral. Like Ingrid, they used a major distribution partner (ADA under Warner Music Group). Although it was released in August of 2012, it didn't actually crack the top 10 on the *Billboard* Hot 100 until January 2013. But it became the second-best-selling song of 2013. And it sold over 10 million downloads in the United States alone. And because they released it independently, the duo got to make the record in the way they wanted and kept the majority of the revenue without having to recoup (pay back) a major record-label advance.

Lorde's song "Royals" also didn't break into America until Sean Parker (of Facebook and Napster fame) included it on his wildly popular Spotify playlist, Hipster International, two weeks after the song was released. Six days after Parker included the song on his playlist (of 800,000+ followers at the time), "Royals" debuted on the Spotify Viral Chart. Less than a month later, "Royals" was #1 on the Spotify Viral Chart. And then a month after that, "Royals" hit alt-radio. And a month after that, it cracked the *Billboard* Hot 100. By year's end, it was the third-most-shared track in the country.

As stated earlier, Halsey self-released her song and music video

"Ghost." Because of her massive Instagram, Twitter and YouTube follow-ing, it quickly went viral. Labels approached only after she was wildly suc-cessful. And her song "New Americana" was an easy sell to radio because she was already a proven artist.

Gotye's "Somebody That I Used to Know" was recorded in Gotye's parents' basement and initially released by an Australian label, Eleven Music, in July 2011. Powered by a stop-motion body paint video, it gath-ered 200,000 views in the first couple weeks. Hip music blogs quickly took notice and shared the video. By December the video had gone viral, with millions upon millions of views. Universal Republic swooped up Gotye and pushed the song at U.S. radio (even though many stations had already begun playing the song). By January 2012, the song cracked the *Billboard* Hot 100, and a few months later you couldn't get away from it. *Glee* was covering it. *American Idol* finalists were singing it. It hit #1 on the *Billboard* Hot 100 and became the longest-running #1 by a solo male artist ever. In 2013 the song won two Grammys. All from a very creative music video (and an incredibly personal, yet ever-so-relatable, song).

But again, radio didn't lead the charge here either. They rarely do. They want something proven. Unfortunately, quality and taste have very little to do with it anymore.

THE MAILING LIST

I remember in 2008 when every band on the planet's entire online pro-motional plan revolved around MySpace. And why wouldn't it? It was the most popular social network in the world. And the band profiles were easily customizable. MySpace profiles became most artists' primary web-site. Artists grew massive fanbases on MySpace, and fans loved the access it gave them to their new favorite artists. MySpace seemed to be break-ing artists left and right, and play counts and "friend" numbers were the new musical currency. Facebook was, of course, rapidly growing, but at the time it was still primarily just used by students. And never for music.

But then, in 2009, something happened. People started leaving MySpace in droves. By 2010 it was all but a ghost town. It became the slums of the Internet. You didn't dare visit.

What's the big deal, right? Well, all the artists who built up their fanbases on MySpace couldn't reach them anymore. Some haphazardly attempted to transition them over to YouTube and Facebook, but most didn't. I went on a national tour supporting a MySpace star after the death of MySpace. Even though this artist had millions upon millions of plays on MySpace, the fans didn't transition to Facebook, YouTube or the artist's mailing list. We grossly undersold our tour projections because the artist didn't have a way to reach the fans and let them know about the tour. The fans were still listening, but now they were listening on You-Tube. To fan-made lyric videos. So this artist couldn't even add annotations to the videos letting everyone know about the tour.

What's the lesson here? Build up your email list! Jamie Foxx told Tim Ferriss on his podcast, "I was social media before there was social media." Jamie built an audience while he was working the stand-up circuit of L.A. in the early '90s. He used to hand out 3 × 5 cards at his shows and asked people to write down their pager numbers so he could text them when he had upcoming shows.

The mailing list remains the best way to communicate with fans. All the contacts on your email list, you own. All the Likes on Facebook, Followers on Twitter, Instagram and Periscope, Subscribers on YouTube and Friends on Snapchat, you rent. Any third party can change their terms, and overnight you could lose access to all your hard-earned fans (like Facebook does all the time). Even though average music email open rates sit at just 23%, Facebook's average Page reach is a dismal 10%. But even if the Facebook user sees your post fly by in their Newsfeed, they didn't digest it or engage with it. The actual average Facebook engagement rate is well below 1%. Whereas when a fan opens your email, they've engaged with it (clicked open).

Make sure your email sign-up on your website is prominent and that there is an incentive to sign up. Signing up on the website from home is very different from signing up at a concert. There isn't the buzzing energy (or a band member's personal encouragement to do so), so incentives like exclusives, raffles and full-quality songs help.

For your shows, use a lined sheet of paper (or print one out) and include two columns. The first, which should take up the majority of the page, is "Email." And the second is "Zip Code." Or, to speed up the process, you can just include one column for "Email" and you can manually add the corresponding zip code (from the city you just played) when you import the names. Always, always, always provide a pen for the mailing list clipboard. If there is no pen, no one will go out of their way to track a pen down to sign your list. And make sure you tie the pen to the clipboard.

Or better yet, get an iPad and lock it on the mailing list sign-up screen. No need to worry about attempting to decipher drunken handwriting. Hand out a free sticker at the show for everyone who signs up.

At every intimate show you play, pass the clipboard or iPad around. Make sure everyone signs up. Especially at house concerts. People are very willing to sign up on your list during house concert experiences. And you absolutely want everyone's email at these shows so you can hit them up for your club appearance when you return to town.

Make sure building your email list is the first priority. Email isn't going away anytime soon and remains the only constant in an ever-changing digital world. Building a grass-roots music career is about gaining fans, one at a time, and keeping them engaged and respected.

As far as who is the best mailing list provider? Well, I haven't found the best yet. I've used a few different services and most have pros and cons.

Things to look out for when you're researching whom to use:

■ **No Double Opt-In**
Meaning, if they sign up on your clipboard at the show, you should be able to import the name to your list online without them having to confirm it. And if you're changing mailing list providers, you want to be able to import your current list without the users having to opt in (again) to the new provider's list.

■ **A Customizable Autoresponse**
Most mailing list providers have this. This means, when someone signs up, they immediately get a welcome email in their Inbox (that you customize) containing links to the incentives. Others enable multiple autoresponders. The provider can send an initial autoresponse to new sign-ups immediately, then another automated response one day later and then another autoresponse a week after that. A stream of welcome emails.

■ **Analytics**
You should be able to see how many opened the email, who clicked on each included link and from which geographic location.

■ **Location Sorting**
Make sure you can add emails by postal (zip) code. Some mailing list providers will grab the zip code automatically when fans sign up online. Having the ability to sort by location is especially important when you're touring so you can send out targeted emails to the cities you are visiting with specific details (and reminders) about their show.

■ **Reuse Past Campaigns**
Considering the template for most email blasts will be very similar, you should have to design it only once and then be able to reuse it (changing out the body info).

■ **Not Using Your Physical Mailing Address**
In America, the law requires that any email that promotes goods or services include the physical address of the "sender," which is the person on whose behalf the email is being sent. For that reason, some providers will require you to put your own, personal address. Others will put their company's address. It's nice if you don't have to give all of your subscribers your home (stalker-friendly) address, even though that doesn't comply with the U.S. law.

■ **Groups**
You should be able to filter your subscribers by location, open history, click history (for album purchases), and then add them to groups to email directly. You should even be able to create a street team group and other filtered groups to mail separately for things that may not concern the entire list.

■ **Customer Service**
This is key. The best services will provide you with a phone number or online chat. It's also good to test customer service email turnaround time. Things come up. Glitches occur. Being able to contact a human is a must.

THE TRIPLE CHECK

This is a tactic you should employ with everything in your music career. The last thing you want to have happen is send out a blast to 5,000 people with a link to your new album, only to realize that your link doesn't work. No brainer, right? Well, I can't tell you how many emails I've received from artists with broken or incorrect links. Always, send yourself a test email (every provider allows this) and open the email on your desktop *and* your phone. It should look great on both. Click each link to make sure it's good. And it's good to click the link in an "incognito" window. Incognito windows are available in Chrome and enable you to create an entirely new session with none of your settings saved (and fresh cache). This is crucial to test your links, because many times links may work for you when you're signed in, but no one else. Perfect examples are Dropbox and PayPal links.

If you edit a blast, send another test. Edit it again, another test. Train yourself to use the triple-check method in everything you do.

6.

PLAYING LIVE

Bands should not be trying to play in front of 1,500 people because they've got one song in heavy rotation and they literally weren't a band a year and a half ago. They might get away with it for a little while, but I can tell you a bunch of bands that I heard on the radio two years ago, you ain't hearing about them now. Because they couldn't bring it live.

—BRUCE FLOHR, RED LIGHT MANAGEMENT

You really don't know how something's going to play until you test it.

—B. J. NOVAK, WRITER/ACTOR/COMEDIAN

People are nervous for no reason, because no one's going to come out and slap you or beat you up.

—JAMIE FOXX

THE PURPOSE OF PERFORMING LIVE

I love playing live. I love connecting with an audience. I love elevating a crowd to new heights. I love creating a beautiful, shared experience that people walk away from inspired, uplifted, invigorated and fulfilled. But I realize not all artists like or want to perform. Many very successful YouTubers I know have no interest in performing or touring. They make enough money for them to live on and that's totally fine. And, of course, professional songwriters rarely, if ever, tour. They cowrite day in and day out and hope their song gets cut by a big star and becomes a hit. All they need is one hit a year and they're set.

However, most artists want (and need) to play live. So ask yourself what kind of artist you want to be. Does playing live interest you? If so, you need to have a killer live show. And the only way to get better at performing is by performing. So, start by playing as much as you can. Anywhere and everywhere. You need experience more than anything early on. Get onstage whenever you can. You won't be getting paid for these early shows, but you don't deserve to be just yet. You deserve to get paid when your act merits it and when you can consistently get crowds out to your shows.

WHEN TO CHARGE FOR SHOWS

There will come a point when there is a shift in your audience's reaction. It will go from a polite, respectful (pity) applause to a rousing, enthusiastic, fervent one. Your friends will compliment you with a hint of disbelief in their voice and people you don't know will start coming up to you gushing about your show. People (if you do it right) will start coming back to your shows and bringing friends. At some point you will look out at the crowd and there will be more faces you don't recognize than those you do. That will be the moment you know you're onto something.

Once people start requesting to book you, you need to know what (and if) to charge. Obviously, you can do benefit concerts for free if you believe in the cause. But always ask if they can give you a "stipend" to at least cover your expenses. Or charge them a very reduced rate. And make sure the gig will represent you well and will cover all of your necessary technical requirements. You don't want to take a benefit concert only to find out that you're going to be playing in the corner of the cafeteria, without a stage, through a sound system that only half works, with one mic on a shaky stand in a fluorescent-lit room. Or worse, a completely unlit "stage." I've done it all. So, if you take a free gig, send your tech rider and compromise on less.

We'll get into negotiating techniques, price points and tech riders in the next chapter, but don't undervalue yourself. If people are asking you to play, and you've proven yourself over and over and over again, then you can ask to be paid. If you're still green and need the performance experience, ask if there is compensation, but if there's not, you probably should still just play it.

THE PERFECT 30

Put every show you play to the Perfect 30 test:

    Payment = 10
    Career building = 10
    Enjoyment = 10

The Perfect 30.

You don't want to play any shows for less than a total of 15 on the scale. If the payment is incredible (10), but there will be very little career-building potential (3) or enjoyment (2), that equals 15. If there is decent payment (5), but will bring great enjoyment (9), but little career building potential (1), that also equals a 15. Take these shows. The shows you shouldn't take are the ones for little to no money (1), very little career-building potential (3) and very little enjoyment (3) = 7. Pass!

But, career-building potential doesn't just happen. You have to *make* it happen. If you play a show outside at a beer garden for 2,000 people, it could be a 10 for career-building potential if you have volunteers walking around with flyers/business cards and a mailing list sign-up sheet/iPad. It could also be a 10 on the payment scale if your volunteers walk around selling merch, holding a tip jar, and you have a manned merch table set up.

A funk/reggae band I used to manage got a chance to open for Damian Marley at Summerfest in Milwaukee in front of nearly 3,000 reggae lovers. We employed this exact approach, and not only did their roaming volunteers sell $2,400 in merch during their ninety-minute set; they sold tickets (and passed out flyers) to an upcoming Milwaukee show which ended up selling out. This Summerfest show was the Perfect 30.

THE POWER OF THE TAG

Before you play your next show, make sure every piece of your gear is labeled with your name on it. Every pedal, every cable, mic, mic stand, amp, everything. I use white duct tape and make a two-inch tag on every cable and then write my name on the tape with a Sharpie. You can even get craftier and print out your name on a sheet of paper and then cover it with clear packing tape. Whatever you do, make sure all pieces of your equipment (especially cables) are tagged. This will save you a tremendous amount of money (and stress) in having to purchase all the cables accidentally stolen by other bands or the club. The last thing you want to have happen is to show up at a club the next night and realize your one-of-a-kind power cable that powers your mixer was grabbed by the previous night's sound guy, mistaking it for his own, and you have to play tonight's show acoustic. (This may or may not have happened to me . . .)

BEHIND THE BANTER

Practice what you're going to say in between songs. Rehearse stories and jokes and write notes on your set list for what you are going to say. Come up with "safety stories" just in case the crowd doesn't give you much energy to play off of in between songs and you need to pull these stories out.

The Grammy-nominated folk duo the Milk Carton Kids, have some of the best live banter of any working act today. Fun fact: Their first tour was supporting me for a string of shows in the Midwest. They reciprocated and gave me my first California tour supporting them. I've seen their banter evolve over the years. Lead story teller, Joey Ryan, has an extremely dry sense of humor. And he plays it up. Who you are onstage should be a heightened version of yourself. Or, if you've created a character, it's the best version of that character. I saw the Milk Carton Kids captivate the 1,600 in attendance at the Theatre at Ace Hotel in L.A. The show was equal parts music and comedy. Joey with his dry wit and subdued stage persona had the entire theater rolling. Joey and Kenneth played off of each other effortlessly. It felt fresh and spontaneous, when in reality much of it had been worked out over hundreds of shows. None of it felt rehearsed—that's when the banter is the best. There were definite moments when the banter was actually spontaneous, like commenting on the theater, the audience or responding to a heckler.

Eventually you will become so comfortable with any crowd that you will effortlessly be able to switch between old jokes, rehearsed stories and spontaneous jokes and comments. Once you have the audience in the palm of your hand, you can virtually say anything and they will go along with you for the ride.

THE BRIDGE
When Greeting Fans, Never Say "Nice to Meet You"

When you're at a show, you are onstage from the moment the doors open to the moment they close. Even if you're not physically standing on the stage. You are the artist and there is a spotlight on you, even if you're hiding in the corner trying to get ready. If you're being loud and obnoxious at the bar during the opener's set, people will notice. If you make out with your girlfriend by the stairwell, yeah, you're gonna lose a few fans. PDA not OK! People are watching you and judging your every move. If they talk to you, your little twenty-second interaction will remain with them for a very long time.

I still have fans who come up to me after shows and remind me of the conversation we had three years prior. Of course I can't remember it (or them), but they retell it like it was yesterday. To me, that was hundreds of shows and thousands of postshow conversations ago. To them, it was the only conversation they've had with one of their favorite artists.

You're going to meet fans after shows, on the street, in coffee shops and at other bands' concerts. Greet everyone like you've met before. Replace "nice to meet you" with "nice to see you." Because, if you've met once (or four times) before and you say "nice to meet you," they will, at best, feel bad that they aren't memorable enough to remember or, at worst, be so offended that they will turn on you, bad mouth you around town and never return to one of your shows ever again (it can happen, trust me).

There's no way you're going to remember every fan, every conversation or even every show. So fake it. Pretend like you remember them. It will make their night.

1) We're Having Technical Difficulties Even if your guitar just caught fire. Well actually, that would be hilarious if you said it then. But when bands sheepishly admit it into the mic, it's uncomfortable and kills the vibe. Technical difficulties are your fault. Even when they're not. Your amp will crap out, your guitar cable will short, your batteries will die, your tuner will get dust in it and short out, the DI will die, the mic stand will fall apart and all of this you're going to need to know how to deal with on the spot, in front of your audience.

It's your stage. It's your show.

I once had a venue's DI die on me during my first song in front of a sold-out show in San Francisco. I had just built up a 12-track loop with beat boxing, trumpets, bass, keys, guitar, the works. So when it crapped out, it felt like Satan had just burst through the floor, grabbed my sound and bust out the back door leaving only awkward silence.

However, because I knew my setup so well, I quickly went through the checklist of everything it could be and realized within four seconds it was the DI. Without missing a beat, I got the crowd 1 2, 1 clapping while I told the sound guy I needed a new DI. He ran up, switched out the DI, the sound came back and joined the crowd's 1 2, 1 claps almost right on beat where I left off.

I could have smiled awkwardly at the crowd, pissed myself, then curled up in a ball on the center of the stage crying "There's no place like home" while clicking my heels, but that wouldn't have accomplished anything. That's basically the same as saying "Uh, we're having technical difficulties" while looking awkwardly at your band members hoping someone will fix it for you.

2) I Forgot the Lyrics If you can't memorize your lyrics, then bring a lyrics sheet on stage as reference. Or get good at making them up on the spot.

The only thing worse than bad lyrics is forgotten lyrics.

Don't ever step on stage unprepared. Not at an open mic; not at a talent show, not at a songwriters showcase and especially not at a show where your name is on the bill. The stage is not a time for you to "see how it goes" or to practice. Rehearse on your own time.

3) I Want to Thank My Significant Other It's like having a one-on-one conversation with someone in the audience off the mic. Uncomfortable for everyone else in the house.

Leave your lover out of it. If he or she did something truly awesome, then you can say something like "We'd like to thank our friend Sarah for getting this song into the hands of the music supervisor at *The Fosters*."

If your significant other needs to be publicly thanked as your significant other, then you have bigger issues you have to work out.

4) **I'm Sorry** Don't ever apologize onstage. It makes you look weak. I don't care if you just dropped a baby. Don't apologize.

Making excuses for your lack of preparation makes everyone in the house uncomfortable and feel bad for you. I hear it all the time: "I forgot the rest of the song. Sorry." "I'm sorry if this song sucks, we just wrote it." "I'm sorry there aren't more people here." "We haven't rehearsed this much, it might suck."

Own the stage. Own the room. Own your set. Or don't show up.

5) **Your City Sucks** Should be a no-brainer, but I can't tell you how many touring bands I've seen make fun of the city they are in—onstage. It may be fun to joke about in the van, but your audience takes pride in their city. No matter if you think their city is cool or not.

Never say anything negative about the town you are in while onstage unless you want a beer bottle thrown at you.

6) **This Song Is About My Grandma Who Died of Cancer. Love You, Nana.** Don't depress your audience. You can play a song about your dead grandma, but you don't need to tell the audience that's what it's about.

People don't pay money to come to shows to be sad. They come to be happy. To have fun. To be enlightened. To be inspired.

If you can't communicate the power of your song by just playing it, then maybe the song isn't really that good. That being said, telling stories about songs—especially at folk shows—is extremely important and impactful. Work out your stories so you don't ramble.

7) **I'm Broke** Don't make your audience feel bad for you. It removes the mystique and coolness factor. You can say "Pick up a t-shirt and help us get to the next city." That offers an emotional appeal in a positive light.

Guilting your fans into buying your merch never works.

8) **You Guys Suck** Even if 95 out of the 100 people are screaming above your acoustic set while smashing glasses and vomiting in the corner, 5 people are engulfed in your set. Never insult your audience. They always have one ear to you—even if you are just background music.

9) **Any Requests?** You're never going to get the songs that you actually have prepared, and there will always be that one a**hole who yells "Free Bird" as if he just came up with the joke.

10) **How Does It Sound?** This is a slap in the face to the sound guy. Never ask the crowd that. It should sound amazing. If it doesn't, then it's either your fault or the sound guy's fault. Either way, you just pissed off the one person not in your band who can actually make you sound worse.

DON'T PLAY TO THE A**HOLES

We've all experienced the drunk a**holes. My first instinct is always to engage. Sometimes you have to. If they're making themselves a part of the show (like yelling at you or talking loudly, disturbing the show for others), you have to engage. It's awkward not to. *But* you don't have to do what they say. Actually, you should *never* do what they say. It only encourages them.

There's a huge difference between taking requests from fans and appeasing drunk a**holes. Drunk a**holes are just there to party and make themselves look cool around their friends. Unless you're a cover/party band, these people are not your crowd. You don't want them at your shows. They are an unwelcome detraction for the people who *are* your fans and are actually there to see you.

Remember, there are always people in the room who want to hear *your set*. They are holding on to every word you sing and every note you play. Don't play to the a**holes, because the show is not meant for them. It's meant for the fans (or potential fans) who are actually into your music and will stick with you for the rest of your career. You don't win fans by appeasing drunk a**holes. You win fans by shutting them up (humorously) and kicking butt with the set you prepared. If the a**holes leave, so be it. Better for everyone.

Take a three-step approach to dealing with loud a**holes:

Step 1: Humorously Engage

If there's a loud conversation going on at the back of the room and everyone else is silently listening, you can whisper through the mic and (politely) discuss the wardrobe of the offending party until they notice and take the hint. If there is someone who is constantly yelling out requests of cover songs you can say, "So I only know 2 cover songs and I already played them. However if you have any (fill in your band name) originals you'd like us to play, let us know!" That should put them to rest. Many times they'll realize that you're not into making the show about them and they leave. Good riddance.

Step 2: Show a Bit of (Reserved) Annoyance

If the humor doesn't work (it almost always does), try engaging in a bit more assertive, albeit still polite, manner. Look them directly in the eye with a "why are you f'ing up my show?" look that they will recognize and others will appreciate. Or if they're close to the stage, you can hop off the mic and ask them to stop. With a smile.

Step 3: Kick Them in the Head

Now, I only know of the Brian Jonestown Massacre actually doing this literally. And I definitely don't recommend it. But take the figurative approach. Stop the show. Make it known that you don't like what they're doing. Get them kicked out (or ask them to leave). Florence and the Machine stopped the show because of a fight. The way Florence approached it was brilliant.

You don't want a**holes at your show. It makes you look bad. People come to concerts for the scene as much as the music. If your shows turn into douchefests, then the crowd you really want will be driven away. Catch this early on. Make every one of your shows *your* show. Take control. Command *your* stage. Play to the supportive faces in the room. Play to those who want to be there. For those who ended up at your show and are working their damnedest to destroy it? Kick them in the f%*&ing head. Figuratively, of course.

DOES THIS MUSTACHE MAKE MY
A$$ LOOK FAT?

It's not cool to your dude friends to fret over your image, but your image is almost as important as your sound. If you look like an idiot onstage, half of your audience will think that you sound like one (and the other half may not care, but you just lost half of your audience before your first note).

They say that 80% of what the audience remembers is visual. So even if you sounded like Led Zeppelin, if you looked like Weird Al, that's what they're going to remember.

Image is extremely important in music. You won't hear most musicians talk about this because it's not cool to talk about how much time went into their outfit or hair. Fans love thinking that your outfit is just what you normally wear and is an artistic expression of who you are.

Your image should represent your sound appropriately. When was the last time you saw a folk artist get up on stage looking like Kiss? If you want to be taken seriously, then look, act and sound serious.

I can't tell you what your image should be, but I can say it is extremely important.

You should have a look that separates you from everyone else. If you look like everyone else, then you're admitting that your sound has no originality and you should get written off as just another pop/jam/acoustic/blues/college/rock/hip-hop/whatever act.

You know how when you're at a concert the band stands out from everyone else? They didn't always have "the look." They grew into their look. Clothes are an expression of who you are and so is your art. This should be taken into consideration. However, sometimes a group of artists who all have a similar external way of expressing themselves get together and form a band and they never discuss or need to think about their image because it all just clicks. This is ideal. Eventually when you mature into yourself, your onstage and offstage look will be the artistic expression of who you are and it will feel comfortable.

Or if you create a persona, like a Lady Gaga or Lana Del Rey, you embody a character when you step on stage or into the studio. You're like an actor, in costume, playing the part.

It's quite rare for young artists to wear outfits that are different. It's uncomfortable to stand out, and even very talented artists succumb to peer pressures and conform. Be an outcast! Some of the best artists of all time were outcasts and weren't really comfortable with themselves or anyone around them and they expressed this through their art.

Also, many music reviewers will (believe it or not) start by reviewing your image and the culture surrounding your music before (if ever) they review your sound.

HOW TO HIRE FREELANCE MUSICIANS

As a singer/songwriter or musical director, there are a few very important things you need to understand about hired guns:

- ■ **Freelance Musicians Aren't Playing Your Music for Fun**
  Sure, all musicians love the art. Love the craft. Have a passion that bleeds out of their eyeballs. It's the only reason they chose such an unstable career.

  But musicians, like all other humans, need to eat. Just because they're holding a guitar instead of a hammer, you shouldn't value their craft any the less. Just like a carpenter isn't going to build your fence for the love of the craft, don't expect a professional freelance musician to play your gig for free either.

  Young musicians will tend to take gigs for free, however.

For experience. Some friends might even agree to play your gig as a favor. Or because they believe in you. They may even say "for fun." But be very cautious about getting a volunteer band together. If they get offered a last-minute paid gig the same night as your show, you may be left without a drummer hours before you hit the stage.

By paying your musicians (regardless of the amount), you can demand (politely) a level of professionalism. If they're playing "for fun" or as a favor, prepare yourself for flakiness.

However, "sitting in" is an honored tradition, and many artists sit in with friends all the time—for, of course, no pay.

■ **Discuss All Details Up Front**

You can't just ask someone to play the gig for $100 and then spring three rehearsals on them the week of the show and assume they'll be OK with this. Make sure you discuss all details up front: rate, rehearsals, show date(s), per diems, sleeping arrangements (if it's a tour), how many songs you want them to learn, rehearsal length (three hours is typical), show length, and anything else you'd like from your musicians.

■ **Get the Scene's Going Rate**

In L.A., the typical going rate is $100 for the gig and about $50 per rehearsal. This varies depending on the musician's reputation and experience. Some ask for more and some will accept less. If you've never hired musicians before, ask other singer/songwriters in your scene what they pay their players.

Don't be afraid to ask musicians what their rate is. But keep in mind their "typical rate" might actually be their "ideal rate" and they would accept less. Make sure you set your own budget before getting into these discussions.

■ **Send Streaming and Downloadable Links**

I hate downloading music. When I freelance, I want practice tracks sent as streamable links. I want to listen to them when I'm driving. I want to dedicate a few minutes here and there to run them in my home studio. I don't want to spend fifteen minutes downloading, importing, labeling and syncing to my iPhone. Box.com and Dropbox allow you to stream the song online *or* download it if you want. They're the most flexible for your players. SoundCloud also has this option, but you have to enable it. Some will prefer to download, others only want to stream.

Give your players options.

■ **Be a Leader**

You need to lead your rehearsals. Your players have agreed to play *your* gig with *your* name on the bill. They may be the lead songwriter and front person of their main project, but for this gig, they defer to you.

Make sure you show up to rehearsals prepared. Know what songs you want to rehearse in the order you want to rehearse them. Don't spend ten minutes in between each song deliberating over the setlist. This is your responsibility. You can ask their opinions if you want, but you know your audience, act and songs best.

You should be familiar with every player's part. Be able to answer every player's question decisively. Confidently. Don't say, "I don't know. Do whatever you think." Yes, you can trust their talent, expertise and craft, but it's your gig and your songs. Know your songs and know your show.

■ **Set Expectations**

In addition to discussing all details up front, make sure you let your players know what you expect from them. Will you have charts available, or do you want them to learn the parts on their own?

Let the players know what to wear to the show.

It's your responsibility to lock in a rehearsal space, but feel free to ask if they have suggestions.

Are you religiously against alcohol? Make it known that the tour will be dry. Don't wait for show number three on a fifty-date tour to bring that up.

■ **Have the Check at the Gig**

This is the most important rule. Don't make them hunt you down for the check. If you become known as someone who never pays (or delays payment), you're going to have a very difficult time finding players. Hand them the check before they hit the stage.

If you can't afford to hire a band, you can't afford to have a band

I never recommend singer/songwriters split the door with their freelance players, because it's a slippery slope. If you somehow get your musicians to agree to split the crappy door cuts with you, they're going to expect the same when you get the huge check.

It's your name. Your image. Your reputation. You are making all of the management decisions and you are setting up the shows. If you get a $2,000 check, then you should pay your players a fair wage and then invest the rest in the career. If you get a $100 check, then you take a loss and pay your players the same fair wage.

You're the entrepreneur. It's your project. And your career.

Early on, your gigs will not pay for your band and you'll have to take losses. But those early investments in your career will pay off when you're selling out venues with the same players who have felt respected and cherished from day one.

As much time as you spend in your rehearsal space perfecting your sound, it won't mean anything if it's botched coming out of the P.A. All the money you spent on new pedals, amps, guitars and strings doesn't matter if the mix is off in the club.

The sound guy (or gal) is the most important component of your show that most bands don't really think about. He can break your set (few sound guys can actually *make* your set if you suck). First off, they like being referred to as front of house (FOH) engineers. So, this is a good place to start.

You have to know how to approach sound guys right and get them on your team for the short amount of time that you have with them.

1) **Get His Name** The first thing you should do is introduce yourself to the sound guy when you arrive. Shake his hand, look him in the eye and exchange names. Remember his name—you're most likely going to need to use it many times that night and possibly a couple times through the mic during your set. If you begin treating him with respect from the get-go, he will most likely return this sentiment.

2) **Respect Her Ears** All sound guys and gals take pride in their mixing. Regardless of the style of music they like listening to in their car, they believe they can mix any genre on the spot. However, most front of house engineers will appreciate hearing what you, the musician, like for a general house mix of your band's sound. Don't be afraid to tell her a vibe or general notes ("we like the vocals and acoustic very high in the mix" or "we like keeping all vocal mics at about the same level for blended harmonies" or "add lots of reverb on the lead vocals, but keep the fiddle dry"). She'll appreciate knowing what you like and will cater to that. She is most likely a musician herself, so treat her as one—with respect. She knows musical terms—don't be afraid to use them.

3) **Don't Start Playing Until He's Ready** Set up all of your gear, but don't start wailing on the guitar or the drums until all the mics are in place and the sound person is back by the board. Pounding away on the kit while he's trying to set his mics will surely piss him off and ruin his ears. Get there early enough for sound check so you have plenty of time to feel the room out (and tune your drums).

4) **Have an Input List** Print out an accurate, up-to-date list of all inputs (channels). A stage plot can also be very helpful, especially for bigger shows. Email both the stage plot and the input list in advance. The good sound gals will have everything set up before you arrive (this typically happens only at BIG venues). If you're at a line-check-only club, then just print out the input list/stage plot and hand it to the sound gal right before your set.

There are some great stage plot software options, like StagePlotPro, that allows you to simply create a graphic stage plot without needing image-editing software. At the very least, though, print out an input list like this:

Channel 1—Kick Drum mic
Channel 2—Snare Drum mic
Channel 3—Hi Hat mic
Channel 4—Tom 1 mic
Channel 5—Tom 2 mic
Channel 6—Drums Overhead mic
Channel 7—Bass Amp DI (upstage right)
Channel 8—Guitar Amp mic (upstage left)
Channel 9—Fiddle DI (stage right)
Channel 10—Acoustic DI (center)
Channel 11—Keyboard DI (stereo-L) DI (stage left)
Channel 12—Keyboard DI (stereo-R) DI (stage left)
Channel 13—(lead) Vocal mic (center)
Channel 14—Vocal mic (stage left)
Channel 15—Vocal mic (stage right)
Channel 16—Tracks DI

5) **How to Insult Your Sound Guy** Address him as "yo, sound man" if you want to piss him off. You got his name—use it. Or ask him politely again if you forgot. Don't tell him that the house mix is "off" or "bad." Everything is subjective. It may not be what you like, but it's obviously what he likes. He most likely has much more experience mixing than you do. So get specific about what you like and don't like for your band's house mix from the beginning or keep quiet.

6) **Know Your Gear** Know how you like your vocals EQed generally so you can say that. You can say, "Can we drop some of the highs on the vocals in the house?" You shouldn't say, "The vocals sound piercing—they hurt my ears." You should know how your gear works inside and out, so if anything goes wrong, you point to the sound gal last. Pointing to her first is a sure way to piss her off.

7) **He's Part of the Club** The sound guy, door guy, bartender, booker, managers and servers are coworkers. They hang out, have work parties, hit the bars together and they talk. If you're a d**k to the bartender, he'll tell the sound guy and the sound guy may then decide to ruin your set out of spite. Or just not put any effort into mixing you.

8) **Everyone Wants a Great Show** Believe it or not, your sound gal wants to perform at her best just like you do. Make her job easy by showing up prepared and not sucking. She most likely has her sh*t together so make sure you have your

sh*t together as well. Remember, the stage is not the time for you to "see how it goes" and try stuff out. That's what rehearsal is for. Show up prepared.

9) **The Chip** There are sound guys out there (we've all worked with them) who seem like they have a massive chip on their shoulder from the moment they step into the club. These guys are typically older, failed musicians who have been at this club for decades. They are hardened from years of working with holier-than-thou musicians who not only suck, but believe they are rock stars and that the sound guy is a peon—and treat him as such. You may not be able to change his outlook on life, but treat him with respect and dignity from the get-go and he may lighten up just enough to put some effort into mixing your set.

Even though it should go without saying, apply the golden rule. If you treat your sound guy as you'd like to be treated and work with (not against) him on putting together a great show, you most likely will have one.

THE ONLY WAY TO PREVENT BAD SOUND

The only way to make certain you won't have a bad-sounding show is to bring your own sound engineer. Find an FOH whose mixes you love, get her rate, and treat her like a member of the band. If she's your only call, then book shows around her schedule. Pay her like you pay a freelance musician. Most going rates for one-off sound guys is $100 a night. It's worth the investment. Unfortunately, too many clubs around the country employ very terrible sound guys. So remove the variable, hire your own.

And, no matter how nice the sound guy is, the only thing that really matters is what his mixes sound like. So just because you love working with your church sound tech, he may not be that good. And he may not know how to mix any system other than the church board. You want someone versatile who can work with any system, digital or analog, in any venue. Someone who knows how to tune a room and can rewire the entire system if necessary. Because you will run into issues—especially while on tour.

So get out to shows around town and find someone whose mixes you love. Compliment her at the show on the mix, ask her if she freelances and get her number. A great sound technician is very hard to come by.

If you absolutely cannot find someone just by going to the local clubs, check on SoundBetter.com or AirGigs.com. Many live sound engineers have profiles on the service, and you can filter by location to find one in your town.

HOW TO PUT TOGETHER A LOCAL HEADLINING SHOW

When you're just getting started in your local market, most gigs won't be technically "headlining" or "opening" (no matter what number you are on the bill) because most local bands typically start off on a level playing field.

It may feel like once you are officially anointed as a "headliner" for a show (or tour) that you have made it. The worst thing you can do is act like a headliner and treat the openers as unworthy peasants.

If you're headlining in your local town (and actually headlining—not just playing last) it's your job (if the talent buyer doesn't do this) to tell the opener(s) their set time/length and ask them to stick to it. You have earned rights to the best merch location, but definitely leave room for all other bands to set up their stuff as well. If you're running the night, you'll want to make sure that the openers know their load in/sound check times and know what the drink/food deal is. Don't expect them to know this info. Give them an allotted sound check time—to make sure everyone gets enough time to check. Be courteous of their time and don't run your sound check overtime either. If you're paying them a flat amount, come to the venue with your checkbook just in case the venue pays you in a check. Or ask them if they're cool being paid via Venmo or PayPal, and if the answer is yes, do it from your phone, right there. There's nothing worse than having to track down a check, especially from fellow musicians. If you're giving them a cut of the door, then make sure you get a rep from each band to settle up with the venue at the end of the night so there's no confusion on what was brought in and what was paid out).

You'll most likely be in charge of promo if it's "your" show, but it's totally acceptable to ask the openers to pull their weight in promo as well (especially if they are getting a cut of the door). However, if you're paying them a flat amount, you can't expect them to go all out with promo (because they have no financial interest in this show's success). So, it may be to your benefit to give them a cut of the door.

HOW TO HEADLINE ON TOUR

Now, if you're headlining on tour with local openers, it's a little different game. The promoter or venue that booked the local opener will most likely negotiate the deal with them. Confirm with the talent buyer (promoter or booker at venue) the opener's set times/length and make sure your pay is not affected by theirs. I always like to get the local opener's contact info and touch base with them a couple weeks in advance and get them excited for the show and help promote it. Remember, you'll most likely need some of the local opener's audience to fill the venue.

When you're at the club, make sure to introduce yourself to the local openers (sometimes they'll be huge fans and too nervous to come say hi). The short amount of time you have with them will leave a huge, lasting impression of what kind of person you are. They will either turn into life-long fans or vocal haters. Hang out with them in the green room. Get their story. Take a photo together, post it on Instagram and tag them. Do it in the green room and I guarantee they'll get all their friends to check out this photo on *your* Instagram account. Snapchat some fun backstage shenanigans.

And, above all, watch their set. It's totally reasonable to hang out on the side of the stage and not in the house, as most people in the house will want to talk with you (which takes them away from the opener's set—and you should preserve your voice if you're the singer), but watch at least a couple songs and compliment the local opener on their music. It means a lot more than you may think.

It's also a good idea to have your tour manager (or you if you don't have one) to go over the set times again (just to make sure everyone's on the same page and make sure they won't go over their time). I've had headliners in the past (when I've been the local opener) ask me before the show to not hang out by the merch table when the headliner is performing. If it's a small club, this will be very noticeable (and quite annoying) to the headliner if the opening band is taking photos and chatting with fans during your set (especially if it's a quiet singer/songwriter show). It's fine during set breaks, but once the show starts, the opener should go hide at least for a few songs. Be polite about this and feel it out. If it's a big club, this is probably not necessary to mention and the openers could take this the wrong way.

Every band believes that once they become a headliner they will always remain one. This isn't the case, no matter who you are. So, make sure you treat your openers with respect—they may be your headliner someday very soon.

HOW TO BE A GREAT OPENING ACT

Being the opener for a more established act can be one of the best ways to make new fans. I can pinpoint specific opening gigs where I gained a large number of fans who are still incredibly supportive to this day. I love opening slots for more established acts because I get to win over new audiences. I sometimes prefer playing in front of a room of people who've never seen me before rather than a room full of fans. Sometimes.

When you get an opening slot for a touring or established act, make sure you approach it right. *The number-one rule about opening is to play one minute less than your allocated time slot.* Meaning, if you get a 45-minute set, play 44 minutes, pack up your gear quickly and get off the stage. I don't care how good you think you are or how much the audience is loving you, never play long. And especially if it's a local show with four bands on the bill, it's just disrespectful to play longer than your time slot. This signals to the other bands that you think you're better than them and the audience prefers to hear you more than them.

You have to understand the purpose of being selected to open an established act's show. The main reason you are on the bill is to bring people out. Even established acts that can get a few hundred out still would like an additional fifty that you could bring as the opener. You're expected to pull your weight somewhat when asked to open. It also looks good to the headliner's fans if your fans are in the crowd singing along and enjoying themselves.

Sure, the promoter or venue chose you to open the show because you have a similar sound or vibe, but the reason touring acts ask for a local opener and don't bring one themselves is because they need the audience buffer with the local's draw. Local promoters have their ear to the ground; they are living in your city and they know the pulse of the scene. If you go all out and promote the show that they asked you to open, they'll see this and appreciate it tremendously (because it's unexpected) and they'll ask you to open more shows and give you more opportunities. They'll also be much more willing to help you if you need a venue in the future or a festival spot or something.

When I was just getting started in Minneapolis, I was asked to open a show for a U.K. star right when she blew up in the U.K. (but was virtually unknown in the States). The promoter told me point-blank that I needed to bring people because tickets weren't really selling. This promoter was the biggest promoter in Minneapolis and this was the first opportunity he gave me. I went all out. I printed up 200 posters (on my dime) and plastered downtown Minneapolis and the University of Minnesota campus (and near where the promoter's office was, of course). I made it sound like the biggest show of my career. I talked it up to everyone. I got about 60 people in there (that was really good for me at the time). The promoter was very happy, and you know what show I was asked to open next? The sold-out 800-person Joshua Radin show.

PLAYING LIVE FROM YOUR BEDROOM

If you've built up a following online but aren't ready for a full-on tour, you can set up shows right from your bedroom. Platforms like Stageit, Concert Window, YouNow and Busker make the at-home concert experience not just possible, but actually quite fun. You can sell tickets to the show (however, many shows are "pay what you want") and both platforms encourage tipping. You can set up incentives to get fans to tip more. Or set up higher-priced exclusives. This can allow you to actually bring in some pretty decent income without ever leaving your house.

You can also use live broadcasting platforms like Periscope, Facebook Live and YouTube Live to hold live Q&A sessions, access your rehearsal or studio space or just check in from the road.

You should make sure to schedule your load-in as early as the venue is comfortable with. If you're a solo act, two hours before the doors open is sufficient. If you're a band, you'll want at least three hours.

Most musicians don't understand everything that needs to get done before the doors open. The obvious necessities of loading your gear in and setting it up is understood. Many bands don't fret over sound checks, with an "it'll be fine" attitude.

1) **Leave Enough Time for Sound Check** Fret over sound check! It's incredibly important. Sure, there will be shows with venues that are so put together that everything runs smoothly and sound check takes ten minutes or the engineer mixes you on the fly with no major issues, but you can't plan on that. Always plan for something to go wrong. Even if the equipment all works flawlessly, every room is different and responds differently to your sound. The room wasn't built for your band so you have to allow time to let the engineer feel out your sound in the room. You don't want the first three songs of your set to sound like butt, cluttered with feedback, because the engineer is attempting to mix you on the fly (giving the audience an unsettling opening feeling about you).

   You want time to feel it out on stage and get comfortable with the space. I've played too many shows where a sound check wasn't possible or was cut too short and I hated performing because it felt awful on stage and I couldn't settle in to my performance and therefore put on a bad show. This can be overcome by setting aside enough time for the sound check.

   And yes, of course, there are venues that just do line checks—especially in L.A. and NYC where they book bands every night on the hour. Nothing you can do about that! Bummer.

2) **Set Up the Merch** Once the sound check is finished, your night has just begun. Setting up your merch is the next step and almost equally important as getting a good sound check. If you aren't touring with a tour or merch manager, you should designate one band member who will be in charge of the merch for the entire tour. She should be responsible and decent at math. She'll need to count in and out the money and inventory every night, and she should also be friendly enough to train your merch seller (fan) for the night. And make sure your display is big, organized and in a prominent section of the venue near the door (or the place the venue has designated). You should bring lights for the merch display because many times venues will not have well-lit merch tables.

3) **Get a Merch Seller** You see touring bands tweet about this all the time: "Need someone to sell our merch tonight in Lincoln. Get into the show for free. email

merch@ourband.com" Until you're packing theaters, you most likely won't be able to afford to bring a merch manager on the road with you, but you *must* have a seller at the table before, during and after the show. Not having someone by the table while you're playing will cost you. If someone wants your t-shirt or CD but has to leave early and glances at the merch table on his way out and there's no one there, he'll leave without buying anything. No one's going to go out of their way to try to pay you. And they definitely won't go online and buy it once they leave the venue.

4) **Park** Many venues will allow you to load in near the stage door but won't have a spot for you to park and will need you to move your car from the load-in door. This can be a huge hassle if there isn't a free, dedicated parking spot. I've had to spend up to thirty minutes finding parking and walking back to the venue. Be mindful of this and plan accordingly. And to make sure you avoid this hassle, always go over parking when you advance the show with the venue a week or two beforehand.

5) **Set Up the Room** This is typically overlooked by most artists. It's your night at the club and you want your fans to have a good show, so look out for them. Many venues (and especially colleges) will be able to set up their room multiple ways. Sometimes the way a room is set up needs to be changed for your show. For instance, if you want people to dance, but the room is full of chairs, all it takes is asking your point person at the club if you can get rid of the chairs or shift them around to clear a dance floor.

Nearly every college I've played (over 100) I've had to rearrange the room to make sure people would be comfortable. No one knows your show experience better than you. Take initiative and work with your point people to rearrange the room to fit what's best for your show and your sound.

6) **Hand Off the Guest List** You then need to make sure the door guy has your guest list. Some venues require this list to be emailed well before the doors open. Make sure to go over this information when you advance the show.

7) **Settle Up** You should also find out who you are settling up with at the end of the night. Hopefully that person is the same person you advanced the show with. Before the show, go over the other agreed-upon details that are in your email confirmation and that you advanced: drink deal, food deal, lodging, door cut or guarantee, set length, curfew, etc. And *always* count the cash in front of the manager. It's not insulting, it's expected.

8) **Dinner** It may seem like musicians NEVER forget to eat, and most of the time you'd be right, but I can't tell you how many shows I did when I didn't actually schedule time to eat, got caught up in all the other show prep, and felt light-headed by the end of my set because of my growling stomach.

7.

BOOKING AND PROMOTION

Some people believe that musicians live in this romantic,
fairy-tale world where only artistic integrity matters and trying to
make a buck where and when you can is "selling out." In reality,
these bands have to make a f%*&ing living and apply
some real business strategies to survive.
—ANDREW LEIB, ARTIST MANAGER

If you don't care about the money, always give the money
away [to charity] because then you can get anybody
to [play your show].
—B. J. NOVAK, WRITER/ACTOR/COMEDIAN

HOW TO BE A STAR IN YOUR HOMETOWN

As important as establishing yourself online is, everyone has a local community they come from. You don't join a NASCAR race before you've
earned a driver's license; similarly you don't book a sixty-date tour before
playing your hometown. I'm a strong believer in establishing yourself at
home before you hit the road.

Supporting your local music community is the single most important thing you can do for your career. When you're not playing a show,
you should be out seeing a show. If you're in a fairly big city, there should

be various local shows happening around town nearly every night of the week. Get out to these shows and meet the community. You'll soon figure out which venues cater to your style of music and which don't. Start to frequent the clubs where you want to play. Get to know the staff and the patrons. The more you show your face, the more the regulars will warm up to you. Meet the other musicians and hang out at the after-parties. When you're establishing yourself in a scene, you need to be out in the world, often.

We hear all the time about artists who start to break online who have played only a few shows locally. These artists completely ignore their hometown and believe they are above it. They may see some initial success in other communities (or overseas) where blogs and local tastemakers have taken a liking to their music. Don't be like them. If you don't lay the groundwork, eventually people may lose interest and then you'll have no one to go back home to. You'll have no support group. No hometown following. No home.

Start local.

Your Scene

I want to make clear that the tactics I'm laying out to approach your local scene do not really apply to L.A. or Nashville. Or New York, to some extent. These towns operate completely differently (as described in Chapter 5) and the ways to approach them are different than most other cities. That being said, even if you do live in L.A., Nashville or New York, keep reading, as you will gain some perspective.

How to Crack the Local Gatekeepers

No digital message or phone call can replace the electrifying experience of a physical encounter.

Every scene has them. The bloggers, the radio DJs, the music editors, the local Twitter stars, the club and festival bookers. Gatekeepers are an elusive group of somebodies who once were nobodies.

What they all have in common is that they love the culture of music. They're typically not musicians and have very little actual music (theory) knowledge. They know what they like and know what they hate. But becoming a local star requires that you crack this inner circle. At least somewhat.

■ **Hang Out with the Cool Kids**

This isn't a lesson middle school guidance counselors would ever reveal, but cool begets cool. Most gatekeepers respect other gatekeepers. The radio DJ will meet up with the music editor and grab drinks with the club booker. They are a tightly knit group who see each other at the buzz shows.

So, find out what those buzz shows are and go there. Find a mutual friend of a friend to introduce you to someone in that crowd.

The way you're going to work your way in is not by handing them a CD or sending a cold email, it's by being welcomed in by a fellow insider.

■ **Follow Them on Twitter**

You want a newspaper review? A blog review? A show at their venue? A song played on their local show? Step 1 is to get on their radar. You're not going to break this crowd in a day. Or a month. It takes time. You have to start somewhere. Follow all of the local music journalists, club and festival bookers and radio DJs, and learn. What shows are they frequenting? Who are they tweeting? Most likely it will be other gatekeepers. What is their personality?

Anyone is flattered when they are followed on Twitter. After some time, start to interact with them. Favorite a tweet here and there. Retweet them once in a while. Reply to tweets with something witty or brilliant.

Above all, don't creep. Following on Twitter is totally acceptable. Friending on Facebook is not. You can search for mutual friends on Facebook, though, and ask for an intro the next time you're all at a show together.

■ Comment on Their Blog

You want something from them? Give something *to* them first. Read the reviews and comment (occasionally) on the articles. Most of the time they won't get any comments, but if they see your name giving insightful (or just praiseful) comments to their articles, they will remember you when you meet in person. But don't overdo it. Keep some level of mystique. Be flattering, not gushing.

■ Go to the Spots

After you've been following them on Twitter for a bit, you'll know where they hang out. Where they like to see live music. So go to those spots. And if you're trying to get a show booked at a venue, frequent it. Go hang out and be a pleasant presence in their club. Tip the bartenders. Buy the band's merch. Pay the cover price. Meet the door people and bartenders. If you get known as a positive energy in their club, they will be much more receptive when you eventually ask them for something (like a show or a review). Which brings me to my next point.

■ **Meet Them in Person**

Again, no digital message or phone call can replace the experience of a physical encounter. Even just a thirty-second interaction with a few jokes (or shots) will get you further than twenty beautifully crafted emails. So get out often. The way you're going to be a member of the scene is to get out into the scene. Physically.

■ **Don't Bad-Mouth Anyone**

The worst thing you can do is trash-talk. They may do it, but don't stoop to that level. If you get caught up in the negativity, you will eventually talk sh*t about the wrong person or band, which could turn *you* into the punch line of their next meetup. Rise above and be a positive presence in the scene.

■ **Ignore Them**

Or, you can disregard everything above and make killer music, draw big crowds and make them come to you. There's nothing they love more than befriending the hottest band of the moment.

Don't be sleazy about any of this. That's a quick way to ruin your reputation. If you can be a supportive, positive presence in the scene, then word will get around. They'll eventually want to meet you.

The Venues

Believe it or not, venue owners, talent buyers and bookers want you to succeed. The reason they are in the line of work they are is the same reason you are: love of music. If they didn't love live music, they wouldn't have it. It's too damn tough to run a music venue. Talent buyers (bookers), who many times are the owners of small venues, want to host great talent. But, more than that, they want a packed club of drinkers. A venue owner's best night is a packed club, record-setting bar sales, a lineup of acts she loves, a respectful audience and no major catastrophes.

Always look at booking a show as a partnership between you and the venue. It's never you versus them. If you have a great night, everyone wins. Put yourself in the venue owner's shoes. If she books too many shows where no one shows up, she will go out of business. You must remember this every time you're corresponding with venues. They are always on the defensive because they've been burned too many times. They assess the risk for every show they host.

If you convince a booker to give you a night at their club and no one shows up, they will never have you back. Everyone loses. So don't book a show until you have a promotional plan set out.

THE BOOK SHEETS: PICKING YOUR SPOTS

Open a Google Doc spreadsheet, invite all your band members, your manager and anyone else on your team, and title it "Our Venues." This will be a living doc that can be updated by all members on your team. The best resource to find venues in your town is IndieOnTheMove.com's (IOTM) Music Venue Directory, which has some of the most complete lists of venues around the country. You will see all venues within your selected location listed by capacity, genre and ages. When you select a venue, the week's upcoming shows will be listed (along with how to book the club with name, email and phone numbers of the booker). You should also use Songkick and Bandsintown apps to see the hot upcoming concerts in town.

On this spreadsheet, add all of the local venues that you want to play.

Make 3 headings: This Year, Next Year, 3 Years. Like your 26-Year Marathon goals sheet, you are customizing a local venue goals doc. Make 9 columns: Venue/Festival, Website, Capacity, Ages, Booker Name, Email, Phone #, Bands, Notes. The first 7 columns can be filled out from the information provided by IOTM. Under the Bands column list other local bands who have played the venue. Under Notes, list any thoughts you have about the club from when you've visited or played it, or what the word on the street is about it (like "Brad and Angela both book. Brad is friends with Alex from Roster McCabe. Angela is friends with George from This World Fair. The bouncer's name is Joe and his wife is Alicia from All Eyes.) This information is important, for when you visit the club, you can ask Joe at the door how Alicia is, and if you go with your buddy George, ask him to introduce you to Angela. This is how you get to be known as a positive presence in the scene, make connections and get it done.

THE BOOK SHEETS: FINDING LOCAL BANDS

Make another shared spreadsheet and title it "Local Bands." Make 6 columns: Band, Members (include email and phone numbers), Website, Facebook, Draw, Venues/Festivals, Notes. All the local acts you meet, see, play with and hear about, add to this list. Check out the Songkick and Bandsintown upcoming show list for your city, note all of the bands and include every local band on this sheet. Of course the draw is an estimation and fluctuates, but if they headline a 400-cap club and sell it out, you can safely say their draw is 400, even if they had a couple openers. List all the venues and festivals they've played within the past year (or have upcoming on their calendar). Under the Notes section, keep it positive. Even if the drummer of the Future Antiques slept with your girlfriend, you don't need to list it or call him names (God help you if this doc ever gets out). Reiterate to your band members to keep the notes positive. You can invite other artists in town to help collaborate on your lists and really start to build up a community of dedicated artists like you.

How to Book Local Shows

The best way to get in at a club is through another band. From your Book Sheets, pick out a few bands with whom to put a show together at a club they've played before. It's best to hit up the bands you have an established relationship with. That's why it's so important to meet them in the scene. *Never email a band and ask to open for them.* This signifies that you have no idea how it works. There are no real openers or headliners in your local community. Sure, there are the outliers who are very established and are headlining the biggest clubs in town, but you're not concerned with them. You want to approach the artists who regularly play the clubs you want to play. Once you have rehearsed your a$$ off, have a 45-minute set that is solid and undeniable, have played a myriad of free shows in town, and have a solid online presence (more on this in a minute), you are ready to start setting up real shows at clubs in town. So, start with your friends' bands. Talk to them about putting a show together. What this means is that you put a complete bill together (three or four acts) and take it to the booker at a venue. Know what the typical club deal is (your friends who have played it will let you know). Since you're organizing the show, you can hit up the club (unless another band on the bill has a strong connection). But this will give you a good opportunity to make the connection with the club. It's best if you've met the booker at their venue. And, if you've done your job right, you will have.

Email Pitch

Email the booker and put in the subject line: Dates—bands ("August 5, 6, 9, 15—The Alarmists, White Light Riot, This World Fair, Ari Herstand"). Lead with the band who is most established at the club. Since it's a local show and you're not routing a tour, you can give a date range or a few dates. First check to make sure the dates work with your lineup (and that they are open at the club). Keep your email short and to the point. Your email should not be more than eight sentences. You don't need to include your bio or all of your accolades. Just hit the booker with the important points: How many people you expect, a few promo tactics you're going to utilize and your previous show turnouts in the area.

Your initial email can read like this:

Subject: aug 5 , 6, 9, 15—the alarmists, white light riot, this world fair, ari herstand

Body: hey eric, great meeting you last week at the debut's show. i'm putting together a show with the alarmists, white light riot and this world fair (link them) and we're calling it The Unknown Order where we will draw names out of hat right before each set to see who will play. I brought 70 to my show june 12th at the whole, the alarmists just played the Rock the Park (last week to 500), wlr brought 200 to their fine line show in may, and this world fair just had 150 at their last varsity show with you. we expect to get 500 out for this show. we will be promoting with posters, handbills, a street team, facebook ads, heavy instagramming. andrea at 89.3 has agreed to help us push it and we're sending out press releases. bauhaus beer is down to help with promo through their networks if we can work out a beer special that night. looking at august 5, 6, 9 or 15th.

> let me know if we can lock in a date
> ~ari
> http://ariherstand.com
> http://facebook.com/ariherstand

new vid: http://youtube.com/ariherstand

**News:

* songs featured on How To Get Away with Murder, Pretty Little
Liars, Microsoft Surface ad

* opened for Ron Pope, Ben Folds, Matt Nathanson

* played KCRW's Morning Becomes Electric

Boom. Eight sentences. Put your accolades in your signature. And yes, you should use all lowercase letters. It's less formal and how most in the club booking world communicate. Use proper spelling and proper grammar, but all lowercase. All lowercase is more approachable, friendlier and signifies you're too busy to use caps.

If you haven't heard anything from the local booker after a week, your follow-up email can read:

Subject: Re: aug 5, 6, 9, 15—the alarmists, white light riot, this world fair,
ari herstand

Body: hey eric, checking in to see if i can grab one of these dates for this
Unknown Order show. we'll get 500 out for this. thanks!

~ari

http://ariherstand.com

http://facebook.com/ariherstand

new vid: http://youtube.com/ariherstand

**News:

* songs featured on How To Get Away with Murder, Pretty Little Liars,
Microsoft Surface ad

* opened for Ron Pope, Ben Folds, Matt Nathanson

* played KCRW's Morning Becomes Electric

Always reply from your initial email so the booker can just scroll down to see the details. For local shows you can definitely follow up every week. If you haven't gotten a response after the third email (or sooner depending on the timeline) pick up the phone and give a call. This seems so obvious, but so many musicians are deathly afraid of the phone and have gotten so accustomed to just interacting over email, text and Facebook that they sometimes forget that phones actually function as spoken communication devices. And, believe it or not, some bookers still only book over the phone.

I've actually called a venue after four emails with no response and the phone call went like this:

"Warehouse."

"Hi, is Steve in?"

"Speaking."

"Hi, Steve, this is Ari Herstand, I'm looking to get into the Warehouse on June 10."

"Oh yeah, I think I got a couple emails from you about this. So what's the show? What's your history in the area?"

"I just played the college down the street for 300 students and want to follow this show up. I have a student street team ready to promote this show."

"OK, let me see, June 10. Yeah, it's open. OK, sounds good. Let's do it. $8 tickets? 7:00 doors, 18+. We do 70/30 split. Cool?"

"Yup, that works."

"OK, it's confirmed. Send me a promo photo and bio that we can get up on the website along with links."

Boom! Show booked at a venue I'd nearly given up on because of no email response.

We've all been there. You're attempting to manage your business, but one extremely necessary party isn't responding to your emails.

I know this can be awfully frustrating when you're contacting clubs for potential shows, music supervisors for placement, other musicians for favors, press for reviews, or festivals for booking and no one is getting back to you. So what do you do?

Follow up. *The key to this industry is polite persistence.*

I've gotten nearly everyone to reply to my email through this method (even rock stars and big-time managers). If after three beautifully crafted emails they still haven't gotten back to you, don't get discouraged. They'll scan your email each time—if not just the subject line or sender field—and each time they'll make a mental note (always Reply from the original email so they can see the thread and the subject line says "Re:___"). If they see a seventh email from you with each one more polite than the last, they'll eventually write you back.

If people don't respond to your email, it isn't because they hate you. It isn't because your music sucks. It isn't because they found out you slept with their ex (well . . . maybe).

It's because they just don't have the time. Right. Now.

I know it's tough to say the same thing over and over again, but find a way to be just as kind each time with different wording. And above all, *Keep the emails short.* One of the reasons people don't respond is because they open your email and see it's a mininovel. No one has the time for that. And remember, keep your initial email under eight sentences. "But Ari, I just spent three weeks crafting the most poetic, perfectly worded essay explaining why there has never been a band more ideal than us to play this club." Don't care. Delete. Rewrite. Eight sentences! No more!

It's also about timing and luck. Some days they're putting out fires, and other times they're staring aimlessly at their computer screen when your email comes in and reply right away.

Also, to help curb your neuroses, install the email add-on HubSpot to see who has, in fact, opened your email (synchs with Gmail, Outlook and Apple Mail). You'll at least know if the other party was interested enough to even give it an open. If not, maybe you should update your subject line (but still reply from the original email with the "Re:___." But even if they do open it (as noted above), they may just not have the time to respond or deal with it. So, again, follow up.

Once you do get an email response, *you* should reply *right away.* Do *not* make them wait (like they made you wait). This is not a dating game via text. If they've finally taken the time to devote the mental and emotional effort it takes to fully concentrate on your issue in this moment, every passing minute from when they hit Send to when you reply, they will increasingly lose interest. And if you wait too long to reply to their response, you may have to play the follow-up game all over again.

On one occasion, I had been trying to get into a club (that will go unnamed) for months (years). One day I finally got a response. I *immediately* replied back, and then the booker immediately responded back to me. And we basically had about 20 back and forths within the span of 10 minutes. I was top of mind, so it was super easy to just continue the conversation. Show booked, negotiated, locked down (with some jokes thrown in for good measure), in 10 minutes (+ 3 years).

WHAT DO YOU MEAN WE DON'T GET PAID?!

The Confirmation Email

Once you have a show confirmed, you should send one final email that includes all of the necessary details. This acts like a contract. Most venues with capacities under 600 don't typically work with contracts, especially when booking directly with the artist. Even if they do work with contracts, it takes way too long to send one over, have them sign it, send it back and confirm everything. Most venue bookers won't take the time to do this. Just send them an email that looks something like this (see below). Fill in all the information that you are certain of (what had been discussed in previous correspondences) and highlight the areas they need to fill in.

Attach a stage plot/tech rider and a promo photo or event poster with this email. Note that your band's promo bio is included at the end.

Date:
City:
Venue:
Bill title:

Ages:

Cost:

Capacity:

Venue website:

Artist websites:

Advance tickets link:

On-sale date:

Tickets available at box office?

Box office phone #:

Box office hours:

Box office location:

Guest list #:

Door time:

Set times/length:

Curfew:

Compensation:

Drink/food deal:

Number traveling in band/crew:

Load-in time:

Sound-check time:

Advance with: (name)

Phone: Email:

Venue day-of contact phone #:

Production contact #/email:

Artist day-of contact phone #:

Venue address:

Load-in directions:

Parking:

Other instructions:

Promo bio:

PERFORMANCE DEALS: FROM THE WORST TO THE BEST

When you start booking shows locally and around the country (or world), you'll come to experience all of the various deals venues and promoters work out. From booking over 500 shows around the country myself over the past ten years, I've experienced virtually everything a small-to-mid-level artist deals with. Here are the worst to best deals currently being offered at clubs around the world.

The Worst

Require bands to purchase tickets up front.

What Is It?: Typically this happens with "promoters" who scour ReverbNation (they used to use MySpace) and Facebook, find naïve bands and promise them slots at well-known venues. All you, the band, have to do is sell 35 tickets (which you must purchase in advance). But hey, you get to keep $3 for every ticket you sell. What a deal! Except you have to buy the tickets for $7 and sell them for $10. If you do the math, you are making 30% of the cover from the people *just* there to see you—which is the sh*ttiest deal in the history of sh*tty deals. Or, I've also seen scenarios where you must buy 50 tickets up front for $10 a pop ($500) and then you get to keep 100% after you sell all 50 tickets at $10. So, if you sell 60 tickets, you walk with $100 (and the "promoter" walks with your $500 plus all of the other bands' $500 for the night—ouch). These "promoters" usually present about 5–15 bands on a night, who each play about a 20-minute set. And the bands almost never fit together musically. And many times they won't give you a set time and tell you that set times will be figured out the night of the show based on who sold the most tickets.

So, of course, your fans must get there at 6 P.M. and may have to stay until 1:30 A.M., when your set time actually comes around. And these "promoters" don't actually do anything to promote except post the event flyer on their Facebook Page. Pass!

Is This Fair?: No! How these "promoters" get away with this is by preying on young bands who don't know any better (now you do!) and will do anything to just play the venue, including paying lots and lots of money for this. As tempted as I am to name the names of these promoters who do this (and boy would I like to), I will not and hope that enough of you band together and collectively tell these promoters to politely go f*&k themselves when they contact you (as I have many, many, many times).

Fun story: My final year in Minneapolis, one of these promoters kept hounding me to play a club I had actually headlined many times. I told them that I typically get 500-plus people to my headlining shows and I'm not interested in their offensive deal (as I had a very good relationship with the club already). They responded explaining how much money I could make with their horrendous deal if I brought 500 people (duh). I responded by telling them no thanks and to please not contact me again. I was then hit up by the same "person" with the same form email multiple times. Each time my responses got more and more annoyed, until finally I contacted the owner of the club and told him what was happening and how it was giving the club a bad name and that they should stop working with this promoter. The owner canceled the promoter's upcoming show and hasn't worked with them since. *Boom!* More bands need to do this in more cities.

LESSON LEARNED: Don't pay to play cool venues. You will be paid (a fair amount) to play these cool venues when you are ready and can draw a substantial crowd.

Bad

Venues charge a "rental fee."

What Is It?: Music venues that also host private events like weddings got smart to the fact that they were making a boatload more money when they got wedding parties to rent out the venue than if they book a night of music. So, these venues figured, "why not ask bands to pay nearly the same amount to book a night in our beautiful venue?" They'll make you rent the place for, say $1,500. You can charge whatever cover you like and will make 100% of it (if you're lucky). You are essentially acting as the promoter. Oh, you play music too? Eh.

Is It Fair?: Well, it's not ideal. The venue is basically completely covering their a$$ and will make out on this deal regardless of whether you bring anyone. The venue is basically admitting they have zero faith in your draw and they are doing *you* a huge favor in letting you play their club (for an exorbitant fee).

LESSON LEARNED: I would say pass on this deal typically. Play a different club that gives you a fair and standard deal. Or, crunch the numbers, and if you think you will bring enough people to make this deal worthwhile, then go nuts. It helps to fill a promoter's shoes once in a while.

Sneaky

Venues only pay you after a certain number of people come to see you.

What Is It?: I've only really seen this kind of deal in Los Angeles and New York (some other cities are catching on though). Basically, the door guy has a tally sheet with each band's name on it. The venue works out a separate (standard) deal with each band. Typically, you get paid *only* if a certain number of people (I've seen 15–75) pay to see you (and not the others on the bill). You then get a cut of the door after the minimum number of people come. Meaning if the minimum is 35 people at $10 a head and you bring 33, you walk with $0 (and the venue takes your $330—and all the drinks your fans buy). However, if you bring 35 (and your deal is 70%) you walk with $245. However, I've also seen requiring a minimum number of people and only getting paid a cut after that minimum show up. So if your minimum is 35 and 36 people show up at $10 a head, you walk with $7 (if your deal is 70%). If you bring 35 you get $0.

Is It Fair?: Kind of, but not really. On the surface it looks like they are just covering expenses, but if they have 5 bands on the bill and each one is required to bring 35 people at $10, the venue is getting way more than just the amount to cover expenses. If every band brings 30 people, the venue makes $1,500 (30 people x $10 x 5 bands) and each band makes $0. Yikes!

LESSON LEARNED: I don't like these deals because it encourages competition among the acts and not a "we're all in it together" approach, which I stand by. You have zero incentive to work with the other bands on the bill to make it a great night—encouraging fans to stay from beginning to end. Because of this, bands in L.A. and New York don't get to know each other that well and typically show up right before their set and leave shortly after. "Hit it and quit it." Which rubs off on the fans too. It's very unique to see fans in either city come for a full night of music (because of this practice). Venues don't realize that if they stopped working their deals this way and started encouraging complete bills and promoting the entire evening of music, they would get more people in their club for a longer period of time (i.e., more drink sales). But hey, I don't run the clubs.

Standard

Venue takes expenses off the top.

What Is It?: A venue will take an amount off the top to cover expenses before they split the door with the organizer of the show (the headliner—you). The standard is about $50–$350 depending on the size of the club. A club that takes more than $350 for an under-300 capacity room is screwing you. And this isn't $50–$350 off the top per band. It's $50–$350 off the top of the total, and the rest is split with the organizer of the show, who then pays out everyone else on the bill.

Standard door splits after expenses:

> 70%–100% cut (in your favor) for 21+
>
> 70%–85% cut (in your favor) for 18+
>
> 50%–70% cut (in your favor) for all ages

Is It Fair?: Sure. They wouldn't need to hire a sound guy or a door gal if you weren't playing that night. This money (typically) does directly go to those people and then the venue splits the remaining money with you fairly. But, just remember, they are making bar sales, from which you don't get a cut. So if they take more off the top, you should negotiate for a higher cut after expenses. The reason the split is lower for all ages vs. 18+ nights is because venues typically need to hire more security for all-ages shows and enforce an earlier curfew (less drinking time for the drinkers).

Good

Door split from dollar one.

What Is It?: Many venues are happy to have you and will split the door with you from the first person who pays a cover. This is ideal.

If 10 people come at $10 a head and you have a 70/30 split with the venue, you walk with $70.

Is It Fair?: Absolutely. I see this deal occasionally, but most will at least take $50 off the top for the sound guy.

Great

Guarantee + % of door (whichever is greater)

What Is It?: Venues will do this to get you to play their club (and not the many other options in their city). Because of your proven history, they feel confident that with the amount of promo that they will do, they will be able to get enough people out to your show to make it financially worthwhile for them.

Example: $1,000 or 80% of the cover—whichever is greater. So if 500 people come at $10 a head, you walk with $4,000 ($10 × 500 × 80%). If 50 people come at $10 a head, you still walk with $1,000 (the guarantee). *But, if this actually does happen, give some money back to the club/promoter.* You don't want your low turnout to get them to default on rent that month. They'll never forget you did this and will absolutely have you back.

Most of the time only promoters offer these kinds of deals. They then work extremely hard to promote your show. They have serious skin in the game now.

Is It Fair?: Absolutely. You earned this!

There's a fine line between what is acceptable, ethical, smart business, and career advancing.

Look at it from the venue's standpoint: They are taking a risk every time they open their doors for a show. If no one shows up, then they do lose money (door guy, sound guy, bartender, electricity, heat, AC, on and on). If they are strictly a music venue and don't open unless they have a show, then they really are losing money the moment they open the doors, until people (ideally drinkers) enter their club.

The biggest misconception bands have about venues is that the venue is supposed to promote their show and bring people to the club. Venues think bands should promote the show and bring people to the club. In the end, neither end up promoting the show and no one shows up.

The reason all the clubs in L.A. and New York can create such horrible deals for the bands (and fantastic for the club) is because there are so many bands willing to take these unfavorable deals. If one band refuses, there are ten more waiting in line that will take the deal. Venues in smaller cities tend to create better deals to lure in the good bands who will bring a crowd. They realize that if they offer insulting deals and enough bands pass on the deals, there will be no bands left to play their club and they'll go out of business.

The most important thing to remember is: *Don't play a big venue if you can't fill it.* Take shows at smaller clubs and fill them. Open for bigger bands at bigger venues to build your crowd. Keep selling out the small clubs and eventually you'll be able to move up to the big clubs with enough clout to get a fair deal.

WHAT ARE PROMOTERS?—AND HOW TO GET OPENING SLOTS FOR TOURING ACTS

Most cities have local promoters. Promoters are booking agents' go-to people in town. These promoters are not to be confused with the pay-to-play, shady ones who prey on local bands—like the "Worst" deal from a few pages ago. The legitimate, local promoters know all of the venues and have great relationships with all of the talent buyers at each venue. When agents book tours for their artists, they rarely go directly to the venue; they typically work with a local promoter in town to set up the show. The promoter will typically rent out the venue or work with the venue to put together a favorable deal. Much of the risk and responsibility falls on the promoter. But, if the show is a success, the promoter has a lot to gain. Venues like working with promoters because they are proven and trusted. There is very little risk to a venue when they work with a promoter.

As I said earlier about my experience working with a local promoter to open for the U.K. star, promoters also know the local talent. Many times national booking agents will ask the promoter to find local support (opener). There is one and only one reason for this: crowd buffer. If all they wanted was a great opener, they would bring one with them on tour. Promoters will build up relationships with local artists and know how hard each artist works on show promo, what kind of crowd they draw and what kind of music they play. A promoter will not put a local metal band on to open for a touring singer/songwriter. The lineup still has to make sense.

The promoter is typically in charge of ticket sales and will know if tickets aren't selling as they should. The promoter will find local acts who can help promote the show and increase ticket sales. Typically, promoters will pay the local opener a set guarantee (like $100). *Don't value these shows based on the amount you receive in a guarantee, but rather the fans you will gain and the merch you will sell.* This show can be a 30 on the Perfect 30 Scale (even with a low guarantee) if you do it right and sell lots of merch.

And when you get an opening slot for a touring act, this is your moment to shine. Make sure you bring your A game. This is a chance for you to win over a ton of new fans. Push your mailing list and merch. Have volunteers at the door handing out flyers for your band as people leave.

And maybe, just maybe, if the headliner happens to check out your set and likes what she sees, she may invite you to open future tours.

1) **Add the Show to Your Tour Calendar** You can embed a Bandsintown or Songkick calendar to your website. Even if you don't, you need to add your shows to these sites. Bandsintown and Songkick have each built up communities of active users, over 10 million members each, who use the apps to track artists and get notified when they come to town (via push notifications and customized emails). If you're routing a tour, you can schedule the shows to go public at a certain time. Triple-check the ticket link and don't publish the show until you have the ticket link included (because if fans get a notification about your show and click through but find no link to the tickets, they won't be able to buy and may forget about the show). Songkick and Bandsintown have partnered with many digital platforms like Spotify and Shazam. If you're wondering why your concerts aren't being listed on various platforms online, it's most likely because they aren't on Songkick or Bandsintown.

2) **Create a Facebook Event** If you're playing a one-off local show, a Facebook Event is crucial. If you're going on a 60-date tour, don't worry about creating Facebook Events for each show—an embedded Bandsintown "Tour Dates" tap on your Musician Page is sufficient. Maybe have your local street team in each city create a Facebook Event—send them the graphic for the tour though. Don't leave it up to them to find one.

3) **Create a Show/Tour Poster** Hire a graphic design artist to create something truly eye-catching and interesting that represents your image and vibe.

4) **Create a Show/Tour Video** Make a long one for YouTube and Facebook and make shorter ones to roll out on Instagram and Twitter.

5) **Print Up Physical Posters and Flyers** I've found that Nextdayflyers.com has the cheapest and highest quality options for 4 x 6 (or 5 x 7) postcards. Disc Makers can create high quality 11 x 17 full-color posters on the cheap as well.

6) **Send Posters to the Venue** Bandposters will print, label and ship five very-high-quality, full-color (no-bleed) posters to each venue for $15 a pop. Totally worth saving the time, Sharpies and hand cramps.

7) **Send an Email Blast** Include the ticket link and show promo video.

8) **Write a Press Release** See Chapter 15.

9) **Restock Your Merch**

10) **Split Up Promotional Duties** Work with the other bands on the bill to figure out a cohesive promo plan and delegate jobs to your other bandmates and street team members.

HOW TO DOUBLE YOUR INCOME

When you're on tour, merch can be your number-one income generator. Believe it. Bands stress over their guarantees, door splits and turnouts. If you want to survive financially with your music, you must understand the importance of merch sales. I've played shows where 10 people showed up, but they had such an amazing time and I so stressed the merch to them that all 10 people bought something averaging about $15. That's good for any night.

The tour merch tracking platform atVenu has calculated that for 500–1,000-cap venues, the average dollar per head (DPH) is $3.65. Meaning, if 200 people show up, you can estimate to make $730 in merch. However, this doesn't just happen because you offer merch. The dollar-per-head number will fluctuate based on how well you sell your merch, how attractive your merch items are to your audience, how attractive the merch display is and how good your sellers are. Ingrid Michaelson's manager, Lynn Grossman, stated that they have "become much smarter" about what merch items Ingrid's fans like. She stated that by adding vinyl they increased their dollar per head quite a bit. Her fans also buy songbooks for piano and ukulele—which obviously may not do as well for a hard rock project. Ingrid's dollar per head fluctuates just as much as that of the next act, and Lynn stated that their range has been as low as $2/head all the way up to $8/head. Even though Ingrid is playing to an average of 2,000–5,000 people a night now, she still goes and checks her merch display every night to make sure it is set up just right.

AVERAGE DOLLAR PER HEAD PER GENRE

GENRE	AVERAGE	MAX
SINGER/SONGWRITER	3.52	7.35
INDUSTRIAL	6.23	8
JAZZ	3.15	6.66
HIP HOP/RAP	3	4.51
GOSPEL & RELIGIOUS	4.18	10.87
HEAVY METAL	3.08	6.67
METAL	4.75	7.28
REGGAE	3.95	6.49
SPOKEN WORD	4.46	5.85
CHRISTIAN & GOSPEL	3.51	13.1
COUNTRY	3.18	16.25
HIP HOP/RAP	3.59	10.76
BLUES	3.17	7.01
R&B/SOUL	2.1	4.25
INDIE ROCK	2.13	4.34
HARD ROCK	7.16	9.53
PUNK	4.38	5.63
ELECTRONIC	2.05	8.84
ROCK	3.77	19.32
ALTERNATIVE	4.08	44.81
WORLD	5.33	10.08
FOLK	4.58	7.57
POP	4.47	17.34
R&B	4.28	7.74
ELECTRONIC/DANCE	2.25	7.79

*atVenu 2015

The Display

You should have an impressive merch display. It needs to be big, attractive, professional and well lit. For all intents and purposes you are traveling salespeople. So make your displays as appealing as possible. If your display consists of CDs tossed in a dimly lit corner of the room, you aren't going to sell anything. Bands complain that their fans don't buy merch. Bull. Every fan buys merch. If you sell it right, they'll buy.

The Pitch

Musicians are traditionally horrible businesspeople and that's why managers exist. Most musicians hate having to "sell" to their fans. The most charismatic front person who can captivate every single person in the room while singing can be the most introverted, bland, unimpressive and embarrassing salesperson when having to talk about the merch.

You have to get over this. Getting your merch pitch down is almost as important as getting your live performance down.

Combos

Make combo options. For example, "Each CD is $10, but if you want to buy both, you can for $15," and then not only announce this but emphasize it. I spend about forty-five seconds every show to explain what I have for sale. You may say this is a vibe killer and stops the flow, but on the contrary you can make it a part of your show. My stage banter is a big part of my show, so I incorporate it into my banter and turn it into a joke. For one tour, I titled the 3-CDs-for-$25 combo my "Midwest Combo" because, I say, "I'm born and raised in the Midwest and we love bargains there, so I like to pass along the Midwest bargain wherever I go." People came up to me after the show and, with a smile on their face, handed me their credit card and said "give me the Midwest bargain."

Take Credit

Ever since I got a credit card swiper (for my iPhone), my merch sales have about doubled. Say onstage that you take credit. And print off the credit card logos and put them on your merch display. You will sell more merch if you take credit, especially if your merch seller is a pro. It's so easy to just keep adding on items when you're paying with a card.

Square, PayPal and Amazon have free swipers and take a very low commission (around 2.7%). They work on an iPhone, Droid or iPad. Square now even takes Apple Pay.

Depending on how attentive your audience is, you may need to stress the merch a few times during a show. But don't overdo it. There are classy ways to do it and annoying ways to do it. This takes practice and feeling out the audience.

The Merch Seller

Bringing a merch person on the road with you is best, but expensive, and you probably won't be able to afford that for a while. Not having someone sell your merch, though, is not an option unless you play very short sets and are certain people will stay for the entire show and you can run over and man the table yourself after you finish playing. But most likely, not everyone will stay the entire time, especially if there are multiple bands on the bill or you're playing a late-night, four-hour bar gig.

Bands think that if they didn't sell any merch it was because people didn't want to buy it. But what if they *really* wanted to buy something but they had to leave at 11:00 because they have to wake up at 6:00 and you didn't take the stage until 10:30 (when you advertised 9:00) and you are playing a 90-minute set. They glance at the table on the way out, but no one is there to sell them something so they leave.

You will double your sales by having someone at your merch table during your set. Find a couple fans in each city to help you with this for free admission.

If you push your merch from the stage, take credit, and have a merch seller at your table, you will absolutely increase your yearly income. Doubling your sales by taking credit and doubling them again by having a seller at the table during your set can take your yearly income from $10,000 to $40,000. And now you're a full-time musician.

Your pitch for them to buy your stuff starts with a killer performance and ends with you standing by their side after the show with a Sharpie out ready to sign your record.

Keep It Organized

I once toured with a band who put a lot of money into creating a lot of merch. They played after me, so after I finished my set, I hung out by the merch table during their set. People came over to me wanting to buy the other band's t-shirt. However, all of their shirts were tossed with no rhyme nor reason into several bins. I put in solid effort sifting through hundreds of shirts attempting to find the correct design in the right size, but eventually, with a line piling up, I had to give up and apologize that they either didn't have the size or I just couldn't find it. I told them to come back when the band finished and they could spend more time searching. Sometimes they'd ask if I had their size in one of my designs. Eight seconds later I pulled out their size, swiped their card and just made $20 for being organized.

A good way to keep your shirts organized is to roll them up, put a strip of painter's tape around the rolled shirt and write on the tape the size. Place the shirts in a long, clear bin from Target with the sizes ranging from XS to 3XL left to right. If you carry women's shirts (I recommend it), put the women's shirts in one bin and unisex shirts in another. Label the women's shirts "WS" for women's small and the unisex shirts just label "S."

Sell Quality

Merch is an incredible money-maker and should be looked to as such, but it's also a promotional tool. You want to sell fans shirts that they'll actually wear with your band name displayed on them to promote you to their friends. It's a conversation starter. I've gotten tweets from people saying they met new friends from wearing an Ari Herstand T—and someone actually got a first date out of it once! True story.

Order brands that are comfortable and hip. You're not just selling a design; you're selling a feel and the vibe. If people get your shirt and after one wash it gets deformed and becomes uncomfortable to wear, they'll associate your band with that discomfort.

Offer Creative Options

Use your creative talents to offer items that are unique to you. Are you a painter or photographer? Sell your artwork. Are you a calligrapher? Sell lyric sheets handwritten by you. Can you screen print? The more unique the merch item, the more it will sell (and be talked about). Nikki Lane is a visual artist (in addition to being a musician). She visits thrift shops and rummage sales while on tour and creates art pieces and customized merch items from her travels. Visiting her merch table is an experience in and of itself. I've seen artists sell paintings, framed photographs, coasters, jewelry and everything else you can imagine.

Make a shared doc with your band and keep a living list of creative merch items you can offer.

Have the Right Sizes

Make sure you never run out of a t-shirt size. Keep good inventory and reorder when you're running low. If someone wants to buy a shirt, but you don't have their size, they will leave without buying anything. They aren't going online when they get home to order it from your online store. The energy is at the show, while you're at the table so you can sign the shirt.

Stand by the Table After the Show

Until you're headlining gigantic theaters, you should be back by the merch table after the show meeting your fans, getting mailing list sign-ups and signing merch. Fans will remember their twenty-second interaction with you by the merch table for the rest of their lives. If people see you are there signing merch, they'll want to buy something you can sign. And if they meet you, they'll become lifelong fans.

GOING RATES FOR TOURING BANDS PLAYING UNDER-500-CAP ROOMS

T-shirt (American Apparel or equivalent) = $20

Offer and display female-cut shirts. Ladies will appreciate (and buy) them if they are displayed properly.

CD = $10
EP = $5

It's worth mentioning that a "pay what you want" pricing for CDs can work very well for indie artists with the right crowds. It's all in the pitch. Colorado-based Mark's Midnight Carnival Show uses this method, and band leader Mark Bush mentioned that, on average, people end up paying $15–$20 and some come back at future shows and pay more because of how much they love the CD. But the effectiveness lies with the onstage pitch. Mark explained that his pitch goes something like "This is a commercial-grade CD. We didn't just make it ourselves in our basement. We made it in someone else's basement, and it was a professional basement, too." A charming pitch can go a long way.

Vinyl Record = $20

Double LP Vinyl Record = $20–$25

Large Screen Print Poster = $15–$25 (depending on size, quantity, limited edition, etc.)

Standard Tour Poster (11" × 17") = $5–$10

Sticker = free with mailing list sign-up

Hoodie = $40

USB sticks (with album(s), artwork, videos, extra goodies) = $15

If you're selling these, make sure you have a large, clear display of all that is included:

INCLUDED

▪ Both of our albums (22 songs)

▪ Full liner notes and artwork

▪ 2 music videos

▪ Exclusive studio documentary (not on YouTube!)

▪ Super, special, hidden, secret goodies

Combos:

T-shirt + Vinyl = $35

CD + T-shirt = $25

All 3 CDs = $25

1) **Spread Out Your Shows** Even if your favorite band played in your city every week, you wouldn't go to every show. What makes you think your friends and passive fans will want to come see you every other weekend at various bars around town? They'll just think, "Eh, I'll catch the next one. They play all the damn time!" So don't play all the damn time. I recommend setting up a big show every 6–12 weeks locally and 4–6 months nationally.

2) **Get a Street Team** The greater number of people who work on the show, the greater number that will be invested in its overall success. I used to get a street team of 10–20 people for all my big local shows to hit the town at night, in smaller teams, with staple guns, tape, black winter caps and secret code words. I called my team "The Street Stand" (play off of Herstand) and I sometimes provided pizza or took them out to hot chocolate after a cold Minnesota postering evening, but they always got into the show for free and were, of course, invited to the after party. In addition to the postering evenings, I gave them flyers to hand out at their work, on campus, at the bars, and some nights we had Facebooking parties where we all promoted the show video and Event on all our friends' walls.

3) **Show Videos** Create a 1:00–2:00 video specifically for that show and upload it directly to Facebook. Have all the band members (and street team) share the video. Include clips of music videos of the other bands and impressive (high-quality) live clips. If bands don't have high-quality video, then at the very least run a photo stream with each band's music. Make sure you showcase all the bands on the bill and work with each band to promote the video. Making a show-specific video legitimizes this specific show and turns it into an event.

   You should also create a few, 15-second promo videos for Instagram and Twitter. You can post one or two a week leading up to the show. Make sure for the month that you're promoting the show you put in the Instagram description "ticket link in bio" and you actually put the link to purchase tickets in your Instagram bio. You can include the ticket link directly within the tweet.

4) **Shows Sell—Events Sell Out** Make each show unique. Why people will come out to this show versus a random four-band-bill Wednesday night show is because this is an *event*. Giving the show a title automatically turns it into a talked-about event. "Are you going to the Unknown Order show?" Versus "Ari is playing Room 5 on Thursday. Want to go?"

5) **Create a Show Poster** Get a graphic design artist to create a special poster for this one show (with the show title, of course). You can find a designer on 99designs, Guru or Fiverr if you don't have any in your local community who

are great. Depending on your budget, you can screen-print a limited number and get all the bands to sign a few. Then either sell them or get ticket holders to win them. This show poster should be used everywhere: Facebook Event, Instagram, Twitter, posters, flyers, Facebook ads, etc. The more people who see the poster image, the more they will talk about it and the more likely they will actually attend the event.

6) **Sell Tickets in Advance** Always try to sell tickets in advance whenever possible. Getting people to purchase tickets in advance ensures they will actually come. It also gets them to encourage their friends to buy tickets so they can all go together. Having advance tickets also legitimizes the show and makes people feel more comfortable coming out.

7) **Run Contests** As you ran contests for your release, run various contests for promo efforts and advance ticket purchases. For one show, I gave advance ticket holders goodie bags containing a poster, stickers and other random fun knickknacks from each band. It might be good to give out the bags after the show, though, as people are leaving—biggest complaint was that they had to hold on to the bag the entire night. Also, run contests on Facebook, Instagram and Twitter to encourage people to share the show video, poster and ticket link. On the Facebook Event you can explain the contest: "Share this Event (or Video) on your Timeline, invite all your friends to this Event and then write MISSION ACCOMPLISHED on this Event's wall. Everyone who does this will be thrown into a drawing to win a t-shirt and poster at the show. Must be present to win." Then onstage at the show, announce the winner.

8) **Include Other Buzzing Bands** Maybe you got 50 people out to your last show, the Alarmists got 80 to their last show, White Light Riot got 70 and This World Fair got 40. If there's no overlap, that's 240 that will most likely get out to this show (because it's an event). Those in the local music scene will also love to see four buzzing bands on one bill together. Get together bands who are good and buzzing. If they aren't buzzing yet, well, get bands who are hardworking and who will work just as hard as you on promo. Don't bring on a band unless they are willing to follow the promo necessities.

9) **Contact Local Media** Because this show is now an event, you have the ammunition to get the local media's attention. If none of the bands could get more than just a mention in your local newspaper, bringing them together for this talked-about event will get the paper to write about it. More on this in Chapter 15.

10) **Get a Sponsor** Find a local company (like beer, wine or gear), brand, newspaper or radio station that will get behind the event. This is a partnership for the evening. What the sponsor gets is being associated with a hot event and getting included in all promo, and in return, what you get can be anything from airtime, ad space

in the newspaper, a write-up on their (high-traffic) website, alcohol, cash, printing and so on. The best show-specific partnerships deal in trades, not cash. We got a wine company to sponsor the Unknown Order show and they printed all of the full-color posters (some 400 to be put up around the city), donated a case of wine per band (which was nearly finished during the show—glad I didn't perform last!), an ad in the weekly variety newspaper, some air time and other promo. This show sold out 10 minutes after the doors opened, with 200 people turned away. We'll dig into how to approach sponsorships in Chapter 10.

THE BRIDGE
9 Things to Consider When Choosing a Venue

1) **Capacity** Every booker wants to know what your draw is. Locally, once you're experienced and have a name around town, when you book your big shows every 6–12 weeks, you'll have a pretty good idea of the number of people you can bring consistently.

   When you can, always book a venue slightly smaller than your draw. Meaning, if you can draw 500, book a 450-cap room. If you can draw 50, look for 45-cap rooms. It's better to sell out a 200-cap room than play a 500-cap venue and have it two-thirds empty. Sure, it's cool to put well-known venues on your tour calendar, but it's better for your overall career to pack people in and give the best possible show to a full house, regardless of the size. Those who get in will be buzzing with excitement that they can experience an exclusive (to ticket holders) event and those who get turned away will know that, your next time through, they'll need to get tickets quickly.

2) **Ages** If you're a YouTuber with a target demographic of 12–19, you don't want to play 21+ rooms. If you're a bar band and need a bottle of Jack on stage with you at every show, you don't want to book the all-ages (dry) teen center. I try to book all ages or 18+ shows whenever possible. I remember what it was like before I was 21 and couldn't get into clubs to see my favorite bands.

3) **Reputation** You should use both Indie on the Move and Yelp when doing venue research. Indie on the Move has band reviews for most venues (and full contact, capacity info). Yelp has mostly customer reviews. You can get a great sense of the venue by reading reviews. If the customers don't like the place, then you're going to have that much harder a time getting people out. If the bands have

a horrible time there, then you're most likely not going to have a good show. Choose a venue that's generally liked by both the patrons and the bands.

4) **Vibe** Metal bands shouldn't play coffee shops and singer/songwriters probably don't want to play S&M clubs. Every venue has a vibe, and you have to figure out which kinds of clubs will help provide the most enjoyable experience for your fans.

5) **Payment** There are venues out there (typically run by musicians) that make sure their deals are fair and favorable to their guests (musicians). Some venues (typically run by d**ks) try to screw the musician out of any possible money and all but turn each band member upside down at the end of the night and furiously shake them down for loose change. Remember, nearly every deal (outside of L.A. and NYC) is negotiable.

6) **Promo** Most venues will not do anything to promote your show except display a few posters (that you provide) inside their establishment and list you on the website concert calendar. However, some venues take out ads in the entertainment weekly newspaper. Some venues have street teams distributing flyers for upcoming shows. Some venues exclusively work with promoters that handle this (and you'll then have to book your show with the promoter). It's good to know going into the show what promo the venue does and what promo you're expected to do as the band. Some venues have marketing departments that will poster the town, run Facebook ads and get press, but most don't and will expect you to do virtually all the promo.

7) **Advance Tickets** Most venues have a way to set up advance tickets, if it's not done by default. But some venues are stuck in the dark ages and, oddly, do not. Check the calendar on the website to make sure that they actually sell advance tix and get them set up for your show.

8) **Sound** The sound engineer is the most important person for your show. Try to book venues that have a good reputation for sound—or bring your own FOH.

9) **Perks** One of the perks of working with a promoter (instead of the club) is that they will typically fulfill riders (veggie tray, tub of beer, bottle of Jameson, don't ask to remove the brown M&Ms though). They'll also provide parking for your bus, van, car and sometimes lodging. But you have to ask.

Venues rarely provide any of this when booking directly with bands. But some will. Most venues will have a green room, but not all. If you need a space to clear your head, dip away from the crowd, warm up, rub ice on your nipples or whatever weird preshow routine you do hidden from the audience, you're going to want to make sure the club has a green room. So ask.

The venue is a direct reflection on your band. Your fans will associate your band with the venue they saw you in—for better or worse. So don't pick the wrong one.

WEDDINGS, CORPORATE PARTIES, PROPOSALS, BAR MITZVAHS AND THE WEIRD, WILD, PROFITABLE WORLD OF PRIVATE SHOWS

How to Get the Best Deal for the Gig

Around the holidays, musicians are especially in high demand. Playing holiday parties is an entire business in itself. Learn a handful of holiday songs and you will become much more valuable come December.

Whether you're doing a holiday show, a wedding, a bar mitzvah, a lunch-in or any kind of private party, if you don't have an agent, you need to learn to agent (yes, it's a verb—in L.A. at least) a bit.

Never Accept the Asking Price

When a buyer pitches you a rate for a gig, always negotiate this. Never settle for the asking price. This goes for when promoters and other bands offer you a guarantee for a club show as well. You don't need to go all Ari Gold on them, but if they pitch you $100, ask for $300. You'll most likely settle at $200.

Have a "Normal" Rate

More times than not, a buyer will ask you what your rate is. It's good to always have a rate (and set length) you fall back on. You can set your "normal" rate at, say, $1,000 per show up to 2 hours (for private events), with a "normal" set length of 70 minutes. I've done 70-minute gigs for way more than my "normal" rate and for way less, but, by default, I ask for my "normal" rate plus expenses. Remember everything that has to be factored into this price: (local) travel, rehearsal, equipment, years of practice honing the craft, writing the songs, recording the album, creating the website, building your reputation, and so on. And above all, you're better than anyone else they will ask who is cheaper! Sure, the buyer could get his brother to play, but he only showers once a week, gets drunk before his shows and is kind of racist.

Also, the further out you lock in a gig, the higher your price should be. If you reserve a date, that means you have to turn down other (potentially higher-paying) gigs.

Price Points

Set different price points depending on time:

> 0–2 hours = $1,000
> 2–3 hours = $1,500
> 3–4 hours = $2,000

The reason I say 0–2 hours and not set a specific set length is because once you are set up it's not much of a difference if you play 15 minutes or 120 minutes (if you have the material). You're there, so why not play? The work is getting to the gig. And they will think you're charging based on performance time. They'll try to get extra services out of you. "So since you're only playing for 75 minutes but you're charging for 2 hours, can you give my son a guitar lesson for 45 minutes?" This is how I learned to charge for 0–2 hours—after I gave her son a guitar lesson.

Feel Out the Gig

If a company hits you up to play their holiday party, you can bet they have a large budget. Pitch them your "normal" high rate. They can always come back at you and say that's more than they have budgeted and you can negotiate from there. If you ever pitch a rate and they immediately say "sounds good," you undersold yourself. Up your rate.

Get All Details Up Front

Do they provide sound? Lights? Stage? Seating? What kind of event is this? Can you sell your own merch? How many sets? How many breaks? Do they provide dinner and drinks? Lodging? All of this factors into the price. Have a normal rate plus sound, lights, food, lodging and travel. If they don't provide any of that, then factor that into the price and explain that to them. Your rate could be $1,000, but once you work out plane tickets, sound and light rental, hotel, dinner and rental car, it may cost around $2,000.

Have set points of expenses that are factored in:

- hotel buyout = $100 (either they provide one or add $100 to your check—if you have more band members, factor in the extra rooms)
- food buyout = $15 per member
- plane and rental car you'll have to look up and factor in per show basis

The Massage

If you pitch a rate way above their estimated budget, they may not respond to your email. You may need to follow up and ask if your rate is in their budget and if they are "ready to move forward and discuss details." Massage them—metaphorically, of course . . . or in actuality . . . whatever works. If they reply stating that your rate is way out of their budget, come up with an excuse as to why you can be flexible with them (you like the organization, it's last-minute and you're free, you have a close mutual friend, whatever), and ask what they can afford. Then negotiate from that point.

The Perfect 30

Put this gig to the Perfect 30 test and decide if it's worth it. Most private events are going to be around 2–3 for enjoyment and a 2–3 for career potential, so your compensation better be a 10.

Send a Contract

For these private gigs, always send over a contract that lays out all the details, including the performance fee. It makes them feel like you are professional. It's best to have a lawyer write something up for you, but if you can't do that, at least have something that simply states the facts of the event and makes sure everyone is on the same page.

ARI HERSTAND
Road Contact: Amy Dray | (612) 555-5555 | amy@proudhoneybee.com

PERFORMANCE AGREEMENT
This Performance Agreement is made this 30th day of January, 2017 between Ari Herstand hereinafter referred to as "Artist," and Joe Schmo hereinafter referred to as "Buyer"

Buyer Joe Schmo   **Name of Venue** The Pause
Mailing Address Joe Schmo, Podunksville, PA 19610
Address of Venue 103 St. Olaf Drive, Podunksville, PA 19610
Contact Joe Schmo Email jschmo_85@email.com
Title of Event (All promotions shall be written exactly as stated)
     Ari Herstand concert
Indoor/Outdoor Indoor   **Rain Site** N/A

Load in instructions Drive into alley behind main building. Call upon arrival.

Day of Contact Name: Shayna Rox Cell Phone# 608-555-5555

Artist Road Contact Amy Dray Email and Phone 612-555-5555

Day of Show: Wednesday, March 21st, 2017

Solo or Band? Solo   **Load in Time:** 5:00 PM

Sound Check Time 5:30 PM

Name and Phone # of sound engineer Gremlin: 414-555-5555

Door Time 8:00 PM **On Stage Time** 9:00 PM **Set length** 70 minutes

Other acts on bill ReadyGoes   **On Stage Time** 8:15 PM

Open / Closed to Public? Closed   **Ticket Price** N/A

Sound and Lighting Provided by Rapid Productions

Contact Name and Phone number Joe Le | 763-555-5555

Contract Price $1,500

Hospitality Dinner provided by Buyer

Travel Cost $475   **Lodging** $100 buyout

Total Cost To Buyer: $2,075

Cancellation. If the Buyer cancels the engagement less than five weeks before the performance, Buyer will pay Artist 50% of the contract price (**$750**) If Buyer cancels the engagement less two weeks before the performance, Buyer will pay Artist 100% of contract price (**$1,500**). The parties agree that such payments are reasonable in light of anticipated or actual harm caused by the cancellation—and the difficulties of proving the actual damages—to Artist. If any of the aforementioned stipulations—or stipulations listed in the Rider—are not met by the Buyer, Artist has the right to cancel the engagement without advance notice. If Artist is forced to cancel the engagement because of Buyer's refusal to meet an agreed upon stipulation, Buyer owes Artist the full cancellation fee (**$750/1,500**). Artist may cancel the engagement for any reason not explicitly expressed to Buyer no less than 30 days prior to the engagement. Artist may cancel the engagement less than 30 days prior to the engagement if unforeseen circumstances occur that prevent Artist from attending.

Payment. 50% of the guaranteed payment shall be given to Artist at least 30 days prior to the Event. The remaining 50% shall be given to Artist directly following the Event. All payments shall be given in check form or PayPal.

Make checks out to ARI HERSTAND.

Send check to:

Proud Honeybee Productions

1234 My Street

West Hollywood, CA 90046

Or PayPal to: ari@ariherstand.com

Force Majeure. If because of: Act of nature, inevitable accident; fire; lockout, strike or other labor dispute; riot or civil commotion; act of public enemy; enactment, rule, order or act of any government or governmental instrumentality (whether federal, state, local or foreign); failure of technical facilities; failure or delay of transportation facilities; illness or incapacity of any performer; or other cause of a similar or different nature not reasonably within either party's control, either party may cancel the engagement with no penalty.

General. Nothing contained in this Agreement shall be deemed to constitute either Buyer or Artist a partner or employee of the other party. This Agreement exhibits express the complete understanding of the parties and may not be amended except in a writing signed by both parties. If a court finds any provision of this Agreement or the accompanying rider invalid or unenforceable, the remainder of this Agreement shall be interpreted so as best to affect the intent of the parties. This Agreement shall be governed by and interpreted in accordance with the laws of the state of California. In the event of any dispute arising from or related to this Agreement, the prevailing party shall be entitled to attorney's fees.

Ari Herstand	Date	Joe Schmo	Date

Cancellation

And make sure you always have a cancellation stipulation in the contract. I always require 50% of the money up front as a deposit (that is not returned no matter what), and if they cancel the performance less than 30 days prior to the event, the remaining 50% is required.

How to Get Private Shows

If you build up a hefty cover repertoire, sign up for GigMasters and Gig-Salad. These platforms allow buyers to shop for talent for their event. The most popular gigs on GigMasters and GigSalad are weddings (ceremony and reception), corporate events, parties (graduation, retirement, quinceañera, bar/bat mitzvah, holiday) and, believe it or not, marriage proposals. A few singer/songwriter friends of mine have played quite a few proposals (surprise her in the park; as the couple walks by, a busker just so happens to be playing her favorite song as the dude [the buyer] drops to a knee). There are literally hundreds of various kinds of events that hire musicians through GigMasters and GigSalad. GigMasters boasts over 3 million events secured through its site. The more gigs you play and the more reviews you get, the higher your ranking will be on the site. The higher your reviews, the more you can charge. It costs about $100–$300 a year to become a member (depending on your membership level). But you will typically make back the fee after one booking.

HOW TO MAKE OVER $100 AN HOUR STREET PERFORMING

The downside of being a street performer is the perception that you're either homeless or you suck.
—KATIE FERRARA, AWARD WINNING,
WORLD-TRAVELING STREET PERFORMER

If you're a singer/songwriter and don't want a 9-to-5 day job, it's definitely worth exploring street-performing options in your city. Street performing takes a lot of work to master. Approaching a street performance is very different from approaching a club show. For one thing, on the street you have to grab people's attention as they walk by. In a club, people have paid to be there.

In Los Angeles, the most popular street performance location is in Santa Monica on the 3rd Street Promenade and Pier. It's where Andy Grammer started his career (long before his chart-topping hits and guest appearances with Taylor Swift). One summer I got an acoustic trio together and we busked 4 or 5 times a week for an average of 4 hours a day for about 4 months on the Promenade. It was definitely a learning experience. And, actually, a pretty decent way to make money. The Santa Monica Promenade is incredibly regulated. You need to get a permit (which only costs $37 for the entire year), and you must follow all of their guidelines to a T. Because if you don't, you will get ticketed by the "Promenade Ambassadors" who walk around with decibel readers (I kid you not) and rulers to measure your volume. On the Promenade, there are designated performance spots (you can't set up closer than 40 feet to the next performer), and nearly every performer uses amplification (less than 85db measured at a foot away). The Promenade, though, is unbelievably saturated with street performers (mostly break dancers who have so many in their crew that they crank up their volume (way past 85db) and one person's job is to just be the lookout for Ambassadors. This is one of the reasons many singer/songwriters have fled the Promenade for other locations around L.A.

Wherever you decide to perform, check the rules and regulations. The easiest way to do this is just ask other street performers who are there already or the manager of the event where you're thinking of street performing.

In New York, to perform on the subway platforms, you must follow the MTA's Rules of Conduct. Also, the Music Under New York (MUNY) program auditions and books performers at the most popular subway platforms, like Grand Central Terminal, Penn Station and Atlantic Terminal. You have to become a member of MUNY to apply to get booked. But you don't have to be a member of MUNY to perform on other subway platforms. And you don't need a permit, even with amplification (as long as it is below 85db measured at 5 feet away). To perform in New York City parks with an amp, you need a permit that costs *$45 a day*—yikes! So the subway is your best bet.

Regardless of where you perform, here are a few tactics that will help your earnings.

- **Nothing Draws a Crowd Like a Crowd**

  If you've ever walked down the Santa Monica Promenade, Hollywood Boulevard or explored the New York City subway system, you've no doubt been drawn to . . . wait for it . . . a crowd. Sure, they're surrounding a street performer (or group of ten break dancers), but the reason they have such a big crowd is because they started with a little crowd. When people see a crowd nearby, they want to see what all the fuss is. If nothing very interesting is happening, but there's a big crowd, they'll hang out longer than they normally would because they think the others there must know something they don't.

  The best street performers spend the first few minutes of each set getting a crowd—however possible.

- **Short Sets**

  The purpose of street performing is to make money. Plain and simple. People aren't hanging out at your set to go on a musical or spiritual journey. They have stopped to tune in for a couple minutes because something you said or sang caught their ear. They will not stick around very long, however, so the best way to sell more CDs and make more tips is to engage with them after your set. And the more set breaks you take the more opportunities you will have to cash in. Try playing sets of just five songs. Once you're done, leave your guitar case open by your performance area and go around the crowd with your CDs and a tip jar.

■ **The Performance Space**

The thing that sets the pros apart from the amateurs is the performance space. Setting your space up to feel cozy and unique to you should not be underestimated. Bring a rug to designate "your space." Set up a card table for your CDs, mailing list and a tip jar. Hang a large poster with your name, a professional live shot (of you looking amazing under the lights in a club), and your social links (and Snapchat QR code).

■ **The Sound System**

You don't want to street-perform unplugged. No one will be able to hear you. Get an amp or portable PA that is loud enough for your space. The louder the better—but, of course, stay within the regulations. Katie Ferrara recommends the Roland CUBE Street Ex and the Mackie FreePlay.

■ **The Tip Jar**

It's best to have a clear plastic tip jar. Plastic because with all the traveling you're doing a glass one will most likely shatter—ours did. And fill it with lots of $5s, $10s, $20s and a few $1s. Believe it or not, you will make more tips if the jar is full (because those who want to tip will be encouraged by how many others have tipped you as well—they'll think they have good taste). Having an empty tip jar is just sad. People will not tip you out of pity. They'll just keep walking. It's exciting to see a load of cash. They'll happily be a part of the action.

■ **The Mailing List**

Make sure every person who buys your CD also signs your email list. And at each set break, encourage those who have stuck around to also sign your email list. Even though they only heard a couple songs, they may become lifelong fans if you lock them into your list. And then they may buy tickets to your club show.

■ **What My Friend the Banker Taught Me**

One of the members of my acoustic trio worked at a bank during the day. Don't worry, he got out and is now doing music full-time. But what he explained to us was that the $20 bill is the most popular bill in rotation. It's the bill you get from ATMs. It's the bill everyone has on them (if they carry any cash). So create $20 merch options. Sell a 3-CD pack or a USB stick loaded with music, videos, lyrics, and other special goodies for $20. Just create a $20 option. Oftentimes, though, many regulated street-performance locations will not allow you to sell merch other than CDs, so always check.

■ **Have a Seller**

Having someone walking around with your CDs, mailing list and tip jar will drastically improve your earnings (and email sign-ups). Make sure this person is very charismatic and outgoing. You can cut your helper in on the sales too. Give her 20% of everything you make that day.

■ **Have a Cajon Player**

The thing I learned from Andy Grammer when I picked his brain about street performing was that having a cajon player makes it an event. It becomes a true performance. Two performers is much cooler than one. A million people play acoustic guitar and sing, but very few have a rocking cajon player with them. The cooler your cajon player looks and the more animated he is, the better. Give him or her 20% of your earnings or $50 for the day, whichever is greater.

■ Covers

And, of course, having a healthy cover repertoire will help increase your tips (and traffic). Learn the current hits, but also mix in your favorite oldies. And also learn some more obscure songs that you love, because the few who actually know the song you're playing (and similarly love it) will absolutely stop and enjoy and most likely give you a big tip, buy a CD and become a lifelong fan. That being said, Clare Means has been street-performing on the Promenade and Pier for eight years and plays very few covers and has made a solid living doing just this. She started Periscoping her street performances in September 2015 and in just under a year built up tens of thousands of (paying) followers who became fans of her original music. More on how she did this in Chapter 11.

■ Competition

Katie mentioned that she left the Promenade because there were just too many street performers and loud break-dancing crews. She found that it's best to seek out more obscure locations like farmers markets and malls. Talk to the market manager of the farmers market about setting up and performing. Some even have a budget to give performers a stipend of $100 or so. So definitely inquire.

- **Keep It Fresh**

  The biggest thing you need to look out for if you're planning to street-perform regularly is to make sure you don't burn out. You should challenge yourself to learn a new cover every week and retire the songs that you're bored with.

- **The Ego**

  The most difficult part of being a street performer is dropping your ego. Sure, most people who walk by you will think you're a struggling artist, but what they don't know is that you're pulling in $50–100+ an hour.

And if you're ever feeling down on yourself that no one is stopping by or giving you tips, just remember that Joshua Bell, one of the most famous violinists in the world, played a $3 million violin in a D.C. subway station for 43 minutes (incognito), and only made $32 from 27 people (as 1,070 others hurried by, ignoring one of the greatest living violinists playing some of the most challenging pieces ever written on one of the most expensive instruments in the world).

FESTIVALS ARE NO LONGER JUST FOR HIPPIES, MAN: HOW TO BREAK INTO THE FESTIVAL CIRCUIT

Festivals are a discovery mechanism—a live version of streaming.
—BRUCE FLOHR, RED LIGHT MANAGEMENT

You've heard of Coachella, Bonnaroo and Lollapalooza. But so has everyone else. Getting into a huge festival on your own is nearly impossible. If you don't have at least a manager or agent on your team (and serious online buzz), you're going to have a very difficult time breaking into one of these huge festivals. But you don't want to play such a festival until you're ready.

Festivals can break artists to the next level. There are always one or two bands that nobody expects that breaks from Bonnaroo or Coachella.

If you have an opportunity to play one of the huge festivals, you have to approach it right. Aside from putting on a great show, your online presence needs to be fresh. "You've got to make sure the looks you want line up to when you're peaking," artist manager Bruce Flohr advises, "otherwise, you're playing a festival that's really important and you're not quite where you want to be." When a big festival finishes and 80,000 music lovers disseminate and get home, they'll be asked what their favorite shows were. They'll say, "I saw My Morning Jacket and Radiohead, and there's this new guy." Make that new guy you.

But if everyone starts checking you out online all at the same time and you have an album that's three years old, no upcoming shows and a stale social media presence, that was a wasted opportunity.

So, despite what you think, you don't want to play an influential festival until you're ready—until you have a big fall tour set up, a new album to promote and a team of passionate people ready to push you hard.

That being said, there are a zillion little festivals around the country that you can play. Getting in at smaller festivals is far less difficult than getting in at a big one where everyone is competing for the spot.

Friends Like Helping Friends

Most cities have festivals of some sort over the summer where either music is the main attraction or a featured component. Whether it's the 400-person Folk the Park or the 100,000-person Brat Fest, start with your local festivals. Put the word out that you're looking for anyone involved in your local festivals, and track down how to play. Oftentimes there will be an open submission, but other times you just need to know the bookers.

The conference FestForward held in Santa Barbara, California, is also worth attending to learn more about how to break into some bigger festivals and network with the movers and shakers of these fests.

When They Book

Many of the big festivals begin booking the following year's lineup the day after the festival finishes, and the big ones get 80% booked up less than a month later. The rest of the year is spent finding all of the hot up-and-comers and securing the big headliners. It's a good rule of thumb to start your outreach for summer festivals right after the festival finishes.

It's definitely worth looking into winter cruise-ship festivals like Jam Cruise, Rock the Boat, The Moody Blues, and 70000 Tons of Metal. Festivals skew younger and cruises skew older. It's good to keep that in mind when planning how you want to build your audience.

If you think playing the festival circuit is the best way to go for your project, create a shared Google spreadsheet and make nine columns: Festival, Location, Dates, Attendance, Other Bands, Submission Process, Contact Name, Email, Notes. Some festivals take submissions via Sonicbids or ReverbNation. Some have applications directly on the website. And the big ones are only booked via connections. So you'll have to get scrappy. Submit through the front door, but also hunt down personal email addresses of the organizers. And try to find mutual friends to make intros.

Music Festival Wizard has the most complete listing that you can filter by genre, location (worldwide), type and date. Indie on the Move has a good amount of U.S. listings with links to submit.

Festivals are most interested in what you look and sound like live, so having a very high-quality live video is crucial. They also want to book buzzing bands. So gather up all of your accolades. Getting featured on hip blogs (like the ones cataloged on Hype Machine) definitely increases your chances of being selected. We'll dig into this more in Chapter 15.

The Street or the Ground

There are two main kinds of festivals out there: the Street and the Ground. These are my terms, by the way.

The Street festivals work with local venues, like bars, cafes and, of course, music venues to host music from open to close where music typically wouldn't necessarily be hosted. The most popular Street festivals are South by Southwest (SXSW) in Austin and CMJ Music Marathon in New York. The official SXSW-sanctioned clubs require badges or wristbands to gain entrance, but because of the influx of fans, musicians and industry to the area during SXSW, more and more venues unofficially host live music in the same area and only require an ID to get in. Walking 6th Street in Austin during SXSW, it's hard to tell which clubs are official and which are unofficial. Most artists play multiple "showcases" throughout the festival. Street festivals are becoming more popular around the world and many, like the Mile of Music festival in Appleton, Wisconsin, are popping up all over the place.

The Ground festivals require you to purchase entrance to the grounds. Once you're inside, you can see any act you want. Many times there will be multiple stages hosting music simultaneously. Often there is a camping section and the majority of attendees camp. The most famous Ground festivals hosting all genres of music are Bonnaroo and Coachella. Cruise ships also fall into the Ground category and they take place—you guessed it—out at sea.

Summerfest in Milwaukee, which boasts it's "The World's Largest Music Festival" and Lollapalooza in Chicago don't allow camping (and kick people out every night), but have multiple stages set up throughout the grounds where you can see any act you choose once inside. Brat Fest in Madison, Wisconsin, hosts over 100 bands on 4 stages and is actually free for all attendees.

There are genre-specific festivals like EDC and HARD for electronic music, WE Fest and CMA for country and Jam Cruise and Summer Camp for jam bands. And hundreds more.

Once you get booked at a festival, there are ways to maximize your appearance. For Ground festivals, if you're playing early in the day or on a small stage, you'll want to promote your slot to attendees so you're not playing to an empty lawn. Make sure you print up a bunch of flyers (you can get 5,000 full-color, two sided 4 × 6 postcards from Next Day Flyers for about $150) and walk around the campgrounds meeting people and passing out flyers. Be friendly and make sure you're chill about this process. Don't be sleazy. Festivals are all about the vibe and the hang. So make sure you're keeping a cool vibe when you do this. Enlist the help of your friends, fans and street team members who are at the fest to help you promote your slot. If you're the first act of the day on the small tent stage but you pack the tent to the brim, the festival organizers will take notice and most definitely have you back the following year for a much better slot.

It's much more difficult to promote your set for Street festivals. At SXSW everyone and their mom (literally) is promoting their showcases. You can't walk five feet without seeing a poster on a pole or being handed a flyer. To promote your sets at Street fests, you'll want to do all the heavy lifting well in advance of the festival. Most people will have all of the acts they want to see planned out before the festival starts.

Pay-to-Play Festivals

Every legitimate festival will pay you to be there. Many think that SXSW doesn't pay. They do, but it's not much. No matter who you are. SXSW offers artists (of every level) two options for payment. They can either get paid $250 (for a band) and $100 for a solo act, or get artist wristbands which lets band members attend all festival activities. But SXSW never requires artists to pay to play. There are some unofficial "festivals" that occur during the same time as SXSW that require bands to pay to play. You should never, never, never, never, never pay to play a festival. No exceptions. I have to mention it and emphasize it with five nevers because these kinds of festivals exist around the country and unfortunately are gaining in popularity. Let's band together to crush them. OK?

The way many pay-to-play festivals work is, organizers of the fest first secure fairly well-known headliners (who, of course, get paid). Once they've secured the headliners, the organizers hit up young bands and offer a "great slot near the headliners" if they sell a set number of tickets. To get your (physical) tickets, you have to purchase them up front. They require you to PayPal or money-order the money up front. And before you're allowed inside the grounds, you have to turn in all of the tickets you didn't sell. The closer your set is to the headliner's is based solely on the number of tickets you sell. Note, that "near" is a very loose term. I've heard of bands getting slots on a side stage (not the headliners' stage) with a set time *after* the headliner's set and getting their time cut from the typical 25-minute set to 5 minutes because the festival was running behind. There's an amazing video on YouTube of a pissed-off band who got their time cut short being physically ushered offstage by security because the festival was shutting down. Yes, these festivals cram as many bands in who will pay and therefore keep set times and changeovers as short as possible.

In 2015, I was clued in to one of these shady pay-to-play festivals by a musician friend who had been hit up by one of the bookers. This guy was booking the festival via text. So, acting as a young, dumb band, I texted the self-proclaimed "booking agent" (the title is wrong on so many levels) of the festival and said "I want to play the festival." I never gave my name and gave him a fake band name (had he spent 10 seconds to Google the name, he could have called my bluff). This festival, mind you, was taking place in two weeks. Two. Weeks.

We went back and forth over text for a solid hour during which I got the full rundown. By the end, he offered me a slot at the festival—*without ever hearing my music.*

The deal he offered for a "good" slot "near the headliners" was to buy 40 tickets. I got two options: I could buy the 40 tickets up front ("send money via PayPal or money order") at $18 a piece ($720) and then sell them for $20. I would also get 40 more tickets to sell on my own (and keep the dough). Or, if I couldn't shell out $720 up front, I could buy only 10 tickets up front ($180), get 50 total tickets and then turn in the rest of the $720 three days before the festival (via PayPal or money order). Total potential for option number two if I sold all 50 tickets (mind you, two weeks before the show)? $280. That's 28% of what I sold. And that's ONLY if I sold all 50 tickets. If I sold only 35 tickets, I'd be out $90.

Here's a good rule of thumb: If anyone asks for a deposit or asks you to purchase tickets up front (for a festival or club show), run the other way as fast as you can. It's the festival's job to book a mix of talent that will draw the crowds, along with new talent (whom they love) to showcase amid the lineup. And it's the festival's job to promote. Sure, every artist should do their fair share in helping promote through their social media networks, email list and possibly some press appearances, but in no case, ever, should the band be on the hook for unsold tickets.

Legitimate festivals make their money on sponsorships and ticket sales. Not off the backs of young bands who don't know any better. If the festivals are incapable of securing enough sponsorship money to cover their costs, it is their fault. Not the artists.

GIG RESOURCES YOU NEED
TO KNOW ABOUT

In addition to GigMasters and GigSalad, if you have a home studio setup, you should register a profile on AirGigs, SoundBetter and Fiverr. These marketplaces connect musicians with other music pros to help finish a song. You can hire a singer from Australia, a guitar player from London, a percussionist from Brazil and a mixing engineer from L.A. all within the platform. Mixing and mastering engineers and freelance players and singers are the most popular services offered, but recording studios, live sound engineers, top-line writers, beat makers and full-demo production services also exist.

Fiverr's community is by far the largest, as it appeals to mostly non-musicians and advertises services ranging from social media marketing, cartoon making, voiceovers and crowd-funding managers.

Sonicbids and ReverbNation list gig opportunities that you can submit to if you are a member. Some require payment to submit.

8.

TOURING

We never did anything that we lost money at. Driving her mom's
minivan with her friend all over the country and staying at
people's houses along the way doesn't cost very much.
—LYNN GROSSMAN, INGRID MICHAELSON'S MANAGER

WHY HIT THE ROAD

Too many bands go on tour just to say they're going on tour. Yes, it seems
cool to your friends, but do you know what's not so cool? Playing empty
shows in every city, sleeping on beer-stained couches, getting your gear
stolen from an unguarded green room and having your van break down
200 miles away from the nearest gas station.

The road is an unforgiving beast.

Like moving in with a lover, hitting the road with other musicians
will bring out the worst in them. But putting up with five other smelly
musicians, clashing personalities, cramped living quarters, a fast-food
diet and endless miles of nothing but cornfields instantly becomes worth
it when you step onstage in front of a crowd of screaming fans (and, of
course, see your bank account swell).

But what if you step out onstage and instead of a crowd of screaming
fans there's a crowd of 7 playing pool in the back. Less awesome.

The road isn't for everyone. But if you want to be a live artist, taking your show on the road will be a must if you want to grow past your local scene.

Tour revenue has become a lot more democratized over the years, and more indie bands are seeing serious success on the road. In 2000, the top 100 tours captured 90% of all revenue, while in 2015 the top 100 capture only 43%.

The most important thing to remember: *If you don't promote your show, no one will show up.*

Just being listed on a hot venue's website and being a touring band will not get people to show up to the show. Very few venues in the world have built-in audiences. So, step one is to build up a fanbase and tour where those fans are. If you start to gain traction online, make sure you grab email addresses (with zip codes) so you can promote directly to these fans when you visit their town.

If you have very little traction online and are itching to hit the road, it's possible to book a successful tour, but it takes a lot of creative promo tactics. More on this in a bit.

WHERE TO TOUR

Once you have built up a good following online, you need to find out where these fans exist. YouTube, Pandora, Spotify, Bandcamp, Facebook, along with the analytics platform Next Big Sound, provide excellent metrics of where your fans are located (and how engaged they are). You should also check the geographic breakdown of your fans on Bandsintown and Songkick. Make sure to register yourself as an artist (via Bandsintown. com or Tourbox.songkick.com).

You can also set up a button on your website and send out a WeDemand! link to your email list that will track where your biggest fans are "demanding" shows. And Rabbl takes this one step further by making fans put their money where their demand is. You can create a Rabbl event and have fans vote on bringing you to town by purchasing tickets for their city. Once a city reaches the threshold (set by you), the show is a go. You can also give fans incentives to purchase these tickets by offering cheaper advance tickets, VIP access or exclusive merch items. Mikky Ekko was able to route a tour back to Nashville from L.A. by setting up Rabbls. He was trying to figure out whether to play Austin, Dallas or El Paso, and despite what he and his team thought, El Paso had the most advance ticket sales (via Rabbl), so he routed his tour there. Fans are only charged for advance tickets if the show actually happens.

Venues have also starting using Rabbl to figure out which local bands to book. Instead of requiring bands to sell tickets, venues may list ten bands for a night on their Rabbl and the four who get the most advance sales will get the slots (all other fans are refunded).

HOW TO BOOK A NATIONAL TOUR

Timeline

You need plenty of time from beginning the booking process until the first show. For a tour containing mostly cities you've never been to before, I recommend starting this process at least five months out. You should have nearly all of the shows booked two months in advance of the first show so you have plenty of time to promote the tour.

Most likely you're going to spend the first month routing the cities, researching venues and gaining contact info.

Routing

Your routing will never be perfect. Meaning, you have to expect you'll do a little bit of backtracking and have a few off days because it's impossible to get every venue's schedule to line up with yours. You want to keep the backtracking and off days to a minimum though, obviously.

First, on a map (Google Maps works) plot out the cities you want to visit. Try to keep drives shorter than 6 hours on a show day and shorter than 10 hours on a non-show day. You're going to spend most of your time on the road, but spreading out the long drives will save you from burnout (and murdering your band members). You also want to plan for about an hour of stops for every 4 hours of driving.

The more members you have on tour, the less each member's driving burden, but the greater your tour expenses.

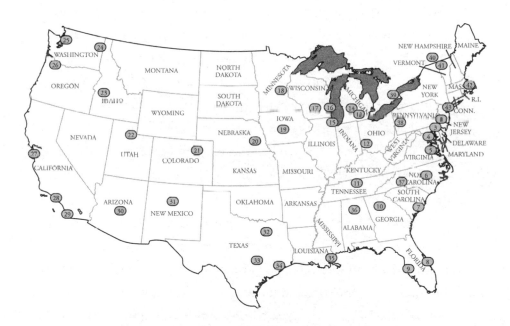

Routed tour using routefast.com.

Open a shared calendar in Google Calendar or iCal and share it with everyone on the tour. Put in "held dates" with city names. When you get a "hold" at a venue, change the color of the "held date" and title it the city along with the venue name. When you get a "confirmation" change that color again and title it the city with the venue, and in the notes of that event, list all details: talent buyer name, email, number, day-of contact, venue address, time of show, set length, load in time, door time, set times (for all acts), compensation, hospitality. This will all get confirmed in your confirmation email. (Remember that? See Chapter 7.)

These held cities will undoubtedly shift, so make sure you keep an updated calendar—especially if you have multiple members booking.

Finding the Venues

Once you have the cities you want to visit, you have to find the venues that are appropriate for your sound and your draw. If you've never been to this city before, it's going to be much more difficult for you to convince the talent buyer (booker) at the venue to give you a night, but it's possible.

First, you have to decide what kind of rooms you want to play. Are you a mellow singer/songwriter? Seek out art galleries, listening rooms, museums, cultural centers, black box theaters and living rooms (more on these in a minute). Are you a rock band? Seek out rock clubs, basement venues, festivals and block parties.

Indie on the Move (IOTM) and Yelp are some of the best resources to use for venue research. Yelp is great for audience reviews of the venue and to get the vibe of the club. Spend time reading these reviews and get a feel for how your project could (or could not) fit in the venue.

Indie on the Move is specifically for bands booking their own tours. They have a great list of venues, contact info and band reviews of the venues. To save time, you can hire IOTM to customize and send out initial emails to venues meeting a specific criterion that you set in each city (like, clubs under 300 cap that are 18+ and host rock music in a 10 mile radius of Atlanta). Currently, IOTM charges 25 cents per venue for this. As someone who has booked 60-date national tours on my own, any way to expedite this process is worth the financial investment. Believe me.

The Pitch

Most talent buyers at venues work over email, but some still work exclusively over the phone. Remember this and don't be afraid of the phone.

Similarly to how you pitch local clubs, your initial email pitch should be short and to the point. Well, all your emails should be short, but especially the initial one.

Make sure you check the venue's calendar first and make sure that date is open.

Keep the email under eight sentences. Write it in all-lowercase letters (if you can stomach it— I know you grammar nerds out there will fight me on this; that's cool—do what feels right for you). Talk about your history in the area (if any) and explain briefly how you're going to promote the show. Most important, say how many people you expect to get out for it. This is what 98% of talent buyers care about.

Sample Email:

Subject: oct 23—pink shoes and thom johnson

Body: hi tony, minneapolis-based pink shoes is passing through on oct 23 with thom johnson. pink shoes recently had a song featured on FOX's So You Think You Can Dance and our new music video (link it) has 254,000 views. our last time through we played the rhythm room and drew 75. we have an active street team on the ground in phoenix, contacting all local media and will be running facebook ads for this show. thom johnson is a

Philly-based singer/songwriter and was a top 10 finalist on The Voice in 2014. we expect 150 for this show. thinking $12/15 cover. can we grab a hold?

pink shoes:

http://youtube.com/pinkshoesawesomevideo

http://pinkshoesmusic.com

thom johnson:

http://youtube.com/thomjohnsonawesomevideo

http://thomjohnsonmusic.com

thanks!

~Ari

**

Ari Herstand

Manager / Guitarist—Pink Shoes

http://pinkshoes.com

http://facebook.com/pinkshoesmusic

NEWS:

- pink shoes named Best Rock Band by City Pages
- songs featured on Grey's Anatomy, New Girl, So You Think You Can Dance, Mindy Project
- performed on the Late Show with Craig Ferguson
- new album Blue Socks 8.7 by Pitchfork

Remember to put a few accolades (not too many) in your signature. It comes off less braggy—especially if you're doing your own booking/outreach.

Local Openers

Most venues will want you to put the bill together, but sometimes they will happily place a proven local act similar to your style on the bill. It's best, though, if you can take a complete bill to the venue.

When Myspace was around, it was very easy to find bands similar to your style in any city and quickly listen to them and see what kind of buzz they had. Now that Myspace is virtually extinct, the closest services that can be used for this purpose are Bandcamp, Indie on the Move and ReverbNation.

Always cross-check these bands on Facebook, Instagram, Spotify and YouTube to check out their numbers and engagement. Once you've narrowed down the list by location and genre, check out their tour calendar. See what kinds of venues they play. Take a look at their past shows by viewing their Bandsintown or Songkick data. See if they tour or exclusively play local. Are they playing local every week or every couple months? If they're playing local all the time, they won't be able to bring many people out to your show. Find bands that have a decent social presence and seem to pull well locally. Shoot them an email and ask them to open your show. Explain all the details up front: time slot, payment and draw request (we need the opener to help get the word out and draw at least 30). Remember to start off with a compliment about their music and how you found them. Give them $50 or 10% of your cut, whichever is greater, so it will encourage them to promote.

If it's getting closer to your tour start and you don't have a show booked, it may be worth searching for concerts in the city and hitting up the bands or the venue listed on the date you need, to see if you can hop on the bill. Pay won't be great, but you will hopefully make up for it in merch sales.

Show Trades

Once you've established yourself in your hometown and can draw decent numbers, you have something to offer. You can team up with other bands from other cities and offer them an opening slot at one of your big headlining shows in exchange for an opening slot at one of their big headlining shows. Ideally, you find similar bands with similar hometown draws.

You have to be careful, though, that you don't promise this to too many bands, as it may take you an awfully long time to fulfill the hometown promise if you play a big local show only every six to twelve weeks.

Payment

Reference the worst-through-the-best deals from the last chapter before getting into negotiations over payment. Most original music clubs will not offer guarantees if you aren't proven in their club (or with the promoter). You don't have much negotiating power if it's your first time through and aren't proven, so you're going to basically take what you can get. But these are good guidelines to stick to so that you know when you should be moving on to another venue in that town. Expect to set (or pitch) your ticket price around the same as most shows on their calendar. Meaning, if you contact a club and every show's cover is $15–$25, don't expect to charge $6 for your show. Most clubs will allow you to set your cover (within reason). I always recommend up and coming touring acts to set their covers around $10–$14. Fans understand that you're on the road and they will pay a little more for touring acts.

COVER SHOWS

If you have a large cover repertoire, it's a completely different ballgame. Most cover bars are located in the suburbs of big cities. If you can play three-to-four-hour cover sets, by all means work these into your tour.

You'll have to do a bit more research to find the bars that hire cover bands, but a good place to start is searching Indie on the Move. These shows typically pay a guarantee, and sometimes they will throw in a percentage of the bar.

The beauty of the cover bar circuit is if the bar is located in a city far away from any major metropolis, the bars are much more willing to throw in a hotel, food and drinks in addition to the guarantee because they want to keep high-quality talent coming to their small town.

Lodging

Once the tour is completely routed and confirmed, you'll want to start figuring out sleeping arrangements. For your first few tours this will mean finding friends in each city with couches or floor space (invest in air mattresses and sleeping bags). Try to figure this out before the day of the show, but as a last resort you can announce onstage that you're looking for a place to crash that night. More times than not this works. Not very rock-star—but neither is sleeping in your van.

TOUR RESPONSIBILITIES

The more successful your tours are, the more people you will be able to afford to bring on the road with you to handle necessary tour duties. Until then, you need to manage everything on your own and delegate when you can.

TOUR MANAGER (TM)

When you're on the road, the tour manager is the liaison between the band and everyone else: venue, promoter, fans, street team. The tour manager should have all of the contracts (or confirmation emails) organized and readily accessible. The TM should either have a physical tour binder with day sheets, maps, directions, addresses, contracts and notes printed out or have all of this organized on the tour iPad. The TM makes sure the night (and day) goes smoothly. She makes sure the doors of the venue don't open until sound check is finished and the band is in the green room. She makes sure the room is set up the way the band likes it (this should be discussed during the advance call). The TM schedules the oil changes and finds laundromats. And of course, the TM collects the money at the end of the night, counts the money in front of the venue manager and makes sure it is exactly what was discussed in the contract/confirmation email and advance call. If there is a per diem, the TM distributes these as well.

DAY SHEETS

The day sheet lists all the info everyone on tour needs to know about the day. It should include:

- Band name | Day of tour #
- TM name, number, email
- Today's date
- Travel
  Starting and ending points with distance and time
- Ending location address
  Typically venue or crashing pad
- Bus (or van) call time
- Venue info
  Name, address, capacity, phone, website, parking info, load-in info, load-in time, sound-check time, door time, onstage time
- Venue day-of contact name/number/email
- Production (house sound guy) contact name/phone/email
- Dinner info and time
     Is the venue providing food? Are they giving you a "buyout"?
  Or are you stopping somewhere before or after sound check.

- Meet-and-greet time and location
- Merch seller's name/phone/email
- Sleeping arrangements

    Hotel info (name, address, phone, website, Wifi password, gym, hot tub, etc.) or crashing pad names/numbers and relationship to band (drummer's friend, found through Twitter).

- Departure time

    Either that night (if you're driving through the night on a tour bus) or the next morning from the crashing pad.

Young Canyon - Almost Famous Tour

Saturday, May 20, 2017
Hi-Dive - Denver, CO - Mountain Time
Venue Address: 7 S Broadway, Denver, CO 80223

Schedule:

Bus Call: 9:00AM

Drive: Lincoln > Denver = 7.00hrs

Time Change: Central -> Mountain (Gain 1 hour)

Load In: 5:00PM

Sound Check: 5:30PM

Doors: 8:00PM

Local Opener TBA @ 8:30PM

Milk Carton Kids @ 9:15PM

Young Canyon @ 10:15

Curfew: Midnight

Hospitality:
Meal tickets for neighboring Mexican restaurant (1 entree)
Draft beer, wells all night
Gram of indica (sativa by request)

Lodging:
Stay with Hutchinsons
1234 Chambers Rd
Aurora, CO
31 minutes from venue
Phone: 720-555-3212
OzarkHutchinson@email.com

Promoter Contact:
Dave@coloradoshows.com
303-555-9752 (cell)

Venue Day of Contact:
Matt@hi-dive-venue.com
303-555-6123

Tomorrow:
Bus Call: 4PM
Denver -> Boulder = 42 min

Example day sheet.

It's best to print these out and tape a copy inside the bus/van and in the green room. The TM should also create a digital day sheet on the shared calendar or a shared Google Doc so band members can view them at will on their phones. Bring a small mobile printer on the road with you to print these (and set lists). You won't be able to make day sheets too far in advance of the show because variables will change (like load-in time, merch sellers, crashing pad, etc.).

ADVANCING SHOWS

One of the most important jobs a TM has is to advance the show with the venue. What this means is calling and/or emailing the contact person at the venue (usually the production manager, bar manager, or house sound guy) at least a week before the show to confirm all details like load-in and sound-check times, how the room is set up (standing or seated show), payment details, who the day-of contact person is, guest list protocol, dinner details and parking info. This information is how the day sheet will be created and finalized. Details change from when the show was confirmed months prior so whether you have a dedicated TM on the road with you or not, every show must get advanced.

Guest List

The TM will handle the guest list and follow the venue's protocol on how to get it to them. You should create a dedicated shared calendar (iCal or Google) just for guest list each day of the tour, so any band member can add names at will. The guest list number will be on the contract (or confirmation email) and the TM should write the number on each day's calendar event so members know not to go over—first come first serve!

Every band, big and small, should organize some form of preshow, VIP meet-and-greet package.

John Legend's touring guitarist, Ryan Lerman offered one-on-one backstage guitar lessons before the show for $75. The Disco Fries challenged fans to a backstage NBA Jam game preshow for $30. Ron Pope challenged fans to Pop-A-Shot preshow for $150. Ryan Beatty offered fans a pizza and a movie date for $500. Parmalee's "All Access Experience" included access to the sound check, Q&A with the band, meet and greet, and swag package for $70. Jana Kramer challenged fans to Ping-Pong and Cornhole preshow for $60. Experiences are a great way to make extra money on tour and get to know your biggest fans on a more intimate level. Wild Child claimed they doubled their net touring revenue (drawing 100–500 a night) by offering experiences at every stop.

The TM will get in touch with each day's VIP guests and arrange all the details. It's fun to make special lanyards with laminated passes that say ARTIST NAME | NAME OF TOUR | VIP. They will cherish this souvenir forever, and it will be a constant reminder of the great time spent before the show.

Believe it or not, many fans will pay good money for VIP experiences. A 2013 Nielsen study revealed that fans would spend up to $2.6 billion more a year on music if "they had the opportunity to snag behind-the-scenes access to the artists along with exclusive content." This study also revealed that 40% of U.S. consumers are responsible for 75% of music spending.

You can offer a portion of all VIP package proceeds to go to the charity of your choice.

LODGING

A TM is also responsible for arranging the lodging. If it's a crashing pad tour, have every artist search Facebook for "my friends who live in City" and go from there. Great ways to save on hotels is by using Priceline's Express Deals or Hotel Tonight. Hotels that have empty rooms will list them for supercheap (like 60% off normal price) a day or two before to try and fill them. I've booked 4-star hotels for $45 using this option.

Airbnb is also a great option to find cheaper lodging in cities. Try not to drive very far after the show (if you don't have a dedicated driver) to the crashing pad or hotel. It will drastically reduce your postshow hang time, bar hopping and overall tour enjoyment. Exploring each city's nightlife is one of the best parts of being on the road.

MERCH SELLERS

You need someone selling your merch every night. Even if you have a merch manager on the road with you, you should still have a few sellers to help out. These can be fans (sought out via Twitter, Facebook, Snapchat or your email list) or sometimes the venue will provide some merch sellers (for a fee). Offer the fans free entrance to the show. The TM will be the point person for the merch sellers and train them on how everything works. The merch sellers should be positioned at the table when doors open until doors close. Hook them up with free drinks and free merch.

PER DIEM (PD)

For bigger tours, each hired gun and crew member typically gets a per diem, which is a daily amount to be spent on food. "Per diem" literally means "per day." It can range anywhere from $5 to $50. Typical per diems sit around $20. But for most early tours, there are no per diems.

As you can see, the TM has a ton of responsibilities and it's crucial that you have a very organized and responsible one. Oftentimes, a sound engineer or merch manager will double as a TM. Or many times, for singer/songwriter tours, hired freelancers will double as the TM. If you're just a 4-piece band on tour with no extra help, have the most responsible member be the TM.

MERCH MANAGER

Many tours will be profitable based solely on the success of merch sales. The merch manager counts in and out all inventory and cash every night, makes sure the "bank" (change pouch) is full of small denominations for change ($5s are best—don't have any of your merch packages cost amounts requiring singles). The merch manager keeps track of inventory and knows when to reorder to make sure you never run out of anything. She should be very organized and very charismatic to be able to upsell each customer.

FOH

FOH stands for "front of house" and just means the sound guy. The first person you hire to bring on the road with you after the musicians should be the FOH. The venue's house FOH does not know your sound and may have completely different taste.

50 IS THE MAGIC NUMBER

Remember, the number-one thing venues care about is turnout. So when booking your tour, you're going to have to figure out how you're going to get people to every single show. Unless you're booking venues with built-in crowds (like restaurants, house concerts, or casinos), you will need to work to promote the tour.

You can book a financially successful tour around the country a lot easier than you think. In pretty much every major city in the country, there will be a small venue with a capacity under 300 that will be conducive to your sound. Nearly every under-300-cap venue in the world will be satisfied with a 50-person turnout on a week night and even some on the weekend if they haven't filled that date with a sure thing. If you tell the club that you can get 50 out, you can probably book the club.

So that's step one. Now that you have the shows booked, how do you actually get the 50 to come? You have to find your niche. Break out that Our Fans sheet again. You should look at groups and organizations as a main target when promoting the show. Sure it's nice to grab one kid's attention from a Facebook ad, but it's much more effective if you get an entire group excited about you.

Does your music appeal to college kids? Line up promo shows at dorms, frats, and sororities in that town a day before or the day of the show and offer them a table at the venue to take donations for their philanthropy project. Are you a chess master? Contact the local chess clubs and offer them discount tickets and run a tournament preshow where the winner will get free merch. Are you Jewish? Hit the local Hillel houses, synagogues, Moishe Houses, summer camps. Are you gay or trans? Hit up the local LGBT organizations. Are you a theater nut? Contact local playhouses and offer them music to play before the show and at intermission and have discount tickets available in the lobby.

Just find a niche or an organization that you can contact locally that you can get excited about your band. Personalize your pitch to them and your reason for wanting to work together. It's a minipartnership for that day (or months leading up to the show), so you should point out how it will benefit them. You should contact a few organizations for each city and not bank on just one—in case the one falls through or doesn't work.

Once you find a way to get 50 people in any city to come to your show, you're now a headliner. Start with your local market and figure out what works there and then take that strategy on the road.

I once booked a 10-city high school tour. I spent a week in each city (most of which I had never been to) and went into the local high schools during the weekdays and then had an all-ages club show booked on that Saturday. I performed a couple songs and talked to the music students about how a music education helped me get to where I was. I offered to visit the high schools for free in exchange for allowing me to sell my merch and promote my Saturday show. I was the talk of the school that week and every club show that weekend was filled with these high school kids who bought lots of merch. I promised every club at least 50 (even though I'd never been to that town before and had no online buzz) and I had 50–250 at every show.

HOW TO MAKE $500+ PER HOUSE CONCERT

A lot of us musicians have big egos and we've all been brought up with this mantra that it's about more tickets and more people in the room and more albums sold. Quantity. I got to a point where I was having these magical experiences that were super out of the ordinary. I connected with a lesser quantity of people, but it was more of a connection.
—GRAHAM COLTON, SINGER/SONGWRITER, COFOUNDER OF FANSWELL

House concerts are not a new thing. There is a long tradition in the folk world that dates back to the '60s. However, they seem to have had a massive resurgence over the past decade of singer/songwriters trading in club touring for house shows. Personally, I've played about 30 house concerts over the past few years and these shows have been some of my favorite (and most profitable) shows of my career. Nothing beats the connection of a room full of supporters sitting merely feet from you, soaking up every note, every word, and every beat. A living room concert is one of the most memorable concert experiences a fan (and artist) will ever have.

And house concerts aren't just for tiny singer/songwriters. Artists like David Bazan (of Pedro the Lion), Jeremy Messersmith, Califone, Mirah, Laura Gibson, Tim Kasher of Cursive, S. Carey, Richard Buckner, Ben Kyle of Romantica, Alec Ounsworth of Clap Your Hands Say Yeah, and John Vanderslice have set up house concert tours over the past few years.

With house shows you don't have to deal with bad sound guys, drunk a**holes, empty clubs, or the headache of promotion. Shannon Curtis has a great book on how to book a house concert tour called *No Booker, No Bouncer, No Bartender: How I Made $25K on a 2-Month House Concert Tour (And How You Can Too)*, which I highly recommend if you're thinking of getting into the house concert game.

The Booking

The beauty of house concerts is that you only need one superpassionate fan per city to set up a house concert. Put out feelers to your email list and on social sites. Set a guarantee plus a percentage of tickets, or you can play for tips.

You'll have to designate Fridays and Saturdays (or Sunday afternoons) for house concerts, since most hosts have 9-to-5 jobs and won't want to organize it for a weekday. Plan your house concerts about two to three months in advance. Give your hosts plenty of time to invite guests and get excited.

You'll want to tour with an amp or PA (and all mics/stands/cords) to plug in your guitar, keyboard and vocal mic. The host will most likely know nothing about sound and have zero sound equipment. You should be able to set up anywhere and play. Don't forget your extension cords and power strips.

The email I send out to potential hosts usually looks something like this (feel free to copy whatever you want):

Ari Herstand Living Room Concert!

What the . . .?
I'd like to set up shows in people's living rooms/backyards/dorm lounges/etc. and have a very intimate experience—something that isn't necessarily possible in many clubs I play. I'm going to play many new, unreleased songs for these performances—many songs that translate very well to the living room, but maybe not so well to the club.

Interested?
If you'd like to host a living room concert, all you need to do is reply and fill in the information below and I'll get back to you with possible dates for your area. I need you to bring at least 20 people to the concert—hey you have home turf advantage!

What I charge.
The concert costs $350 + 80% of admission after $350 is met. This means, if you charge $15 a head (what I recommend) and 30 people show up, that equals a total of $450. I end up with $430 (you end up with $20) at the end of the night. If 20 people show up, that equals a total of $300. I end up with $350 at the end of the night (you have to cover the remaining $50). If you're confident you can bring 24 people at $15 a head, everyone who lives in the house basically gets a free concert because I don't charge the hosts and hostesses. Just so you know, this is much lower than my normal "private concert" rate, but because I want people who really dig my music—dare I call them fans— to be able to afford this and not have to pay an exorbitant amount out of pocket, I've reduced my rate for these house concerts. I used to take 100% after $350, but I've added the 20% to the host idea to give you an incentive to provide simple snacks/drinks for your guests and so you don't lose money.

What to provide.

All you need to provide is a big enough space to hold everyone. Also, make sure my performance space (corner) is well lit with upright bright lamps or something and then the rest of the room can be dim with candles or other lamps. People are most comfortable sitting on chairs, couches, benches, husbands, boyfriends, girlfriends, etc., so it would be great if you had enough seating for everyone. Maybe encourage people to bring a pillow, blanket, or lawn chair to sit on if you don't have enough chairs. Make sure you have a key person who will collect money from everyone at some point.

How long is the concert?

The concert will last about 2 hours. The first 45 minutes I'll play an acoustic, mostly unplugged (chill) set. Then take a 15-minute intermission and the next hour will be a full looping show—plugged in. Make sure your neighbors are OK with this. Won't get too loud, though. I'm looking to start at 7:30 for most places.

Notes for this experience:

Please let your guests know that this is an intimate, private concert by a touring musician. This is not a party. Promote my music to all guests and get them excited about the music if they don't already know my stuff. This is not a drinking party with your best bud providing the entertainment. While alcohol is absolutely OK (and encouraged if somehow a Guinness ends up in my hand), this is not a time to get wasted.

Also, please inform your guests, maybe at the start (because I don't want to look like the bad guy), that talking is very uncool during the performance.

Anything else?

I'll most likely need a place to crash that night, so if you have a couch, that would be fantastic. If you provide dinner for me as well, I'll love you forever.

Please fill in this info and I'll get back to you with open dates:

City, State:

Are you in high school or college (please list where):

If in high school list parent's name:and email:
How many live with you (are they ok with this):
Do you live in a house, dorm, apartment, etc (elaborate):
Expected number of attendees:
Where will this be held (living room, backyard, dorm lounge, etc. please
elaborate):
Exact Address:
Contact Phone Number:

Hopefully I'll see you soon!
~Ari

And once you confirm a date, make sure you send them a confirmation
email. Here's what I use:

Details:
Saturday, March 17
Contact: Mickey Mouse
Phone Number: 612-555-5555
Exact Address:
1234 Beautiful Lane
St. Paul, MN 55104
7:30-9:30 (you can change this if need be)
$15 a person (hosts excluded)
$350 guarantee + 80% of cover after $350
Make public (upon request) or keep private?
Load in: 6:00
Sound check: 6:30
Provided equipment: lamps to light my performance area (corner), mood
lighting for the rest of the room
Sleeping accommodations? yes

**CANCELLATION POLICY
Because I am routing a tour around this show, once this is confirmed,
we cannot cancel it. Please do not confirm this unless you are certain

you can afford the concert and/or can get enough people to attend. If you have to cancel the show less than 3 weeks before the date, I will still need to receive 70% of payment.

Please confirm these details and we're set! Thanks!
~Ari

People have organized pot lucks, birthday, graduation and anniversary parties around these. You will have a lot of fun with house concerts, and even if you're a full band, as long as you tour with a full PA system, you can set up backyard and basement concerts. Customize this for you.

You will build lifelong fans this way. Attendees get a very personal experience, get to hang out with you before and after the show, and typically buy tons of merch.

Make sure you pass around the mailing list clipboard or iPad and get every single person's email who comes. If 30 people show up, the next time through you can book a club and you can estimate that each of them will bring at least 1 more person and now you have a solid 60 for your club show.

Shannon Curtis typically works solely on tips and merch sales for her living room concerts, and it has worked out very well for her. If you're just starting out, you can go this route as well. But make sure the host discusses the importance of the tip jar (she advises not to include a suggested donation because if you say the show is worth $10, no one will drop a twenty in). The tip jar (and merch) should be placed right near the front door so it absolutely cannot be missed.

Companies like Fanswell, Sofar Sounds and ConcertsInYourHome have popped up recently that organize (or help artists and fans organize) house concerts. Sofar Sounds has set up intimate, living shows with oftentimes famous artists like Hozier and Karen O of Yeah Yeah Yeahs.

House concerts are a beautiful, unforgettable experience for everyone involved.

OPENING TOURS

The Purpose of Opening Tours

Opening a hot tour can jump-start your career and expose you to an entirely new audience. It's one of the most valuable things you can do for your career. Many times, openers will not make much (if anything) per show. But, because you're playing in front of mostly new fans, the merch potential is infinite. As long as you work your merch game right and secure as many email sign-ups as possible, you will come out ahead.

Being an opener of a bigger tour has a lot to do with connections. Many headliners (like Ingrid Michaelson) bring only their friends' bands as their openers. Many labels will pair smaller artists with larger ones on the label. Sometimes being the local opener for a touring band can get you on the road with them if they liked your set and you were a fun hang in the green room. There's no one way to get on a big tour. It's best to hit up the manager of the headlining band and ask. Most bands will have their manager's contact info listed on Facebook and/or their website. Send him your draw numbers for every city on the tour and a live YouTube video. Talk about how hard you'll work to help promote the tour. Make it clear you'll be easy to work with.

Buy-Ons

Some mid-level artists charge their openers a "buy-on" amount. Typically, it's a bulk amount of money up front to cover expenses for the bus and hotels. But the opener will make a performance fee for each show throughout the tour (of maybe $150), so in the end you may break even. Artists who charge openers a buy-on rate and provide nothing other than the opportunity to open (no space on the bus, no lodging, no food, no performance fee) are flat out unethical. But you will sell merch and make fans. Remember, the average dollar per head for venues 500–1,000 cap is $3.65 in merch sales. You'll have to crunch the numbers and decide if it's worth it for you.

Getting smart with backstage "experiences" and merch, you should be able to make every tour profitable.

HOW TO STAY SANE ON THE ROAD

I highly recommend setting aside time every morning to exercise. Going for a run before you leave for the long drive will not only give you a fun way to experience the city, but let off steam and prevent you from wanting to murder your bandmates.

Tensions will be high, so keep your tour pranking to a minimal; also execute it in a tactful manner. Waking up on a scummy floor with only your trusty Spiderman duvet for comfort and the house owner's smelly dog licking your face is often a bad start to the day. In such a fragile state, getting shot at with a water pistol full of gravy might just push you over the edge.

—LEWIS WILLIAMS, DRUMMER FOR PRESS TO MECO

1) **Order Merch**
2) **Create the Merch Display** Big. Bright. Bold. Awesome.
3) **Create the Tour Poster** Hire a graphic design artist for this.
4) **Send Posters to Venues** Or have Bandposters do it for you.
5) **Send Promo Packages to Street Team** Posters, handbills still go a long way. Rally the troops!
6) **Write the Tour Press Release** More on how to do this in Chapter 15.
7) **Contact All Local Media** See Chapter 15.
8) **Set Up Credit Card Platform** Square, PayPal and Amazon are all fine options.
9) **Set Up Inventory Tracking Program** AtVenu is proven and excellent.
10) **Get Musician's Insurance** MusicPro Insurance insures musicians, producers and recording engineers (like $250/year for $20,000 worth of gear). Many other insurance companies do not cover nonclassical musicians. Think I'm joking? Try to file a claim with your renters/homeowners insurance plan. I learned this the hard way.
11) **Get a Security System for the Van** And if you're pulling a trailer, make sure to back it up against a wall every night so no one can break into it. And buy the indestructible, uncuttable pad locks. You have to expect that people will try to break in to your trailer. Remove the possibility.
12) **Get the Tour Mobile** Fifteen-passenger van, Sprinter, SUV, bus? Research what is best for your purposes.
13) **Tag the Gear** It's like how your mom put your name inside your undies when you went away to sleepaway camp. Put your name on every piece of gear.
14) **Email List** Set up a landing page that you can lock an iPad on, or a desktop computer that you set at the merch table, or print out enough sheets for the clipboard for the entire tour.
15) **Create the Photo Booth** Set up a desktop computer at the merch table with a webcam locked on a photo-taking program. Upload all photos to Facebook Events every night.
16) **Full Tune-Up** You don't want to break down 200 miles away from a service station in Podunksville, Utah, with zero cell service.
17) **Advance the First Week of Shows** Add Shows to Bandsintown, Songkick Don't forget the ticket links.
18) **Increase Data Limit on Your Phone** You'll be watching a lot of Netflix in the van.

19) **Pack a Cooler** Stay healthy and save some cash on eating out. Swing by grocery stores and make some sandwiches.

20) **Packing List**
- Air mattress
- Pillow
- Sleeping bag
- Laundry bag
- Toiletry bag
- Flushable wipes
- Toilet paper (just in case)
- First-aid kit
- Advil
- Starbucks VIA packets (Coffee on the go! Gas station coffee? No, thank you.)
- Tumbler
- Car outlet converter
- Power strips for van
- E-ZPass
- Trashbags
- Canteen
- Frisbee, football, soccer ball, dumbbells, jump rope
- Phone armband
- Running earbuds
- Fancy headphones
- Phone mount
- Tire jack
- Spare tire
- AAA card
- Duct tape
- Extra phone charger
- Nuts
- Protein bars
- PA system (to be able to set up and play anywhere if need be)
- King-size sheet if you're touring in an SUV (to cover your gear at night)
- Laptop
- Passport (if you're crossing borders)
- Visas/proper paperwork (if you're crossing borders)
- Tour binder

- Printer (for day sheets, set lists)
- Printer paper
- Cash for merch change
- Credit card swiper (bring 2 or 3 to be safe)
- Windshield washer fluid
- Sriracha (my comfort food)

21) **Plan Out Oil Changes**

22) **Secure a Tour Sponsor** More on this in Chapter 10.

23) **Get a Car Topper** If you're touring in an SUV or plain ol' car, I recommend getting a storage component for the top of your vehicle. Throw all of your merch in there. You'll definitely need the extra storage.

24) **Try Not to Tour with a Trailer** You'll save a tremendous amount of gas and you won't be as much of a target for thieves. Take out the back row of your 15 passenger van or fit all your gear in the back of a Sprinter van.

9.

HOW TO MAKE REAL MONEY PLAYING COLLEGES

Ow CAN AN UNKNOWN SINGER/SONGWRITER MAKE $1,800 OR AN unknown band make $2,500 for 60 minutes of original music? For some of you, you just hit the jackpot. As someone who has played over 100 college shows around the country, I can tell you firsthand how amazing (and simultaneously awful) this really is.

WHAT IS THE COLLEGE MARKET?

Playing colleges is unlike any other performance experience on the planet. Before the dollar signs start to blind your vision, you have to understand what the college market actually is. Nearly every university in the country has a campus activities committee, board and/or advisor. Some smaller schools just have one or two people in charge of setting up programming and booking entertainment, and the larger state schools may have an activities committee of 50 students. Most activities committees have subcommittees for music, comedy, homecoming, freshman orientation, Spring Jam, Big Concert, Welcome Week and so forth. These committees plan programming for their students around the year. This includes everything from a hypnotist for freshman orientation, a magician and a rock band for homecoming week, a singer/songwriter for coffee shop night, a comedian just because and a lecturer to mix in some brain juice substance. But they also program activities with moon bounces, sumo costumes, climbing walls, mechanical bulls, Guitar Hero tournaments, laser tag and cotton candy machines. Nearly every university has a budget for these kinds of programs. Most programming budgets range from $10,000 (for the tiny, community colleges) to $200,000+ (for big state and private schools) a year. A year. Wonder where all that money from tuition goes? Now you know.

The Campus Activities Board's (CAB) main job is to provide meaningful programming for the students. The activities have to be diverse enough to appeal to the entire student body. And the entertainers cannot offend anyone. There's a big difference between edgy and offensive. Colleges buy edgy, but very few buy offensive. Of course whether something is offensive is subjective, but when you're competing with a zillion other acts (not just musicians), you want the best possible odds.

Before you go any further, let me make this easy for you. If you are a hip-hop artist who swears a lot, a punk band or really any band that screams, a political folk act, or if you play music that may be considered offensive by anyone, skip to Chapter 10.

CABs, unlike college radio stations, will not book offensive entertainment. Whereas college radio gets off on pushing the envelope, CABs have to be absolutely certain the acts they bring to campus will not get the school sued.

WHO IS ON THE CAB?

The people in charge of booking entertainment are not music aficionados (snobs). They don't know the hippest indie band of the moment or the newest underground emcee to break out of Minneapolis. They know top

40. And they are on the board because they like organizing events (or are looking for a résumé builder). They don't typically know anything about the music industry and aren't interested in your Tom Waits cover. They've never heard of him. But these are some of the friendliest, sweetest, kindest and generally fun-loving people you will meet. And yes, remember, they are 17–22 years old. They don't have any real-life business experience. More on this in a bit.

After playing so many college shows and meeting so many CABs, I started to notice a trend. A type. It's so interesting how similar CABs are in every region of the country. I guess campus programming attracts a certain kind of person.

But let me repeat, the people on the CAB, in charge of the $200,000 annual budget, aren't looking for the next Jack White; they're looking for the next Taylor Swift. If you want to break into the college circuit, you have to understand this and market yourself as such.

MUSIC INDUSTRY VS. COLLEGE INDUSTRY

The college industry is not the music industry. There's only a small overlap. Understanding this is key to your success. You cannot approach college shows like you approach club shows. You cannot approach college booking like you approach club booking. You cannot approach advancing shows with colleges like you approach advancing shows with clubs. You cannot approach sleeping arrangements for college shows the same way you approach sleeping arrangements for club shows (unless you want to get arrested or sued by Daddy). These are completely different industries.

You should look to college shows for one purpose: to make money. These are typically not career-building opportunities—unless you're looking to be a career college musician. Because the money is so good, many musicians get stuck in the college circuit. It's hard to go from making

$1,500 a show with all expenses paid to making $50 a show and a single drink ticket when you start touring clubs again.

Club Shows		College Shows
	$	
less up front, more long-term potential		more up front, less long-term potential
couch	LODGING	hotels
Subway	FOOD	Applebee's
lifelong	FANS	semester
venue works with your schedule	TOUR	you route to school's schedule
oftentimes own venue, older	BOOKERS	changeover every 1–2 years, 17–22
expected to be done by artist	PROMO	done exclusively by school
run by professional	SOUND	run by student
career	PURPOSE	money

Club shows vs. college shows Venn diagram..

CAREER BUILDING VS. MONEY-MAKING

It's counterintuitive, I know, to say that you can't build your career within the college circuit. Let me tell you a little story. My first NACA showcase (more on what NACA is in a minute), was in the spring of 2008 at the Northern Plains conference. I booked 50 dates on the spot (a record at that conference). My entire 2008–2009 school year was filled up with colleges around the Northern Plains region (Midwestish). I promoted the bajeebers out of every show (via Myspace—that was hot at the time). And most shows were totally packed. I sold tons of merch. And the CABs were thrilled. I followed up a few of these shows with a club show a couple months later. Take Drake University in Des Moines, Iowa. I remember this show very well. There were about 200 students at the show, I sold a ton of merch, got a bunch of mailing list names, signed autographs, took photos, the works. The head of the CAB even came up to me with a burned CD (those were big in 2008) of a remix he did of one of my recordings. Man, I hit the jackpot. Or so I thought. I followed up the Drake show with a date at Vaudeville Mews in Des Moines (just a 10-minute drive from campus or a 15-minute bus ride) a couple months later. I emailed the list, promoted it to the students. Everything. The night of the show, 5 people showed up. Ouch.

What happened? I'll tell you (because I've analyzed this ad nauseam after so many failed follow-up club shows).

There's a huge difference for college students between a free event on campus for which all they have to do is fall out of bed, roll down the hallway and they're there and a show off-campus where they have to find someone with a car to drive them, get dressed, and pay money. Getting college students dressed or asking them to part with their money is nearly impossible.

When you play these campus-sponsored events, that's exactly what they are: events. They're not typically concerts. Sure, you look at them as concerts, but the students are constantly going to campus-sponsored programs like comedians, hypnotists, magicians and lecturers. You're just another visiting guest. They love you in the moment. May even buy your CD and t-shirt. They'll give you a Like on Facebook. But they've forgotten about you in two weeks' time. You're done. They've moved on.

Not to say that none of them become true fans, but if I had to guess, I'd estimate about 2% of each audience became lifelong fans whom I saw at future club shows. But often these 2% were on the board that booked me.

The best way to approach your music career with college shows is to book the college dates first and route club shows around them. Promote the club dates. Not the college shows.

One of the best parts of the college market is that you don't have to promote. You get a guaranteed payment whether 500 students show up or 5. You still walk with a fat check. And, oftentimes, the school actually doesn't want you to promote because these are closed shows (only offered to students).

I learned very quickly that spending effort promoting these shows independently was a waste of my time. Sure, work with the school on coming up with creative promo tactics for them to use on campus, but don't feel you need to do anything other than have a conversation or two with the CAB.

THE "SHOWS"

As a singer/songwriter playing colleges, I've played every possible kind of venue on campus you can imagine, from on-site rock clubs, beautiful theaters and arenas opening for huge stars down to student unions, cafes, outdoor grassy malls, dorm lounges and cafeterias. Actually, cafeterias are probably the most common "show" I've played. And usually it's at 11 in the morning playing to hungover kids' backs as they down a cheeseburger while occasionally looking over their shoulder confused as to why this guy with the goofy hair is blasting a trumpet at them at 11 in the morning.

I used to worry a lot about the kind of show I was playing and urged the CAB to create the best possible experience for me and the students. Waste of time and energy. Now I just show up and roll with it. Want me to play in a hallway in the student union during welcome week while incoming freshmen and their parents walk past me with goofy smiles on their faces? Fine. Want me to set up next to the cotton candy machine, across from the moon bounce and kitty corner from the magician who is five times louder than me? OK. Want me to stand behind the pool table and next to the Ms. Pac-Man machine and plug into a sound system without any monitors with the only speakers built into the ceiling? What-ever. Sure. I'll take my $2,000 check and be on my way, thank you very much.

Remember, the purpose of college shows is to make money. Yes, you want to put on as entertaining a show as possible. And you want to be accommodating, easygoing and all-around fun to work with. But you must completely drop your ego if you want to get into the college circuit. Don't tell the CAB that you require a 16-by-16-foot stage if you're a solo act. If you're a 4-piece rock band, don't say you can't play your show without a 48-channel mixing board. Let's be honest—you could play with a 12-channel board if you absolutely needed to.

Now, this isn't to say that you shouldn't put any effort into the per-formance. Of course, bring your A game (always), but just know that you have to be flexible. You're going to have to perform in very uncomfort-able situations with a damn smile on your face. Sure, help the CAB know what works best for your show, the size of the stage, the sound system, the performance space and environment, and how you think the room should be set up, but if they organize something completely different for you, you have two options: Tell them you refuse to perform unless your specifics are met to a T or do what you can to make it work, take the check and be on your way.

WHAT ACTS DO BEST IN THE COLLEGE CIRCUIT?

Male singer/songwriters tend to do very well and get lots of bookings. Pop/rock bands do well for big Spring Jam and homecoming kinds of events. That being said, CABs want to bring diverse talent to campus. Genre doesn't matter as much as performance. Can you put on a fun, interactive, entertaining performance? Is it "safe" for colleges? Then you're golden.

NACA AND APCA

Now that you understand what college shows are and have a better idea of whether you want to make a go at the circuit, you need to know exactly how to approach this. Believe me, if you make a go at this blind, you will waste a ton of money and get nowhere. I've seen it happen to far too many bands.

NACA (National Association for Campus Activities—pronounced *naca*, not *N.A.C.A*) and APCA (Association for the Promotion of Campus Activities) are the two biggest organizations in the United States for college booking, and they organize annual conferences for colleges to scout out talent and diverse programming to set up for the coming year. NACA has seven regional conferences and one national conference. APCA has five regional conferences and one national conference. NACA is the bigger of the two and has been around the longest. It is a nonprofit. APCA is for-profit. NACA typically draws higher-budget schools (four-year state and private schools). APCA caters more to the two-year community colleges. However, they're not exclusive. Many community colleges go to NACA and many four-year institutions attend APCA. And some go to both.

The colleges that attend these conferences will send members from the CAB to scout out talent to book for the coming school year. These CAB members are called "delegates" at the conference.

I've showcased at both many times. NACA is much larger. Typically thousands of students representing hundreds of universities attend both the national and regional conferences. APCA typically has hundreds of students representing fewer than a hundred schools attending. The conferences last two to five days depending on the region and the number of attendees.

They both operate fairly similarly though. They both have showcases and marketplaces.

SHOWCASES

At the conference, there are designated showcase times where every attendee piles into a ballroom for a couple hours to sample the showcasing talent. Each act gets exactly 15 minutes to show the audience what they can do. The conferences are incredibly strict about the time frame and will shut off the sound and lights if you go over. You get 15:00 on the dot. There's actually a clock on stage that counts down from 15:00 the moment the curtain opens.

There's typically a comedian emcee that introduces all the showcasing acts (the comedian has also been selected to showcase). And the acts range from jugglers, magicians, comedians, hypnotists, singer/songwriters, bands and, for lack of a better term, variety acts. I once saw two guys covered head to toe in skintight black body suits, wearing masks with programmed light pads all over their bodies. They didn't speak. They didn't sing. They didn't dance. They pressed play on an iPod and ran around the audience hyping up the crowd. For 15 minutes. They booked five shows.

Every attendee from every school gets handed a packet at the start of the conference. In the packet is every showcasing act with a photo, bio and cost.

If you get selected to showcase, you set a price that is not negotiated at the conference. The school either decides to bring you for the listed price, or not. There are, however, discounts that can be applied. More on these in a bit.

The main showcase categories are Showcase High, Showcase Low,

Club, Sampler, Roving, Lecture and Emcee. All the showcases take place in the main ballroom except the Sampler, Roving and Lecture. The Sampler showcase has the same kinds of acts as the Mainstage (Showcase High/Low/Club) showcases; however, instead of getting 15 minutes, you get 5 minutes. The Roving showcase doesn't get a room. They are the conference buskers and can set up in the hallways of the convention center. But instead of playing for tips, they're playing for high-priced bookings. More on these categories in a minute.

The showcases are top-notch production events. They are run by professional sound, lighting and staging companies, and there is a stage manager and helping hands (usually students from the attending schools). The showcases are extremely impressive. They make you look like a star. Even though when you play the campus you may be set up in a corner with a sound system that only half works if you duct-tape the master volume knob just so, at NACA and APCA conferences, you perform on a giant stage, with a pro sound system and a sexy light show in front of hundreds or thousands of students. It's definitely an unforgettable and exciting experience.

How do you get a showcase? Keep reading.

BLOCK BOOKING

Both NACA and APCA offer block booking discount prices. Every act has the option to give discounts if nearby schools want to go in on booking the act during a set period of time. APCA offers 3 block booking tiers: 2 of 3, 3 of 5, and 5 of 7. NACA offers only 3 of 5 and 5 of 7. This means, that 3 nearby schools (typically within a few hours' drive of each other) come together to book an act within 5 days.

So, if your "Single Date" (SD) price is $1,000, your 3 of 5 could be $800 and your 5 of 7 price could be $600. This encourages schools to coordinate with other schools. They could save a lot of money. And it benefits you because instead of flying out and playing one school for $1,000, you can fly out, rent a car and bang out 5 schools and come home a week later with $3,000.

You can tack onto your price a lot of extras like travel (plane ticket, checked baggage fee, car rental), lodging, food, sound and lights. So, even though your rate is $1,000, you may walk with a $1,600 check which includes the cost of your expenses. Many times, though, colleges will have deals with local hotels or set you up in a guest house on campus. And more times than not, the CAB will take you out for dinner. That's one of the most exciting things for the CAB. Don't skip the dinner. This hang time is vital at winning over the CAB, gaining a great reputation and getting rebooked. More on this in a bit.

HOW TO GET A SHOWCASE

NACA is very selective about who can showcase. There is a panel of 8-12 students (judges) for each region and national conference that goes through every application, one by one, and votes on who gets to showcase. It's an extensive process and sometimes lasts for days. Each region has a different panel of judges. It's very possible to get selected for one conference and not others.

For APCA, however, anyone who registers for the conference pretty much automatically gets a showcase if there's room. First come, first served. So this breakdown on how to get a showcase is for NACA.

The Video

The application process is extensive and requires a lot of paperwork. NACA asks for press clippings, accolades, bio, photos, tech requirements.

But the single most important part of the application is the video. If you have absolutely zero impressive accolades, no press, but an amazing video, your chances of getting a showcase far outweigh a seasoned act with a Rolling Stone 5-star album review, countless headlining tours, but a poorly made video.

Your video should be three to five minutes long and it needs to be live. It's not a requirement in the application, but I'm telling you, after speaking with the advisor of the NACA national showcase selection committee and grilling her on exactly how they chose their talent (backstage before my NACA national 2014 showcase), your video, first and foremost, needs to be live. Not a music video where you're "performing" (lip synching) in a cool warehouse. Live. Live audio and live video. It doesn't, however, need to be from a live show. But it definitely helps to see the audience reaction.

Your video doesn't have to be just one song. And actually, it's recommended that it consist of clips of various songs. Well-known covers of pop songs work best. Classics are always good. Well-known classics that 17–22-year-old, non music aficionados know. Like Michael Jackson or Beatles hits. No deep cuts. You're not going to impress anyone with a cover that only hard-core fans know. The hits. Currently, the late '90s/early 2000s era is hot in colleges right now. Like, *NSYNC, the Backstreet Boys, Britney Spears, the Spice Girls, TLC and so on.

You absolutely should have at least one cover featured in your video. You can include originals, but you will increase your chances if you have well-known covers.

To put things in perspective, I got rejected at six conferences in a row (same year) before I got selected to showcase at NACA Nationals. But after every rejection I reworked my video. And I didn't even change up the footage, I just changed the order of the songs and the way it was edited.

The Selection Process

Each region operates slightly differently on how the selection process works, but for the most part it goes like this: The advisor hits PLAY on the video. At the 90-second mark, she pauses the video and takes a vote of the room "everyone who wants to put this video through to round 2 raise your hand." If the video gets a majority of hands, it moves on to round 2. The committee will go through every submission video before moving on to round 2.

Round 2, the advisor will play 3 minutes of the video and take another vote. At round 3, the members split off on their own with all submitted materials, including the video, and can spend as much time with everything (this is where they can watch all 5 minutes of your video, or even a second video if you submitted two). Each person comes back with their ranked list. And the committee makes a master ranked list.

The judges don't just take into consideration their favorites, however. During the conference, the showcase trades off between High Tech (HT) and Low Tech (LT) acts. Meaning, a singer/songwriter (LT) with just a guitar can perform in front of the curtain while a rock band (HT) gets set up behind the curtain. A comedian, similarly, is LT because she can do her act in front of the curtain, and a magician who may need 10 minutes to setup is HT.

So the committee has to pick about an equal number of HT and LT acts. Similarly, there are, what's called, Showcase High and Showcase Low. At regional conferences Showcase High acts have Single Date (SD) prices at $1,251 and higher. Showcase Low acts are $1,250 and below. At nationals the threshold is $1,500. And at nationals the Showcase Low acts are considered for a Mainstage showcase or a Club showcase, so Showcase Low acts have a better chance to get accepted. Club showcases actually happen in the same room and on the same stage as Mainstage showcases.

When you submit your application, you indicate which showcase you're applying for (Roving, Sampler, Showcase High/Low, Lecture).

Applying to Showcase

The only way you can actually apply to showcase at NACA is by going through a bunch of steps and jumping through many hoops. For one, you have to be a paid member of NACA to apply to showcase. But not just that—you have to purchase a booth at the conference (whether you get selected to showcase or not). There are delegate fees (per day), a showcase submission fee, a showcase fee (if you get selected), a conference fee, not to mention travel costs. When all is said and done, it will cost you about $2,000 per conference. Just the NACA annual membership costs $245 per region or $595 for a national membership, which enables you to submit and attend every region and the national conference.

APCA also has a myriad of fees. The showcase fee, for one, is much higher because everyone gets in.

GET READY FOR THE CONFERENCE

So, let's say you take the plunge, pay all the fees, and actually get selected to showcase at the conference. First and foremost, know that as a first-time attendee you are at an extreme disadvantage just by nature of its being your first time. All the established agencies not only know each other, they know the organizers, most CAB advisors and know how the process runs. It's not as simple as just showcasing, standing in your booth and waiting for people to come and secure dates. There are "co-op buying forms" with levels of interest that a single approved member of the CAB is able to fill out. There are co-op sessions where all the block booking is done in an art auction style. If you don't know how this process works, your head will spin right off.

So, I strongly advise you not to go into these conferences blind. Actually, I strongly advise you not to attend these festivals without an agent.

Agents cover all of the fees (except the showcase submission fee of about $100), have the connections and the knowhow.

Marketplace

Every day of the conference there are showcases and there are marketplaces. The marketplace is held in a huge convention center and is lined with booths upon booths of agencies, vendors, self-represented artists, and, really, anyone who has something to sell to colleges. If your showcase goes well, your booth will be swarmed with college kids wanting to meet you and take photos with you (and hopefully book you). Because, for this day, at the conference, you are famous. Everyone looks like a star on the showcase stage. At my last national showcase, an American Idol winner performed right after me. Acts large and small, known and unknown, perform on the same stage at the same conference. So, just because the students have never heard of you before now, if they liked what they saw, they'll want to meet you and get a photo with you to brag to all their friends back home about all the awesome musicians they met.

But more important, the marketplace is also where business is done. This is where you schmooze your ass off not only to get every student to fall in love with you, but actually to commit thousands of dollars to bring you to campus. This is where you'll get the interest forms, exchange business cards and potentially secure dates on campus. Oftentimes you'll get a handful of interest forms (if your showcase kicked a$$), tons of business cards and hopefully lock in a few dates.

Technically, business can only be done within the confines of the marketplace, but the networking and schmoozing extend through the entire time you're there. And, especially after your showcase, you will be recognized everywhere: in the hotel, at the restaurant, the cafe, everywhere. Remember, thousands of college kids have just descended on a very small area of this city. They're everywhere. So you want to make the most of it. I once ran into a group of kids at the Starbucks a block away from the convention center, sat down and shot the sh*t with them for fifteen minutes, got their business cards, sent one to my agent and was booked by night's end. I also attended a showcase (after mine), sat in the back next to a few kids from another school, talked them up and got them to book me at their school as well. That was $3,000 just from schmoozing.

And know that the cheaper your price, the more shows you will book. CABs have a budget, and if you charge $1,500 but a singer/songwriter who is not quite as good is only charging $1,000, they'll probably book the cheaper act.

Should You Attend NACA Without Getting a Showcase?

No. You will be attempting to drag people into your booth (without crossing your booth exit line—yes, that's a NACA rule). Even if you have a big TV screen with your high-quality video playing on repeat or you play your music on your iPhone and hand delegates headphones to sample, you're competing with all the other acts who they actually saw showcase. Your chances of getting booked without showcasing are very slim. So don't waste your money or time going to the conferences if you don't have a showcase. And really, don't go to the conference without an agent.

FINALIZING THE SALE

Even if you lock in a date at the marketplace, there's still a lot of work to do before you actually show up on campus. For one, every school requires an actual contract. They'll need one from you that contains the details of the performance and the fee, and you'll most likely need to sign the school's form contract as well. These are typically nonnegotiable.

I booked a handful of college shows on my own when I was between agents, and I calculated that there are about fifty emails from initial contact to actually showing up on campus. Multiple that by, say, fifty schools if you absolutely killed your showcase. And that's just the schools who book you. You probably also received hundreds of business cards from the conference. So there's the work of following up and convincing schools to book you postconference. You are able to negotiate more with price once the conference finishes, so this is a negotiating tactic you can use outside the confines of the conferences.

There's the routing of shows, scheduling the plane tickets and lodging (if the school doesn't provide this), so you're looking at hundreds if not thousands of hours of work.

This is why you want a college booking agent. Not only do they have all the connections and know how to maximize each conference appearance, they also typically have a staff that can handle all of the paperwork and play interference for you. They know how to talk to CABs. There are lots of bubbly emails with smiley faces and friendly encouragement. Very little of that, of course, happens during club booking. Whereas you can finalize a club date with a total of four emails, written all in lowercase letters and short fragmented sentences, if you write in lowercase letters to 19-year-old college students and are short with them, they'll think you're not only unprofessional, but mean. There is a completely different etiquette when dealing with CABs and club talent buyers. Remember that venn diagram?

So get a college booking agent.

HOW TO GET A COLLEGE BOOKING AGENT

Most college booking agents solely book colleges. And many represent college entertainers of every kind: musician, comedian, variety, and so forth. Many can also provide the moon bounce and cotton candy machine. You don't hit up college booking agencies like you hit up club booking agents. College agents typically make 15%–20% of your net earnings from colleges. Meaning, if you got a $2,000 check from the college, but it cost you $400 to fly to the show and $100 for your hotel, your agent should take 15%–20% of $1,500. Some agents will actually ask the college to cut the agent's check separately and send it to them directly.

College booking agents won't bring you on their roster simply if you're good. You have to have music that not only will get booked on campus, but get a NACA showcase. You have to be easy to work with. Most agency contracts contain stipulations stating that you won't sleep with any of the students, you won't drink or do drugs while on campus, you won't party with the students and you won't act like a d**k in general. You are a direct representation of the agency. If you mess up, the agency messed up. And this is why most colleges solely prefer to work with agencies. They know that agencies vet their talent. CAB's butts are on the line if it gets out that the musician they brought to campus not only hosted an underage drinking party in their hotel room, but also gave one of the students an STD. So, unless you showcase at NACA, there is virtually no hope of getting booked on college campuses by cold emailing and cold calling. Don't waste your time

Get an agent.

Agencies only really want to bring on talent who can get showcases at NACA. Now that you know how to get a showcase (a killer 3-to-5-minute video), you should get this video together before submitting to agents. If you need examples of NACA submission videos, you can visit any college agency website, click on their music section and browse their artists. Most agencies will have their artists' videos right there on the site, and more times than not this will be the artist's NACA submission video. Cross-reference the artists who got showcases with the videos that got picked.

How to see who got showcases? Visit Naca.org, click on Events, then click on any regional conference or the national convention. If the conference hasn't happened yet, there will be a link to see who the showcasing acts are for the upcoming conference. If the conference has happened, there will be a link to the Final Conference Activity block booking report. This lists every showcasing act from the conference and how many interest forms they received.

So, once you have your video good to go, email the agent with an email like this:

Subject: NACA submission

Body: Hi Scott, I'm a Los Angeles–based singer/songwriter. I'm seeking college representation and specifically would like to submit to the upcoming NACA conferences with you. Let me know if we can discuss possibilities.

NACA submission video: youtube.com/myawesomevideo

Talk soon,
~Ari
http://ariherstand.com
http://facebook.com/ariherstand
NEWS:
**songs featured on One Tree Hill, MTV, VH1, Showtime
**toured with/opened for Ben Folds, Ron Pope, Matt Nathanson, Eric Hutchinson
**performed 600 shows around the country

When to Submit

Six NACA regional conferences happen in the fall. Nationals happen in February and one regional conference happens in the spring. April and May are the best months to submit to agencies. The fall conferences start taking applications in June. If you don't find an agent until August, you have completely missed your fall NACA submissions window. However, you can still hit them up to submit to nationals and the Northern Plains region. Those deadlines are October and December.

Don't hit up agencies in September or October, though. This is heavy conference season, and they are way too busy going to conferences, following up with schools and booking their acts from the interest generated at the conference. So April (at least two weeks after the Northern Plains conference finishes) and the month of May are best. Or all summer is fine, but know that you're missing the fall conference window. December-January is also a slower time when you will get more looks, but you're far away from any conference submission deadline.

THE TOP 8 MUSIC COLLEGE BOOKING AGENCIES

(in alphabetical order)

The Barry Agency
thebarryagency.com
info@thebarryagency.com
(763) 550-0513

Bass/Schuler Entertainment
bass-schuler.com
chris@bass-schuler.com
(773) 481-2600

The College Agency
thecollegeagency.com
booking@thecollegeagency.com
(651) 222-9669

Degy Entertainment (DMS)
degy.com
jeff@degy.com
(732) 818-9600

EVO Entertainment
evocollege.com
marie@evocollege.com
267-606-0386

Houla Entertainment
houlaentertainment.com/
leemayer@houlaentertainment.com
(865) 385-5514

Neon
neon-entertainment.com
scott@neon-entertainment.com
(716) 836-6366

Sophie K Entertainment
sophiek.com
kate@sophiek.com
(212) 268-9583

WHAT TO DO ONCE YOU HAVE A SHOW

Whether or not you get an agent, once you have a show on campus, there are still things that you, the artist, need to do. You must advance every show. It's best to do this two weeks prior to the show to go over all details like load-in, sound-check times, dinner time, lodging (it will be listed on the contract), who is going to pick you up from the airport or if you need to rent a car, and who your day-of contact is with their phone number.

And remember, whenever you interact with anyone on CAB (or even the advisor, who most likely was on CAB when she was a student), be bubbly, friendly and include smiley faces in your emails. One time a CAB member got in touch with my tour manager and requested that I send over 300 CDs that they could use to promote my appearance. My tour manager explained (via email) that selling CDs is how I make my living and that we cannot send them 300 free CDs, however we would happily sell them 300 CDs for a very big discount of 50% off. I got a call from my agent a few days later saying that my TM made this girl cry. After that, my TM included lots of smiley faces and took a deep breath before every email interaction with college students. They're young. They're sensitive. Be gentle.

Fly Dates

Unless you showcase within the region you live in and route tours around your college dates, you'll most likely fly to most shows.

President Obama signed into law the FAA Modernization and Reform Act of 2012, one section of which states that musicians are legally allowed to carry their instrument on the plane if at the time they board it fits in the overhead compartment. Most airlines don't give me a problem, but for some reason, United continues to insist that I gate-check my guitar, even after the infamous United Breaks Guitars viral video. What I do in that case is let them affix the gate-check tag to my guitar, but as I walk down the jetway, I rip it off and put it in my pocket. Then I board the plane, smile at the flight attendants, and pop that sucker into the overhead bin. (Just to be on the safe side, I always carry a copy of the section of the law that covers this. You can find it here: aristake.com/?post=87. So far, this has worked.)

The only airline where guitars do not typically fit in the overhead bins is Delta. Their bins are mostly too short. However, Delta has a coat closet up front and they always allow me to store my guitar in there. And if you have to fly one of those tiny puddle jumpers, it won't fit up top either. So, it's always advisable to get a case that can be gate-checked if absolutely necessary. I recommend the WolfPak Acoustic Guitar Polyfoam Case. Not only is it sturdy as hell, it's lightweight and has a backpack strap, and lots of storage for strings, clippers, tuners and sheet music. I've flown with that sucker around the country with no problems.

I want to give a special shout-out to Southwest Airlines, as they have never once given me a problem flying with my guitar (even before the law went into place), and because of their no-fee flight change policy, I've been able to reroute my travel plans with no problems if I get a last-minute gig. They also allow two free checked bags, which I always utilize what with all of my gear and merch. Southwest for the win!

GETTING REBOOKED

Just so you're not startled when this happens, most colleges will not book the same "event" two years in a row. You can imagine my horror after my first year of playing colleges—during which I booked fifty schools from my NACA showcase and nearly every show was packed and I made special moments and inside jokes with every CAB—when I didn't get asked back the following year by most of them. I thought I did such a good job promoting the shows, drawing such a big crowd, putting on such a good show and being all around a good hang that they'd have to bring me back. However, the CABs patted themselves on the back for putting on such a great event that brought lots of people. Because at the time I was working with an agent who went to only one regional conference, I had no other prospects and no plan B. I had gotten accustomed to the fat pay checks and lifestyle that reflected that. So it was back to the club hustle and PB&J dinners.

Moral of the story: Save, save, save. Even though you're rolling in it today, you may not be tomorrow.

BREAKING INTO COLLEGES

As you can see, it takes a lot of work to break into the college circuit. Lots of time and lots of money—even if you have an agent. Sure, your agent will cover all of the fees for NACA and APCA, but you still have to pay to get yourself to the conferences. You have to pay for hotel rooms at the conference. You have to pay for a rental car from the airport to the hotel. If you can't fly with your gear, you'll have to pay to rent gear at the conference. If you don't know how to shoot and edit high-quality video, you'll have to hire someone to do this. You could spend hundreds or even thousands of dollars long before you see your first check. Let's say you get 3 Fall showcases and it costs an average of $400 per round-trip plane ticket, $100 a night for a hotel and $50 per rental car. You're looking at around $2,000 just to get to and from the conferences. Your first show won't typically be for 6 to 12 months. Or longer. Because schools book for the following school year.

So if you want to get into the college scene, make sure you are willing to stick with it for at least three years. Remember, I got rejected six times before I got a showcase. That was a full year of nothing but rejection. So if you really want to go for it, you have to stick with it. You won't start seeing results (checks) for a long, long time.

10.

SPONSORSHIPS AND INVESTMENTS

*Guys like me are sitting out here just dying to have
the right partners knock on our door.*
—JAMES BOOK, MARKETING DIRECTOR,
NINKASI BREWING CO.

WHAT ARE SPONSORSHIPS?

If you have built up a substantial fanbase, even just a local one, you should seek out sponsors. However, don't think of them as sponsors. They are partners.

The biggest misconception bands have about sponsorships is that the company will give the band a fat check and that's that. Why do you think they're giving you a check? It's not because they love your music and want to support you. That's why your Uncle Joe is writing you a check. Not why Budweiser is.

The reason any company wants to partner with you is because they see value in it. So you must offer value.

It's not about what they can do for you; it's what you can do for them.

The location of your fanbase will determine what kind of sponsors, ahem, partners, you should solicit. Are you drawing 500+ people to your shows in your hometown? Contact local breweries, car dealerships, pizza parlors, nail salons, sandwich shops, clothing stores—really, any local establishment who wants your fanbase to buy their product.

If you're a YouTube, Periscope, Instagram, Snapchat, or Vine star and have a national or worldwide audience, you can think bigger. Who are your fans? Where do they live? What are their ages? You can find all of this info in your YouTube analytics.

If you're killing it on the national club circuit bringing 200–500+ people at every tour stop, with a 50-date tour, that's 10,000–25,000 focused eyeballs and eardrums on their product. These aren't 25,000 views on some banner ad, these are 25,000 engaged audience members willing to do whatever their favorite artist tells them to (and buy whatever he tells them to buy).

So, put together a list of companies who would be interested in marketing to your fan base.

A 2015 study done by AEG and Momentum Worldwide found that 93% of Millenials say they like brands that sponsor live events. And going to a music event that was sponsored made Millennials love that brand more, while those that stayed at home didn't have the same reactions.

The study also found:

- 89% like brands that sponsor a live music experience, compared to 63% among nonattendees.
- 89% perceive those brands as being more authentic, compared to 56% among nonattendees.
- 83% leave with a greater trust for brands that support a live music experience, compared to 53% among nonattendees.
- 80% purchase a product from a sponsoring brand after the experience, compared to 55% among nonattendees.

- 80% recommend brands that sponsor a live music experience to their networks, compared to 49% among nonattendees

If you're contacting a company to sponsor your local shows or tour, this is strong ammunition to use for your proposal.

HOW TO GET A SPONSORSHIP

The Proposal

Once you have your list of companies and contact information, you should put together a proposal packet to pitch the company. In the proposal you should have:

- Your Band Logo Directly Next to the Company's Logo
- A Short Bio of Who You Are (If They Don't Know)
    Include impressive accolades.
- What You Are Asking For (Money, Gear, Van, T-shirts, Vinyl Printing)
    Remember that a sponsorship doesn't just need to be for cash. Often, "trade" partnerships are the best kind. If you're working with a statewide car dealership, see if they will give you a van. You can wrap that van in the dealership's name, and if you tour around the state, they get a touring billboard with a sexy band inside which will be parked outside of every venue you play.
- What You Can Provide for Them
    It can be signage at all your shows. Mentions from the stage ("Bauhaus Brew Labs has been awesome to us and is helping us

tour the country. Everyone go buy a Bauhaus beer. Our favorite is the Stargazer. Cheers!"). Subtle (or not so subtle) product placement in your videos. Shout-outs to them on all of your social media. A creative music video featuring their product (that you film and edit). A jingle for their company to use in commercials, videos, their website. Interactive experiences at your shows (a photo booth with their logo tagged on every photo that gets uploaded to your Facebook Musician Page and emailed to fans to post on their social media). Five Tweets a month mentioning the brand. One Instagram photo a month with product in shot. One Facebook post a month linking to the company's website with a photo. Five Snapchat or Instagram Stories a month that include the product. Get creative with what you can offer. The more you're able to offer, the more you can ask for.

■ The Time Frame

Is this for one local show? A tour? A year? Get specific.

■ The Potential Reach

10,000 YouTube subscribers. Average 50,000 monthly views. 200,000 Vine followers. 8 million monthly loops. 10,000 Facebook Likes. 20,000 Twitter followers. 350,000 Instagram followers. 30,000 Periscope followers. Average of 1,000 Snapchat daily views. 500 people attend every local show. Average of 200 college age kids per show at your upcoming 50-date college tour. Be realistic. But make this look impressive.

■ What the Company Needs to Provide for You

Make sure you include that they will need to provide the promo materials you promise: sign, beer to drink on stage, wrap for the van. If you promise to hang a sign onstage but don't specify that they actually need to provide the sign, they may expect you to create and print one, which may eat into much of the money they give you. It's good to have a sign onstage no matter what, so have them print a big banner with your name on it with a "brought to you by Company Name" below it. Not only does it get their name out there, people will see the company much more favorably because they are "bringing you," their favorite band.

■ Perks

VIP access and seating for all shows. Tickets for all employees for all shows. Studio hang time.

■ Private Performance

Offer to play a private show for the company (they must secure the venue). If you have your own sound and lighting, this can be easy and painless. Say this is a $2,500 value.

Don't attach this proposal to your initial email. Find the person at the company who is in charge of marketing. Get her email and phone number. Call her up and say "Hi, I'm Ari Herstand, manager of the band Roster McCabe. I have a partnership proposal I'd like to send you. The band loves Bauhaus beer and I think there are ways we can work together. Can I send over the proposal?" Let her give you her email. Then send the proposal the minute you get off the phone. If you don't hear back, reply from that same email three days later and confirm that she got it and if she'd like to discuss it more.

You should be realistic about the kinds of sponsors you can hit up. If you're a band playing to 200 people a night, you're not ready for Pepsi. However, a less well-known band like Lagunitas might be interested. Especially if they're trying to break into the clubs you already have booked for your tour.

It's very possible for mid-level bands to obtain sponsors that can help cover expenses. You just have to be smart about it.

HOW TO GET AN INVESTMENT

You never know who's listening. I once helped a singer/songwriter playing a weekly 4-hour cover gig at the local watering hole secure a $100,000 investment from one of the regulars there. You don't need 1,000 fans to pay you $100 a year. You could just have one pay you $100,000. When someone approaches you for something like this, you should know how to go about securing this.

Typically, someone who has this kind of dough to invest in you isn't doing it to make money. They're doing it because they want to help you succeed. They aren't giving you a loan. It's an investment. A risky one at that. And they know this. So the proposal you put together should absolutely indicate that this person could make good money if you explode.

Set it up so that you don't have to pay back any money until your annual net income surpasses a set amount of, say, $30,000 per member (before salaries). Now, this is net income. After all expenses. So, if you have 4 band members, you will start to pay on the investment after your annual net income surpasses $120,000 (so each band member makes $30,000 minimum). This is quite modest and your investor will appreciate that. Your minimum annual income can increase by a small amount every year. So $30,000 minimum this year, $33,000 next year, $36,000 the year after and so forth. So, if your investment is for $100,000 with a term of 10 years, you have to make a minimum of $30,000 net income your first year to pay anything to the investor. If you make $25,000 (after expenses), you pay nothing. If you make $33,000, you pay a percentage of $3,000.

It's fair to pay 25% of your annual net income (above the base). So, in this example, if you made $33,000 net in your first year, you would pay $750 (25% of $3,000). If you also made $33,000 your second year (and

$33,000 was your base your second year), you'd pay $750 your first year, but $0 your second year).

Your investors will want you to succeed, and they also will want to come along for the ride. So in addition to giving the investors a percentage of your earnings (above your base), give them perks like free tickets, VIP everything, shout outs and so forth.

This may sound pretty informal, but you're going to have to enter into a carefully drafted written agreement that sets out all these details and requires you to report to your investors periodically. It is important to understand that any investment arrangement implicates federal and state securities laws. You absolutely should not do any deal like this, no matter how little money is involved, without the help of a lawyer who knows this area of the law.

HOW TO WASTE AN INVESTMENT

Once you secure the dough, don't blow it on dumb purchases like vintage gear or expensive music videos. Approach your career with the income it is currently generating. Treat the investment as a true investment in your career. How can it best grow your audience? How can you use $100,000 to generate $150,000? A $4,000 guitar and $2,000 amp is not how. A $15,000 music video with no marketing behind it will go nowhere. The money would actually be best spent developing your own production studio where, instead of spending $5,000 per video, you spend $10,000 and purchase expensive cameras, lights, audio equipment, editing and recording software, and you become an expert on how to use it all (or have one of your band members learn this) and then pour the rest into marketing.

And remember, the 50/50 breakdown—50% of your budget goes to production; 50% goes to marketing. Whether you're working with $500 or $500,000, this is the ratio.

11.

HOW TO MASTER
THE INTERNET

*A person like Prince or a person like Michael Jackson could have
never survived in today's (social media driven) world.*
—JAMIE FOXX

FROM 2005 TO 2008 A BAND'S ENTIRE ONLINE FOCUS WAS CONFINED TO
Myspace. The only thing musicians had to worry about was about
gaining friends, posting a "thanks for the add" on new friends' comments
section, organizing their top 16 list to give the appropriate shout-outs
without offending anyone by omission, and finding the proper theme
that accurately represented the project. There were entire Myspace marketing books on how to effectively grow an audience. It was an exciting
time for musicians. For the first time in the history of the industry, the
playing field was level. Every artist was on Myspace. The same Myspace.
Major-label artists and 17-year-olds-living-with-their-parents artists had
the same capabilities on Myspace. Mastery of the platform was depen-
dent on how much time you spent on it—not how much money you had.

Unsigned artists were able to mimic major-label artists' Myspace
accounts. And for a while, everyone did. Artists customized their profiles
to match what the labels did. The idea was, "We have to make it look like
we're a professional outfit and can compete with the big boys."

Even though unsigned artists ran their own accounts, most made it look like an entire operation ran it. Artists put up an untouchable façade. They thought it gave them a mystique enjoyed by their favorite rock stars. However, what most artists didn't realize (until it was too late) was that fans craved access and authenticity. And artists who gave this to them were rewarded.

One of the biggest stars of Myspace was singer/songwriter Ron Pope. On the "unsigned" Myspace charts he was always in the top 3. His song "A Drop in the Ocean" went viral on the platform, gaining upward of 60 million plays. I happened to meet Ron right as he was gaining popularity on the platform. I was booking my first tour to New York City and searched for New York–based singer/songwriters on Myspace and saw he had a show at a small cafe in Greenwich Village during the time I was going to be in town. I asked to open the show and offered in return that I'd book him every day on a stage I was running at Summerfest in Wisconsin. Right around the date of our cafe show, his Myspace plays began to skyrocket. Hundreds of "A Drop in the Ocean" covers were popping up on YouTube from teens around the globe. I asked Ron what his trick was. Was he paying these kids to do this to make it look like he was big? He shrugged and said that there were no tricks. He just said that he made sure to reply to every message he got. And his bio was written in first person.

I was shocked. Dumbfounded. "But we independent artists should maintain mystique," I thought. But Ron proved that "shoulds" didn't exist in this new, open world. Artists that did it differently succeeded. Artists that did it like everyone else were ignored. Anonymous. Fans have always craved authenticity, but it was a rude awakening for most artists to realize how authentic they were really supposed to be. Open. Honest. Naked.

By the time most artists realized this, it was too late. People were leaving MySpace in droves and finding refuge on YouTube and Facebook. Different rules. Different game.

Today, artists don't have the luxury to solely exist on one social media platform. Fans are everywhere and expect artists to be as well. As new ones pop up and others evolve, artists have to constantly revise their strategies.

You rent your fans to social media platforms; you own your fans when you have their email addresses. And you own your website.

HOW TO BUILD A GREAT-LOOKING WEBSITE WITH NO WEB DESIGN EXPERIENCE

You absolutely need a dot.com website that you own. Luckily, with template-based website creation services like Bandzoogle and Squarespace you don't have to deal with unreliable and expensive web developers anymore.

WHAT SHOULD GO ON YOUR WEBSITE

■ **Music**
This may seem obvious, but I can't tell you how many musician websites I've visited that didn't have a way to actually play the music. A music player of some sort should be on your home page. Don't make a new visitor hunt around for it either. Within five seconds of visiting the site someone should be able to listen to your music if they want to. But, whatever you do, do not have it autoplay. There is nothing more annoying than visiting a site and being blasted with audio and having to frantically figure out how to turn it off.

■ **Video**

You should also have your best video front and center on your homepage. Do not have it autoplay either. Allow people to click play if they want to. If you don't have any high-quality video, get some. You should also have a video section on your site that features many more videos, but put your best or most recent video right there on the home page.

■ **Mailing List Sign-Up**

Make this prominent. Remember to give visitors incentives to sign up. And make sure there's an option to join the street team as well—it can be in your confirmation email.

■ **Show Dates**

If you want to have your concerts appear on the sidebar of Google when someone searches your band, you have to either embed a Bandsintown, Songkick or ReverbNation widget on your site or use Bandzoogle's concert calendar or the GigPress plugin for Wordpress. It's no longer enough to just list your shows on your website; you have to make sure they get listed on Google as well. And you have to use a Google-approved show calendar and put it on your official website (just adding your shows to Bandsintown or Songkick is not enough).

■ **Photos**

Press outlets will want to quickly grab promo photos for their stories. Oftentimes they will grab something without asking you. So make it easy for them. Feature your best, highest-quality promo photos first. It's best to have the option to download high res-versions easily as well (for print).

■ **Lyrics**

This is a biggie. So many artists forget to put their lyrics online. Don't make it difficult for your fans to find your lyrics. One of your tabs should be Lyrics.

■ **Bio**

Have both a short, promo bio that venues and press outlets can copy and paste, and your longer, personal bio. Reference how to write these in Chapter 4.

■ **Press**

Include impressive press quotes.

■ **Contact**

List email addresses to humans. Don't just have a contact form with a Submit button. No one knows where those go. And they're frustrating. List names and email addresses for everyone on your team. Or just the point person for your band at the very least. Names. Emails.

■ **Social Links**

In addition to links to all of your social sites, make sure you have a Facebook Like button (one click Like), a Twitter Follow button and a Spotify Follow button.

■ **Purchase**

Make sure it's easy for fans to buy your merch and music or to become a subscriber. Bandzoogle and Squarespace have excellent embedded, on-site stores. Shopify is also a great store to embed to your website if you don't use Bandzoogle or Squarespace. You should also have links to BandCamp, Spotify, Apple

Music and anywhere else you want people to stream or download your music.

■ **Extras**

Some people embed an Instagram, Twitter or Facebook feed. That's fine and can give a real-time glimpse into the band. It's much better to have this than a News or Blog section that you only update twice a year. If you're active on Facebook, Twitter and Instagram, embed them. Bandsintown and SongKick trackers are good to list as well to build concertgoing followers.

PLACES YOU NEED TO BE ONLINE

MusicBrainz

If you want that profile sidebar in Google with your photos, mini bio, tour dates, social links, top songs and discography, you need to have your info on MusicBrainz.org. MusicBrainz is the Wikipedia of music. Whereas most musicians have never heard of MusicBrainz, it's one of the most used sources of information for tech companies. So make sure your information is accurate.

Wikipedia

You should get a Wikipedia page if you don't have one, as soon as possible. But, unfortunately, that's easier said than done. Wikipedia only includes pages for prominent figures. How do they determine if you're prominent enough? Press helps. Getting mentioned in other Wikipedia entries also helps. The more press references you have, the higher likelihood your page will stick. Review the guidelines for posting. Your entry must be neutral and factual (it cannot read like a bio). There are companies you can hire to create Wikipedia entries for you. It may be worth investing a little bit of money to hire someone to do this for you. Or, better yet, put a notice out to your fans. There's bound to be an active Wiki User among the bunch who would be willing to help you out for free tickets or a merch package in the mail.

Musixmatch and Genius

Genius (formerly Rap Genius) is the company that powers Spotify lyrics. And Musixmatch app users can display lyrics on their iPhone home screen for the song they're currently listening to in Apple Music and Spotify. So make sure all of your lyrics are there and correct.

WHICH SOCIAL PLATFORMS TO IGNORE AND WHICH TO MASTER

Because technology evolves so rapidly and startups come and go seemingly overnight, by the time you're reading this the social media landscape may look drastically different than it does today. So, to explicitly tell you the platforms on which to focus your efforts would be flat-out irresponsible. The only thing I can guarantee is that what's hot today won't be hot tomorrow. So you have to stay active and realize where your fans are.

THE BIG 10

To help you figure out where to focus your efforts, make a list of 10 artists whom you admire: 5 traditional musicians and 5 YouTube musicians.

Pick one local artist, one regionally touring artist, one indie-label (or no label) nationally touring artist, one major-label nationally touring artist and one worldwide superstar. The reason you want to follow so many YouTube musicians (you may not admire any now, I know), is because they are ahead of the curve when it comes to the Internet and social media. They use social media in more creative ways than most traditional musicians. They have built their existence online and have a mastery of the Internet in a way that most do not.

Research where each artist is most active and how they utilize every platform. This is not something you will be able to do in an afternoon. You'll want to follow them on every platform and note how they use it. Analyze how they Tweet, Snap, Gram, post and live-broadcast. And how often. There is a different etiquette on every social platform. You can't just link them together. Well, technically, you can link a few together, but you shouldn't. Every platform is a community, and if you act like an impostor, you will be ousted from the community (unfollowed). Learn to use each platform the way it is intended to be used. The only thing worse than not existing on a social platform is misusing it.

WHAT IS THE PURPOSE OF THE WEB FOR MUSICIANS?

You can no longer fragment your career between the physical and digital worlds. They don't just overlap, they intertwine. Someone who sees you at a show may Like your Page, follow you on Instagram, Snapchat, Periscope and Twitter before you finish your last song. They'll take a photo with you after the show and within minutes it's seen by all their friends— spreading the word about how awesome you are. You now have the awareness of hundreds more people. A few may follow you solely because their friend whose taste in music they trust tagged you.

FOLLOWERS ARE NOT NECESSARILY FANS AND FANS ARE NOT NECESSARILY FOLLOWERS

People may follow you on Instagram because they think you're hot, but they may hate your music. They're not a fan, they're a follower. And your biggest fans may not even be on Instagram.

Some artists have hundreds of thousands of followers online, but can't get 15 people out to a show in their hometown.

Go where your fans are. If your fans skew young, you need to be active on Snapchat. If they skew old, you need to be active on Facebook. Understanding who your fans are is crucial to figure out where you need to be.

How do you do this? Well, be everywhere at first and analyze the analytics and insights the platform provides. If you notice that your fans are much more active on Snapchat than Instagram, focus more of your efforts on Snapchat. If you notice that people respond very well to you on Periscope but not Facebook, make the necessary adjustments.

PICK YOUR ONE

It's too tough to master every platform. So pick one that you go all in on. This doesn't mean ignore the others; it just means master one. Focus the majority of your efforts on increasing the engagement and growing your followers on the one.

YouTubers became YouTubers because they spent most of their time learning how to grow an engaged YouTube audience. Viners became Viners because they spent most of their time mastering Vine. Snapchatters . . . well, you get the point.

But make sure you pick the platform that makes the most sense to you. The only way to master a platform is to stay inspired by it. You can't force it. It will show. Fans can sniff BS a mile away.

And you should be your authentic self no matter how different you are. Yes, note how successful artists use the platform you choose, but use their method merely as inspiration. You have to set yourself apart. Find your niche. Define your voice.

Just like you define your sound in the studio, you have to define your voice online.

YOUTUBE

People fall in love with content, but they also fall in love with personalities on YouTube. It's important to make yourself accessible that way.

—DANIELA ANDRADE, PROFESSIONAL YOUTUBER, 1M+ SUBSCRIBERS

Most musicians don't understand how to use YouTube. They see it as a video-hosting website. Sure, it's that. But, like every other social platform, it's a community.

As high-quality audio and video recording became more affordable, the quality standards evolved. In 2007 it was totally acceptable to sit in front of your webcam with an acoustic guitar and sing through your crappy built-in computer mic. But by 2011, if you didn't have a professional-looking (and -sounding) music video, you were ignored. The competition had stiffened. And YouTubers upped their game. Most YouTubers became completely self-sufficient, with home recording studios, DSLR video cameras and full lighting rigs. By being able to control every step of the production process, these musicians, or "YouTubers" as they soon came to be known collectively, were able to put out high-quality videos regularly. Most put out a video a week. It's astounding to visit some of the most successful YouTuber channels and see how much content they have created and released over the past few years. Whereas label artists typically put out 10 songs every 3 years, YouTubers put out 10 songs every 3 months. It's become such a standard that if you don't put out high-quality content regularly, fans of YouTube move on to a YouTuber who does.

QVCA

Alex Ikonn, cofounder of Luxy Hair, built his seven-figure business by creating a successful YouTube channel. He explains that the key success to YouTube lies in four simple letters:

Q = Quality
V = Value
C = Consistency
A = Authenticity

If you don't have quality videos that provide value, and roll them out very consistently and authentically, you will not succeed in building a YouTube channel.

YouTube is less about the one viral hit and more about the connection with the audience. And that connection is earned and built over the course of hundreds of videos.

YouTube evolved to become teenagers' primary music-streaming service, TV network and movie studio. So much so that a 2014 study commissioned by Variety revealed that the five most influential figures among Americans ages 13–18 are all YouTube stars, eclipsing mainstream celebrities like Jennifer Lawrence and Seth Rogen.

Like mastering an instrument, to master YouTube takes lots of focus, practice and time. Lots of time. I've collaborated with a few YouTubers to experience their process firsthand. For one, they move extremely quickly. They don't fret over guitar tones or drum fills. It's all about the turnaround time. They know their audience will primarily be watching their videos on their phones, often without headphones. That's not to say YouTubers aren't perfectionists. They perfect what they've found their audience cares about most like vocals and visuals. You may scoff at their order of priorities, but while you're rolling your eyes, they're rolling on down to the bank. You can't argue with success. And successful YouTubers not only have millions upon millions of views, but hundreds of thousands (sometimes millions) of fans—fans who back them on Patreon, support their crowdfunding campaigns, download their music on iTunes, purchase their merch and attend their shows if and when they go on tour.

If you want to be a YouTuber, it better inspire you, because it will take up most of your time. And you better have an alternative income source, because being a YouTuber doesn't pay much for a long time. There are YouTubers with 300,000 subscribers waiting tables.

> YouTube is not the end game, it's the foot in the door.
> —CONNOR MANNING, 70,000 SUBSCRIBERS

There's no one way to approach YouTube. You may think the only successful YouTubers are good-looking teenagers and twenty-somethings playing covers of pop songs. Sure, there are those, but the most successful YouTubers have paved their own way. And done things differently. And many are actually in their thirties.

When Scott Bradlee started his channel in 2009, people had been putting covers up on YouTube for years. Other YouTubers were bubbly and catered to a tween audience. Scott went a different way. He decided to post jazz renditions of pop songs. He went from merely recording solo jazz piano instrumentals from his bedroom to creating an ever-evolving and revolving collective of world-class musicians and dancers performing pop songs in period styles (with the outfits to match). He called it Postmodern Jukebox and his videos have been viewed over 365 million times. Postmodern Jukebox now tours the world playing huge theaters. Scott built such a strong collective of various musicians that oftentimes he doesn't even go on the tours.

Peter Hollens started off singing in an a cappella group he founded at the University of Oregon. After college, Hollens built up a mobile studio business in which he traveled around the country recording, producing and mixing other a cappella groups. He didn't actually start his own YouTube channel until 2011—pretty late to the YouTube game.

Peter Hollens was slowly building his channel posting solo a cappella renditions of classic and contemporary pop standards. He was at about 15,000 subscribers when the violin sensation Lindsey Stirling got in touch with Hollens to collaborate. Their rendition of "Skyrim" got over 38 million views and Peter's channel shot to 80,000 subscribers nearly overnight. He now has over 185 million total views (1.5M+ subscribers) and makes over $8,000 per video from his patrons on Patreon. He has no desire to tour and lives a quiet life with his family in Oregon.

In 2007, Taryn Southern recorded a parody of Obama Girl called "Hott4Hill." It went viral, but Taryn didn't start regularly creating music or videos until three years later. She posted weekly comedy and cover music videos and since 2010 has gotten over 60 million views (from hundreds of videos). Most of her songs and videos were created, start to finish, for just a couple hundred dollars, if that. In late 2015, Maker Studios created a talk show for her called Party Fun Times with Taryn.

Other YouTubers like Boyce Avenue, David Choi, Kina Grannis, Madilyn Bailey, Nicole Arbour, Pomplamoose, Tyler Ward, Julia Nunes and Walk off the Earth each now have millions upon millions of views (and hundreds of thousands or millions of subscribers), but none of them started with a viral video or much of a budget. Even Walk off the Earth, who shot to stardom with their viral cover of "Somebody That I Used to Know" (over 170 million views) had been making creative videos for years prior.

What is the key to the success of all these YouTubers? Consistency.

Collaboration is one of the best ways to gain new fans quickly. When you appear in another YouTuber's video, you are exposed to a completely new audience. The quickest way to gain new followers is through collaboration with other YouTubers. It's like opening for a big artist on tour. You're exposed to a new audience and given the stamp of approval from this audience's favorite artist. One of the reasons many YouTubers happen to live in L.A. is because they collaborate with other creators in town.

YouTube is about the long game. So many musicians put all their effort into one video, and when it doesn't go viral they give up. YouTube is about defining your voice, building a connection, and collaboration. Lots of collaboration.

Because YouTube is still the most popular music-streaming service in the world, and most people turn to YouTube first to check out music, you need high-quality content on YouTube no matter what. Whether you decide to develop a YouTube audience by following in the footsteps of the thousands of other successful YouTubers is up to you

If you want to choose YouTube as your one, make sure you spend some time with YouTube's Creator Academy (creatoracademy.withgoogle.com). They have put together hours' worth of tutorials, with tips and tricks on how to master YouTube along with personal anecdotes and thoughts from some of the biggest YouTubers out there.

Believe it or not, over 10,000 channels have over 50,000 subscribers. With over a billion users on YouTube, there's plenty of room for more creators. And you're not too late.

Excellence is never too late.

INSTAGRAM

Like YouTube, some of the most successful Instagrammers collaborate in some capacity. Whether it's tagging the company who made a dress, tagging everyone in the photo including friends in your Stories and showcasing their handles or giving a shout-out to someone in the comments, despite what it may seem like on the surface, Instagram is very collaborative. And you don't actually have to be in the same time zone as your collaborators. Just tag them and they may Regram and tag you. Their followers are exposed to you and your followers to them.

A relatively unknown 33-year-old singer/songwriter, Rachel Platten, released her single "Fight Song" on February 19, 2015. She had about 35,000 Instagram followers at the time. The song was just bouncing around adult radio (with a push from her label Columbia), struggling to gain traction. On June 6, though, that all changed. Rachel's manager, Ben Singer (also Andy Grammer's manager), contacted Taylor Swift's manager to see if Taylor would be into meeting Rachel backstage after Taylor's arena show in Pittsburgh. Hours later, Taylor Swift Instagrammed a 15 second video of the two rocking out backstage to "Fight Song" with Rachel on guitar. Of course, Rachel was tagged, and Taylor Swift's 50 million Instagram followers wondered A) what song this was, and B) who was Rachel Platten? Within hours, Rachel's Instagram followers doubled. And by the next day she had well over 100,000 Instagram followers. "Fight Song" reached #1 on the iTunes charts. And a month later it cracked the top 10 Billboard Hot 100 and went on to be a worldwide hit. Hillary Clinton also used it as her theme song for her 2016 presidential campaign. All from one Instagram video. And, of course, a great song.

Bands often struggle with how to effectively use Instagram. As the platform evolves, former tips and tricks become obsolete or frowned upon. At one point, utilizing a bunch of hashtags was a sure way to get discovered by new followers. Now, if you use a bunch of hashtags, you look desperate. It is not a welcomed practice anymore. Early on, just throwing a filter on a crappy photo was sufficient. Now many edit their photos by utilizing outside apps like Afterlight or Snapseed. In the summer of 2016, Instagram released "Stories"—which was positioned as direct competition to Snapchat's "My Story" feature. Keeping up with the trends is vital to being a welcome presence on the platform. You shouldn't use Instagram the way you use Facebook, Snapchat, Twitter, Vine or Periscope. It's a different community and there is different etiquette.

To build your Instagram followers, once you have a good amount of high-quality photos with a defined voice (this is going to be a theme), then it's time to start building your followers and upping your engagement. The follow-back method currently works well on Instagram, but make sure you unfollow those who don't follow you back—to maintain a good looking ratio. Work on your collaborations, tagging, descriptions, editing, and always keep up with all new features.

A good rule of thumb for keeping your Instagram feed engaging is to post photos of you and include your face in the majority of your Stories. Your fans don't care what your salad looks like. That's not interesting. But you holding that same salad, in the green room, before you play a show? That's interesting. Following you on Instagram (and every platform), your fan should feel connected to you. Seeing a photo of the empty club pre-show isn't interesting. Seeing you in that same photo makes it a hundred times more interesting and gets your fans to connect with you on a deeper level. You make them feel like they are there with you. Anyone can post a photo of an empty club. How do they know you didn't just pull this from the Internet? Because you're in it! Posting a photo of just your friend's face may be hilarious to the both of you, but none of your fans will get the joke. You just insulted everyone who doesn't know your friend. "Ha-ha, you don't get our inside joke!" The goal on Instagram is to get your audience to identify with you. Sure, post photos of your friends and include them in your Stories, but make sure you're in them as well. Go through your Instagram feed right now, and I bet you loads of money that the photos that have the most likes are ones you are in.

FACEBOOK

The big kahuna. The social network. Where you keep up with friends from high school you don't care about and where your mother Likes every—single—post. The teens aren't as active as the elders, but nearly everyone is still on it. You 100% need a Musician Page. Even if you're a singer/songwriter, you don't want to just use your personal profile. For one, Facebook limits your friends list to 5,000 friends. So, if all goes right, you will surpass this and you don't want to have to start over when you reach the limit. Two, if fans aren't friends of your friends, often they won't be able to find you in searches. And three, the number of Likes your Musician Page has is still a currency used by many. Get a Musician Page and make it look awesome. Customize your photos to the cover photo and profile pic standards. Add the Bandsintown or Songkick or BandPage tour dates tab and the Bandcamp, SoundCloud, CD Baby or ReverbNation music tab. Make sure you feature a video at the top of your page and pin a post to the top of your Timeline. Respond to messages and Like the comments. Don't get creepy with your Facebook engagement. Not every comment requires a reply, but you should reply to every message. Enable the Sign Up email list button. Fill out every field in the About section, especially the bio and contact fields.

Upload videos to Facebook. Let me repeat. Upload videos to Facebook. If you missed the memo, it's no longer acceptable to post YouTube links to Facebook.

It's now less about how many Likes you have and more about how engaged your fans are. So work on posting content your fans are responding to. The more initial engagements you get for each post, the more people Facebook will show the post to. Keep the quality high. Photos (with a description) do well. Long-form, personal thoughts/statements do well. Videos do well. Links to articles without any explanation, not so much. Maintain your identity and your voice. Make sure your voice is defined and consistent on every platform. Don't be bubbly and cutesy on YouTube but rant your a$$ off on Facebook. Consistency and authenticity is key.

Above all, just keep up with your Big 10 (artists, not football teams) and make sure you're not falling behind on the new trends.

HOW TO GET MORE LIKES WITHOUT PAYING FOR THEM

Post content people want to share. This will take lots of trial and error, but you'll soon realize what people are responding to. More specifically, create fun videos meant for Facebook. Show people that it's fun to be a follower of your Page. Keep the high-quality content flowing consistently.

One of the best Facebook Musician Pages is by (DIYers) Vulfpeck. Band leader Jack Stratton creates videos he knows Vulfpeck fans want to see (regardless if they have anything to do with the band). Because most fans of Vulfpeck are fellow music nerds, Jack regularly posts videos that have nothing to do with Vulfpeck. One is an instructional on how to (correctly) play "Superstition" by Stevie Wonder on the clav (that got over 330,000 views). Another is an explanation of what the top 3 snare sounds on recordings of all time are. The videos aren't professionally edited, but rather edited to the Vulf-look. They've created the Vulf brand and nearly every video posted to Facebook has the Vulf-filter (and every song uses the Vulf compressor—which they sell as a DAW plugin). Not only that, Vulfpeck regularly shares videos of fans covering their songs (which naturally encourages more fans to cover them). The most brilliant string of posts happened when, first, Mr. Talkbox posted a video of himself covering Vulfpeck's song "Back Pocket" a cappella. Vulfpeck shared the video and it got 215,000 views. Then MonoNeon took Mr. Talkbox's video, split the screen and added a bass line (in essence collaborating on the track). Vulfpeck of course shared this collaboration. Finally, Jack added some funk guitar to Mr. Talkbox and MonoNeon's creation (and, of course, popped himself funking out in the center of the frame). Vulfpeck fans (myself included) lost their sh*t. Fans continue to regularly engage with Vulfpeck's Facebook posts, which in effect gets Facebook to rank every post higher in people's Newsfeeds. I highly encourage you to browse some of Vulfpeck's Facebook videos and study how they're managing their Facebook Page. It's the best in the biz right now.

TWITTER

Twitter was superhot around 2009–2012. It's technically still growing, but it's definitely not used as actively by common folk as it once was. It's now mostly used by influencers. You're an influencer. So you should be using it. It's how influencers communicate with one another. And non-influencers still use it to keep up with their favorites. It's still celebrities' platform of choice to get their thoughts out. And now that Twitter is pushing video and photos, see how your Big 10 are using it effectively and model it.

But once again, Twitter is a community; if you're going to be a member of the community, be respectful and follow the etiquette. No linking to or from Facebook or Instagram. The only exception is show announcements from Bandsintown or Songkick. Tweet, heart, retweet, appropriately, and you'll do just fine.

Comedians like Rob Delaney and Joe Mande have done extremely well building up their fanbase on Twitter. James Blunt gained worldwide respect when he turned his Twitter feed into a snark fest, publicly responding to haters.

James Blunt @JamesBlunt
And no mortgage. RT @hettjones: James Blunt just has an annoying face and a highly irritating voice.

SNAPCHAT

Snapchat is one of the relatively more recent apps to take over the world. It was launched in September of 2011, and just two years later, the company famously turned down a $3 billion acquisition offer from Facebook. Rightly so, because just two years after that, Snapchat was valued at around $15 billion and was getting over 6 billion video views a day with 100 million daily active users (to Facebook's 8 billion daily video views and 1 billion daily active users). Snapchat, however, boasts that it's used by over half of U.S. teens 15–17. Although Facebook may be your favorite social platform, teens choose Instagram and Snapchat ahead of both Twitter and Facebook. Facebook comes in at a distant fourth. And as of this writing, nearly three-quarters of Snapchat users are under 34.

So if your target audience skews young, Snapchat is where you should be. And especially if you're targeting college-age kids.

Yes, Snapchat started as a way to send disappearing photos to friends (which is why it got the reputation as a sexting app initially), but it quickly evolved into an "as it happens" quick sharing platform throughout the day with the addition of the My Story feature.

Throughout the day, you can take photos and ten-second videos and add them to My Story and your followers can see your story throughout the day as it unfolds.

Instead of bringing a film crew along on tour to document the experience and edit together hundreds of hours of footage and release it long after the tour finishes, keep your fans engaged, in real time, by Snapping everything that happens on tour: loading the van, tour pranks, sound check, the opening act, the merch table hang, the after party, the road, the drives, everything. Take your fans along for the ride. In real time.

Snapchat allows you to follow others by scanning their Snapchat QR code. Every user gets a unique code. Put your code on your stage banner. Or make stickers of your code and place them around festival grounds. People will be intrigued enough to give you a follow just to see who it is, and if they like your Snaps, they'll stick with you.

One of the most interesting ways people use Snapchat is by making the Story actually tell a story, not just a real-time account of what happens during the day.

Unlike Instagram and YouTube, you cannot edit your Snaps (other than adding text, drawings, or built-in filters). These limitations have actually enabled Snapchatters (yes, that's a thing now also) to find an audience.

One of the most well-known Snapchatters is a 40-year-old producer from Miami. DJ Kahled, who has been called "The King of Snapchat," amassed over 6 million followers just a few months after joining the platform in October 2015. He gained a loyal following by regularly posting inspirational catchphrases (and, of course, Snapping every mundane activity throughout his day). He has a personality people are attracted to.

Boston-based Evan Garber (emgarber) got known on Snapchat for his intricate Snap art. All of his creations are hand-drawn in the Snapchat app (without the aid of any third-party applications). Some of his drawings take hours to create. There's no erase feature (except for a simple undo button for the previous stroke), so he has to be incredibly meticulous with his creations—on the first take. He's now a full-time Snapchatter hired by companies to help them with their Snapchat presence and push their brand on his account in creative ways that don't feel like tired advertisements.

Shaun McBride, who goes by Shonduras, is also uber popular on the platform. One of his early Snaps of a grandma on a plane with rainbow hair who he turned into My Little Pony by drawing the pony body and tail, made it to the front page of reddit and helped gain him a tremendous number of followers.

I finally understood the potential of Snapchat when I saw Emgarber, Shonduras, Stuart Edge and Dash Dobro's GoldenEye Story. Remember the N64 game from back in the day? They re-created it from the first-person player standpoint and went around a warehouse holding toy guns, shooting opponents, getting body armor. But first the Story started off by selecting a character. They had the GoldenEye music playing throughout the entire Story. If you don't use Snapchat this might not seem that impressive to you. But consider the fact that Snapchat limits you to ten-second clips that must be recorded by holding your finger on the screen. You can't add sound to the video after the fact—everything must be done in real time. No editing in post. They literally held up another phone playing the GoldenEye music next to the phone that was filming.

All four Snapchatters created their own Story on their channel with different characters and points of view. They nailed the graphic details from the character selection dance, to the awkward camera angle pointed at the gun, the fall-to-the-knees death and the blood that slowly covers the screen when you die.

This elaborate and brilliantly conceived Snapchat Story was only live for twenty-four hours (the Story limit).

That's another thing that older generations have a hard time grasping and accepting—the impermanence. The reason Mom, Dad, Grandma and Grandpa get Facebook is because it's basically their photo albums, home videos and diaries in digital form, saved in perpetuity to share and reminisce over. After twenty-four hours, the Snapchat Story is gone, forever.

Snapchat rolled out paid Geofilters in early 2016, which enables any user to create a custom filter for a designated location and time frame. Artists and festivals now create Geofilters that fans can use at the concert.

Snapchat, like every platform, continues to evolve. By the time you're reading this, there may be a completely new platform etiquette. But one thing is for sure, you can't ignore Snapchat any longer.

VINE

I once acted in a commercial for Samsung that never ended up actually airing (all too common in Hollywood). One of the other actors on set was Andrew. Andrew and I became buddies. He came to my shows around L.A. and we collaborated on goofy YouTube videos. Then one day, Andrew was on the cover of *New York* magazine and being written about by every tech publication out. What happened? Andrew Bachelor, better known as King Bach, became one of the first stars of Vine. He is now the most popular guy on Vine (with over 16 million followers and over 6 billion "loops").

Vine was launched in January 2013 by Twitter as a six-second video-sharing app. As companies, brands and average users fumbled through how to get their message out in just six seconds, a new class of youngens (including Bach and a handful of other L.A.-based creators), not only figured it out, but conquered the platform. They created six-second comedy videos that took the young video app by storm.

Around the same time, the husband and wife musical duo Us the Duo posted six-second clips of their mouths singing pop songs in perfect parallel harmony. Just thirty days after they posted their first #6second-cover of John Legend's "All of Me," they gained over a million followers. They have since grown to 5 million followers, and they got a record deal with Universal Republic. Because of six seconds.

The teen heartthrob Shawn Mendes also started his career on Vine, posting six-second cover videos (when he was just 15). He built up such a rampant following that he promptly got signed to Island Records (with the help of manager Andrew Gertler, who orchestrated the deal). His debut single, "Stitches," reached #4 on the Billboard Hot 100 (and #1 on the Mainstream Top 40 radio chart).

It's a different world. Whereas before, the only way to get signed to a record deal was if you had a killer live show and a great record, now all it takes is six seconds. Well, and millions of followers.

Vine now seems to be a platform of insiders. Vine stars typically collaborate with other Vine stars or other celebrities (Justin Bieber hit up King Bach to help him get his account going). Vine evolved into a sort of entertainment network. And more specifically, a comedy network. The most successful Viners make comedy videos.

It's not necessary to be on Vine, and it's hard to gain followers if you don't use it as the community expects. People don't follow celebrities on Vine to get a glimpse into their lives (like Instagram or Snapchat); they follow Vine accounts that are entertaining, no matter who they are.

But like being a YouTuber, becoming a Viner can be a full-time job. And it is for many of the biggest stars of the platform. Conceiving and executing hilarious six-second videos takes planning, coordination, rehearsal and lots of practice. A single six-second video can sometimes take hours to shoot and edit. And now that Vine allows for longer-form videos (with six-second previews), it has opened up loads of possibilities.

And like YouTube, you don't become Vine famous from one viral video. It takes consistency. And resilience. Top Viners post multiple videos a week. And oftentimes it takes months upon months to see real success.

LIVE STREAMING: PERISCOPE, FACEBOOK LIVE, YOUNOW, YOUTUBE LIVE, LIVE.LY AND BUSKER

Live streaming is the newest wave of social media. It quickly gained popularity in 2015 when most mobile-only live-streaming apps launched. Meerkat took over SXSW 2015 as it was launched just weeks prior. Twitter-owned Periscope barreled in weeks later and quickly eclipsed Meerkat, then Facebook launched Live. YouNow quietly went after the teen market as it rapidly gained popularity. And Live.ly was launched in mid-2016 by the widely popular lip synch app Music.ly.

By the time you're reading this, any one of these live-streaming apps may have died (Meerkat has already "pivoted" out of live streaming) or completely taken over the live-streaming market, as these things move quite rapidly.

Regardless of which platform you use, live streaming should be a part of your fan engagement tools. Matt Nathanson debuted a song off of his new album by live-streaming (over Periscope) the first listen of the vinyl test pressing he got from the plant. Before and after the song debut, he showed off his massive vinyl collection and interacted with his fans, pulling out records they requested (from real-time comments on the screen). Like Snapchat, Periscope keeps the video accessible for twenty-four hours before it disappears forever. But the excitement is in the real-time broadcast, where you can send over your questions and comments directly to the broadcaster.

Clare Means has been live-streaming nearly every street performance on Periscope since she started her account in September of 2015. Because she street-performs nearly every day, she built up tens of thousands of followers who tune in most nights. She includes a PayPal.Me link in her bio (for tips) and a link to her website (to purchase merch), and in just under a year, she more than doubled her income—just from her Periscope followers.

YouNow, however, is Periscope on steroids. It takes the monetization possibilities five steps further—offering in-app tipping and a subscription service (based around YouNow's "bars" currency, which can be purchased in-app). As of spring 2016, Brent Morgan was making $10,000 a month through YouNow, and Hailey Knox's YouNow following was key in getting her signed to S-Curve Records.

One of the newest live streaming apps joining the party is Busker. It launched in April of 2016. Like YouNow, it has in-app tipping. It also has a store feature to sell merch directly to fans, in-app. Some musicians on Busker were making thousands a month (just months after the app's release).

The monetization possibilities over live streaming are virtually endless. Whereas StageIt and ConcertWindow enable you to set up live-streamed concerts (allowing real-life fans, mostly acquired elsewhere, to pay you via tickets, tips, perks and exclusives), these live-streaming platforms are more for spur-of-the-moment check ins and interactive performances.

THE MUSIC-STREAMING PLATFORMS

SoundCloud, Spotify, Apple Music, YouTube Red and Pandora each have their own community of loyal users. SoundCloud is most popular among the electronic, DJ and hip-hop communities. Remixes by up-and-coming DJs have found a home on SoundCloud (as well as Beatport). Unlike the other streaming platforms, SoundCloud is quite social. There are social components to the others, sure, but SoundCloud users are all treated equally. Musician SoundCloud profiles are set up the same way as those of average users. Anyone can message anyone else or comment, like, or repost their songs.

SoundCloud's nonmusician users primarily use the platform for discovering the best up-and-coming talent. Most of the blogs curated on Hype Machine use SoundCloud as their primary embedded music player.

The Seattle-born electro duo ODESZA released their first single on SoundCloud in August of 2012. One half of the group, Harrison Mills, studied branding in college and applied what he learned to everything they released. Their SoundCloud channel was sleek from their first upload. The duo emailed their new track to popular users with similar tastes, and five days after the song was released on SoundCloud, it hit #1 on Hype Machine. And since 2012, 24 ODESZA tracks have hit #1 on Hype Machine. They have over 30 million SoundCloud plays and many more on Spotify. They now play festivals all over the world and sell out nearly every venue they book.

All this from smart networking on the underground music-streaming service.

It's worth mentioning that most of the DJs and producers on Sound-Cloud who use the platform to host their remixes have been under attack from the major labels that represent the artists being sampled and remixed. Despite what many DJs think, every sample used requires a license from the label and the publisher. Very few actually obtain these licenses and have seen their remixes get removed from SoundCloud and YouTube as the labels fight to get paid for these. As the music industry struggles to keep up with the tech industry, the labels sue while the creators truck ahead. Now that SoundCloud has officially been licensed by the Big 3, monetiztion (for unauthorized remixes and original songs) is enabled via ads—similar to how YouTube does it.

Dubset has been quietly negotiating deals behind the scenes with every label and publisher to streamline this legal process for independent DJs and producers who don't have the resources (or knowledge base) to secure every license they legally need to release their remixes online. If you create remixes, look into Dubset.

Spotify and Apple Music are the more "legitimate" streaming platforms which require distributors to send them music. As the two largest music (and video) streaming platforms containing only official, artist- and label-distributed content (no UGC—user generated content), they also have various royalties baked into every stream that get paid out accordingly (more on this in Chapter 13).

Pandora started as just Internet radio and also tightly curates it's content.

Because these are datacentric digital platforms, every stream is tracked and most can be pinpointed to a location. Analytics are available for most (via either the app itself or Next Big Sound) and it's important to analyze these stats and use them to focus marketing campaigns.

Pandora released its Insights platform AMP in October 2014 to artists who had music on the service. It continues to evolve and reveal very interesting and important data about best-performing songs and locations of highest-engaged listeners (to help you route tours).

Spotify and YouTube also have similar insights which are publicly visible.

As Spotify, Pandora, Facebook, Apple Music, Deezer, SoundCloud and others dip into the concert ticket and merch game, an entirely new marketplace opens up for artists, enabling them to monetize their most engaged fans where they spend the most amount of time actually enjoying their favorite artists' content.

DON'T LOSE FOCUS

You're a musician. Not an aspiring internet star. I've been chastised on Digital Music News comment boards for giving advice because at the time my most popular YouTube video only had 40,000 views. I had to take a step back and reevaluate my entire existence. "Man, if I was really good, I'd have a gazillion YouTube views." But then I remembered that

I just played a sold-out show to hundreds of people the night before and was actually making a living with my music, and let the dbag in the comments fall right off my back.

Everyone's metric of success is different. No one can define success but you. Don't fret over your social media numbers as much as the true connection you make with your fans. Fans support you financially. Followers want to be entertained for free. Which do you want to court?

12.

THE NEW ASKING ECONOMY: THE DIFFERENCE BETWEEN ASKING AND BEGGING

N 2009, I WAS CO-MANAGING ONE OF MY FAVORITE MINNEAPOLIS bands with my girlfriend. I was actively touring, playing 100+ dates a year myself, so the day-to-day duties were mostly handled by her. The band had built up a loyal grass-roots following and were selling out venues in a five-state region. They were bringing 600 people to their local shows every couple months and were becoming known on the festival circuit. They were making just enough money to support the five band members' living expenses while on tour, but had virtually nothing left over to invest. They had the material for their next album, but we didn't know where we were going to come up with the funds. No matter how we crunched the numbers, no amount of gigging or merch sales was going to bring in the $10,000+ we needed to make the album.

Then one day, through creative Googling, I stumbled upon this new site called Kickstarter. It had just launched a couple months prior, but a Brooklyn-based musician, Allison Weiss, had raised $7,700 from just 200 people through what this new startup called "crowdfunding." We thought, what the hell, it's worth a try. The band has a loyal fanbase that wants to support it. Could we replicate this other relatively unknown indie artist's success? We got Kickstarter to approve our project (by that point it was invite only) and on December 1, 2009, we asked the fans to help fund the new album. Sixty-five days later we raised $10,455 from 173 backers. We didn't really know what crowdfunding was, but we knew, whatever it was, it worked. It enabled the band to fund the new album.

Two years later, I decided to take the plunge for my album. Through a meticulously organized campaign (more on this in a bit), I raised $13,544 from 222 backers in 30 days.

It's funny to look back before Pono, Pebble, Coolest Cooler, Amanda Palmer, Zach Braff, Veronica Mars, Reading Rainbow and, er, potato salad broke records and thrust this scrappy startup into the mainstream. But not too long ago, asking people to pay for simply an idea was not just unheard of, but inconceivable.

Now crowdfunding is a commonly used practice utilized by hundreds of thousands of creators supported by millions of backers generating billions of dollars.

But for some reason, many artists still feel very uncomfortable with the entire concept of crowdfunding. Taking a fat check from a corporation who wants to own the rights to your creative properties (and your firstborn), no problem. Asking fans for financial support to create art in exchange for nothing more than, uh, art (and some fun rewards), big problem. Artists (incorrectly) referred to this as "begging" and many refused to even entertain the idea. While these artists struggled and starved, their less stubborn counterparts were forging ahead in this new asking economy, funding projects and building successful careers.

Luckily, the negative crowdfunding stigma has all but been removed from most artist communities and now if you don't crowdfund an album, eyebrows are raised. Oh, how the times have changed.

Since inception, over $147 million has been crowdfunded for over 40,000 music projects on Kickstarter—not to mention musicians who have seen success on competitors like Indiegogo and PledgeMusic.

CROWDFUNDING VS. FAN CLUBS

I think everyone is embarrassed about their low [YouTube] ad
revenue dollars because they read stories about people getting rich
off YouTube and they think "Ugh, I'm just not getting enough
views. I'm just not smart enough." And no one wants to speak out
and say "Yo this model sucks! It doesn't work for anybody!"
—JACK CONTE, ONE-HALF OF POMPLAMOOSE,
COFOUNDER AND CEO OF PATREON

Crowdfunding is great for raising a bulk amount of funds for a big project, like an album. It's not so great at generating a livable income. Or
helping constant creators, putting out art, regularly, like YouTubers.
That's why Jack Conte, one-half of the band Pomplamoose (who rose to
fame on YouTube), created Patreon. Famous YouTubers were getting millions upon millions of views, but seeing a minuscule amount in ad revenue from YouTube. Jack knew he (and fellow YouTubers) had fans willing
to support them, they just didn't have an available mechanism to do so.
He was right. Creators on Patreon include musicians, bloggers, podcast-
ers, comedians, artists, comic book artists. Patrons of these creators either
pay per piece of content (like per song posted) or per month.

This ongoing patronage model, or Crowdfunding 2.0, can be looked
at as a fan club of sorts. Bandcamp recently added subscriptions to their
already very popular platform. On Bandcamp, fans can support their
favorite artists paying a set amount per month or per year.

Even Beethoven depended heavily on the patronage of just a few
wealthy noblemen to make a living. At some point in the twentieth century, however, the music business became solely about selling small-priced
items (records) to lots of people. For some reason making $1 million from
100,000 people was better than making $1 million from 10 people. If

you can affect 10 people on such a deep level that they want to support you to this level, accept it. Appreciate it. Welcome it. Respect it. If Beethoven didn't have those few patrons who believed in him, he may have given up composing, become a piano teacher and deprived the world of some of the most beautiful music in the history of mankind.

Amanda Palmer, famously, broke the Kickstarter music record when she raised $1.2 million from nearly 25,000 backers in 2012. But that money was all spent on recording costs, packaging and shipping the rewards. She has since joined Patreon and is making over $35,000 per "thing," as she calls it.

Patreon calls it patronage. Bandcamp calls it subscription. Whatever you call it, you should look at it as a fan club. Make this space a fun, digital hangout for your biggest fans. You shouldn't just set it and leave it, you should give your fans a reason to be members—aside from their love of your music, of course. In addition to traditional fan club staples like discussion boards and access to advance tickets, give your fan club exclusive access to b-sides, demos, live streams from the studio or rehearsal studio. The beauty of the fan club (over an album-driven, one-time crowdfunding campaign) is that you don't have to worry about sending out (and paying for) physical goods. Fans are happy to support and happy to get solely digital exclusive content and behind-the-scenes access.

Crowdfunding 2.0 doesn't have to completely replace Crowdfunding 1.0. Many artists run traditional crowdfunding campaigns on Kickstarter, PledgeMusic or Indiegogo in addition to Patreon or Bandcamp fan clubs. YouTuber Julia Nunes ran a $134,403 Kickstarter campaign and a $1,700/video Patreon simultaneously. Funk band (and Sleepify inventors) Vulfpeck raised $55,266 on Kickstarter and ran a $35/year Bandcamp subscription.

These are two completely different platforms for completely different purposes targeting different subsets of your fanbase. Pull out that Pyramid of Investment. More of your fans will back your album-focused crowdfunding campaign than join your subscription-based fan club. But some will join both.

It's all about how you frame it. Locking all of your music behind pay-walls, and forcing your fans to consume music in a way that no longer makes sense to them, alienates your fans and will turn them off. How-ever, releasing all of your music for your fans to consume in a way that makes sense to them, while inviting them to support you for it (offering bonuses like exclusive, behind-the-scenes content and engagement) will overjoy and delight them.

Fans will pay you for music. Ask them. Don't make them.

Sure, the average pledge amount is $5 (per release/month) on Patreon, but that's not to say you can't court your rich fans and encourage them to support you for a high amount that makes sense to them.

WHAT ARE THE DIFFERENCES BETWEEN KICKSTARTER, INDIEGOGO AND PLEDGEMUSIC?

The three most popular crowdfunding platforms for musicians are Kick-starter, Indiegogo and PledgeMusic. Whereas Kickstarter and Indiegogo are for any creators, PledgeMusic is exclusively for musicians. Creators on Kickstarter and Indiegogo set public, monetary goal amounts and in some cases only receive the funds if they reach the goal. Indiegogo allows "flexible funding" as well, which allows you to receive the funds no matter if you reach your goal or not, however I strongly advise against this model. For one, if you calculate that it will cost a minimum of $10,000 for the album production and $3,000 to fulfill (and ship) the reward packages (not to mention marketing costs), but only raise $5,000, you're still on the hook to fulfill all the promised packages of an album that you now cannot afford to create. And another downside of this flexible funding model is that if you set your campaign to last 30 days and 23 days in you've only reached 60% of your goal, you'll shrug and say "Oh well, too bad we couldn't reach our goal" and take the money you did make and do the best you can with it. Whereas if you ran a campaign where you would receive nothing if you didn't reach your goal and 23 days in were at 60%, you would make damn certain that you made up the 40% the final week.

I can speak to this first hand. This was my exact situation. In my final week of my Kickstarter campaign I kicked it into high gear, sent out personal requests to fans, friends and family, added extra incentives and not only reached my goal, but surpassed it by 35%.

PledgeMusic, however, is a completely different model altogether. Sure, it has a crowdfunding component to it, but what sets it apart from Kickstarter and Indiegogo is that the moment the crowdfunding campaign finishes, the preorder begins. All of the work you put into rallying the troops around the crowdfunding campaign doesn't have to immediately shut down the moment the campaign finishes. All of the rewards, exclusives and packages stay live, but instead of backing the crowdfunding campaign, fans simply preorder the packages. Another major distinction between PledgeMusic and the others is that PledgeMusic hides the dollar amount of the campaign and works on a percentage base. Contrary to what you'd think, fans actually spend more when they don't know how much their pledge will contribute to the goal. The average pledge amount sits at around $55 per transaction. PledgeMusic also approves every project that comes through and sets up every musician with a product manager to help them along with the process. And PledgeMusic's success rate is far higher than Kickstarter's or Indiegogo's. Eighty-seven percent of emerging artists and 90% of "frontline" acts exceed their projected goals. Contrast that with 51% of music projects that reach their goal on Kickstarter and less than 10% on Indiegogo, as journalists have estimated. (Indiegogo doesn't release success numbers because their "flexible funding" model enables creators to get the funds regardless if they reach their goal or not.) And because PledgeMusic has deals with SoundScan, every transaction counts as an album sale that counts toward opening-week numbers. Because of this, over 130 artists have charted on Billboard. PledgeMusic also found that artists' second campaigns almost always outperform the first.

Artists like 311, Ben Folds Five, Sum 41, Weezer, Terri Clark, Sevendust, Joan Osborne, Kate Miller-Heidke, Tokyo Police Club, Lissie, the Lumineers, Guster, Plain White T's, Macy Gray, Rufus Wainwright, Antigone Rising, Lindsey Stirling, Mike Doughty, Kate Nash, and Umphrey's McGee have all run successful PledgeMusic campaigns. However, many of them were set up solely for preorder (not crowdfunding).

So, PledgeMusic has changed the entire concept of the album campaign. Instead of starting the album campaign a month before release date, It begins the moment you launch your PledgeMusic campaign and bring your Pledgers along for the entire studio ride.

THE BRIDGE

16 Tips for Running a Successful Crowdfunding Campaign

1) **Rebrand** Like an album release, a crowdfunding launch is a full-fledged campaign and should be looked to as such. Everything online should be rebranded to reflect the campaign. Come up with a title that represents what the campaign is all about. Create a color scheme and design theme that you use everywhere that directly reflects the campaign. Do a new photo shoot that is released on launch day. Put together a to-do list of things you will do during the campaign to keep it fresh, and constantly release new content to energize your base.

2) **Create the Right Timeline** Don't make the time frame too long. Kickstarter has said the most successful projects are 30 days long, whereas PledgeMusic suggests 45 days. They say a longer time frame makes people lose interest, and when they check your project out initially, they don't feel a sense of urgency. You don't want this to drag on. If you do your job right, everyone who wants to pledge will know about it by the time the 30–45 days are up.

3) Create Attractive Rewards That Make Sense for Your Fans It doesn't matter how big your fanbase is, if you don't go about this right, you won't reach your goal. There are (unfortunately) tons of examples of musicians (and some have massive fanbases) with sloppy videos and unattractive rewards who never reach their goal. You can't just put up a crowdfunding campaign and expect the dollars to start flowing. Start planning out your rewards at least a month in advance of your launch. Bounce your ideas off of friends and fans and only use rewards that are exciting, enticing and things your fans would actually want.

Your backers aren't an elusive group of random nobodies from around the globe. They will most likely be people you know personally, have hung out with and are your biggest supporters. They have come to multiple concerts; they comment on your posts, Tweet you, Snap you and follow your Instagram. You must tailor your rewards to them. These are your friends and fans, you know them best.

Make sure you have a minimum of 12 rewards. Create high dollar amounts even if you think there's no way anyone will give you that much. Someone might! Make it an option to be rewarded for a $1,000 pledge, a $5,000 pledge, $10,000 or more. Even though technically you can pledge any amount, most people don't know this and will only pledge amounts for which there are rewards.

Utilize your unique talents for the rewards. If one band member creates spray-painted t-shirts, then have that as one of the rewards. The reason it's going to be fun to be your backer and not a backer of all the other bands running simultaneous campaigns is that your backers get something that is unique to you and that they can't get anywhere else. You have to be more creative than "Get the album a month before it's released with your name in the liner notes." Sure, that can be one reward, but that should be the least interesting one.

4) Celebrate the Launch This is the biggest day of your year. You should spend the week leading up to the launch getting your fans excited for a big announcement. Release daily photos, videos and hints to what it could be. Start to become much more active on all your social sites and email list. Maybe you've been quiet for a while. Time to reengage! You should clear your schedule for launch day (and possibly a couple days after it). Take off work. Stay home with the band and do nothing but get the word out, all at once, about your campaign. Answer any questions people have immediately. Rally everyone online and get that momentum going. You will most likely raise one-third to one-half of your goal in the first week. This is an extremely important week.

5) Create a Killer Video This is the most important part of your entire campaign. The success rates for projects with and without videos are highly weighted on those with videos. Plan this out. Find someone with a good camera. Or use your phone, but make sure you get lights and create an interesting set. Don't film it in your bedroom with dirty laundry all over your bed. Wow your audience. This is the next phase of your career. Make your video represent this. Are you going to step up your studio game? Step up your video game. Write a creative script. Rehearse it. Use your creative talents to make this video unlike all the other ones out there. If you have any hope of penetrating the general Kickstarter/ PledgeMusic/Indiegogo community, your video needs to stand out among the rest.

6) **Pick a Realistic Goal** If you've only played your local market and have fewer than 100 email subscribers, you probably don't want to set your goal at $10,000. Remember you can always raise more money than the goal, but if you don't reach your goal, you get $0. So make sure you set a goal you will reach. You want to set it high enough so people will help you work for it and spread it around. Once the goal is reached, people seem less willing to help spread it because it doesn't seem as necessary. But make sure you set the goal high enough to be able to pay for what you are promising. Also remember that Kickstarter, Indiegogo and PledgeMusic will take about 8%–15% of everything you raise (including processing fees).

7) **Create Stretch Goals** Create incentives for people to continue backing even after you reach your goal. Create stretch goals like recording additional songs, music videos, longer tours and other benefits if you surpass your goal at various levels. So if your goal is $10,000, create stretch goals at $15,000, $20,000 and $50,000.

8) **Make a Budget** *Before* **the Launch** I learned this the hard way. I promised vinyl, but I didn't do my research to see what the actual costs to create a vinyl package were before I launched my campaign. And I didn't realize that vinyl holds only about 22 minutes of music per side, and my album run time was probably going to far surpass 44 minutes, requiring a double LP, and double the cost. I had to spend about a third of my entire crowdfunding income just to create the vinyl package. You can imagine the horror and the feeling in my belly when I discovered this. You don't want to set the goal too high that you don't reach it, but you have to raise enough to actually deliver on what you are promising without going homeless. Don't underestimate the costs of sending out the packages to the backers either (shipping, supplies, ordering the t-shirts, CDs, vinyl, etc). And remember the 50/50 rule: 50% of your budget is for production, 50% is for marketing. Plan accordingly.

Bill Gates said, "If I only had two dollars left, I would spend one on PR."

9) **Don't Forget the Link** Every time you mention anything regarding your campaign, you must include the link. Don't assume people are going to track down the link or take the time to go to search for your project. They may have missed the past five posts about it where you included the link. If this is the only post/tweet they see and there's no link, they won't check it out. Maybe they've seen all the posts about it and have ignored it, and they see this post and are finally pushed enough to check it out and there's no link—you just lost a backer. You cannot post the link enough. Don't make people work to find your campaign. Link it. Every. Single. Time.

10) **Don't Lose Momentum** The slowest part of your campaign will be week 2 through a week before your last. The urgency isn't there like at the end and there isn't the initial excitement like at the beginning. So, to keep the dollars flowing you need to come up with reasons for people to pledge today. Right now. Contests help. Personal appeals help. And release fresh content often, like demos, live streams from the rehearsal space and live-broadcasted Q&As. If you keep putting out videos and releasing new songs (for backers in the Updates section) then nonbackers will be inspired to get involved and become a part of the process.

11) **Maintain a "We're in This Together" Approach** In everything you do with the campaign, your angle should be that "we're in this together." Succeed or fail. And not just with the campaign. Make them believe they are part of the next phase of your career. This is the next phase of your career, and with their help you will reach the next level. Invite them to join you for this ride. You want them to feel like they are a part of the process. Invite them into the studio (digitally), ask them for lyric help on lines you're struggling with (maybe vote on a line or two—I did this and it worked very well). Just remember to put in writing somewhere that they are not going to be joint copyright owners of the song. That may seem obvious, but better to sound a little anal than to get hit with a joint ownership claim by some crazy fan. Keep them engaged and treat them like they are a part of your team.

12) **Don't Beg** You can't look at the campaign like your backers are doing you favors. You must believe you deserve this. If you don't, why should they? Thank your backers profusely, but keep it exciting and uplifting. Positivity is key. Use phrases like "We just made it to our halfway point! "

13) **Embrace Your Passive Backers as Well** Understand that you will have active supporters who will comment on every update, but you will also have many passive backers who will pledge to support you and then unsubscribe from your emails and don't really care to hear about it again until they receive the package in

the mail. You have to respect them too and invite those people to pledge. Get them to pledge by saying that they are preordering your album. Make it black and white. Sell them on why it's beneficial to them to pledge. They may not care to necessarily be "a part of the process," but they may just enjoy your music and are excited about a new album. They'll pledge to get a discount on it and to get it early. Come up with rewards for these people and target them in your outreach as well. Don't assume everyone who backs you will be following every word you say and are as excited about this project as you and your mom are.

14) **Run Contests** A crowdfunding campaign is already gamified in the sense that everyone is working together to help reach a financial goal. But take this a step further. Come up with multiple contests you can run over the course of the campaign that appeal to the various demographics of your fanbase. I ran a contest on Facebook and said, "Everyone who pledges before midnight tonight, I will record a personal video for you and post it to your wall." That worked a little too well. I believe over forty people pledged that day and I spent the next couple days creating these damn videos. But I'm not complaining—that day brought in $3,200.

15) **Get Annoying** This is the one time in your career that you have a right to get annoying through all your online mediums. Tweet about it all the time. Mention it in every Instagram and Facebook post. Make everything you do about this campaign. This is the next phase of your journey, the biggest thing in your life and your career at the moment. Pledge drives are annoying, yes (if you're an NPR junkie like me, you'll understand), but necessary. Remember, not all of your Facebook friends will see the launch post about it. They may not even see 80% of your posts about it, but then they'll get a glimpse at one post and maybe be intrigued, but then will forget about it. They need to be constantly reminded. Maybe they'll ignore it the first five times they see a post about it, but by the sixth post they'll check it out and maybe on the tenth post they'll actually pledge. Don't get discouraged because your mom says, "Maybe you're selling it a little too hard." She checks your page out every time she logs onto Facebook. She is not a good sampling of all of your fans.

16) **Personalize, Personalize, Personalize** Write personal messages to friends, family, former coworkers and big fans who you may be friends with on Facebook, may have been to your shows, may want to support, but just haven't made the time. This personal appeal works wonders. Personalize the message. Spend a couple days doing this. Yeah it's time-consuming and annoying for you, but if you get $2,000 extra out of it for two days of hard work—well, that's better than any day job out there.

13.

HOW TO GET ALL THE ROYALTIES YOU NEVER KNEW EXISTED (AND OTHER BUSINESS THINGS YOU NEED TO KNOW)

A 2015 BERKLEE COLLEGE OF MUSIC REPORT FOUND THAT ANYWHERE from 20% to 50% of music payments do not make it to their rightful owners. Kobalt calculated that there are over 900,000 royalty streams per song. How do you make sure you register your work properly and obtain all of the royalties that are rightfully owed to you? Keep reading.

As you study more about the music business, you'll see the distinction over and over again between "artist" and "songwriter." It's an important distinction to make because the royalties for "artists" and the royalties for "songwriters" are completely different.

The reason I'm putting quotes around "artists" and "songwriters" is because so many of us are both. And many of us use these terms interchangeably. And back in the day, when labels started signing artists who also wrote their own songs (which, at the time, was quite unique), they put in clauses in the contract to limit the royalties they'd (legally) have to pay out to their newly signed artists/songwriters. One of these clauses is the infamous controlled composition clause. The major labels have always tried to screw artists out of money. They look out for their own best interests and use artists' ignorance (and blind pursuit of fame) to manipulate and deceive. This is part of the reason why so many established artists and songwriters have jumped ship from their major labels (and major publishers) and headed over to independent entities.

To not get into too much history, and really just cut to the chase, before the digital age, royalties were difficult to track, but there were fewer platforms to consume music, so there were far fewer royalty streams to worry about.

With physical sales plummeting, people shifting from downloading to streaming, and the rise of digital radio, there are many more royalties out there, but they can be tracked much more easily. We're not quite there yet, but we're getting closer every day. For indie artists without a label or a publisher, you have to know what these royalties are and know where and how to get them.

So let's break them down.

TERMS YOU NEED TO UNDERSTAND

Artist

Artists record sound recordings. Rihanna is an artist. She did not write her song "Diamonds." So she is not the songwriter. Record labels represent artists. A band is an artist. A rapper is an artist. A singer is an artist. Typically whatever name is on the album is the artist.

Songwriter

Songwriters write the compositions. "Diamonds" was written by four songwriters: Sia Furler, Benjamin Levin, Mikkel S. Eriksen, and Tor Erik Hermansen. Publishing companies represent songwriters.

Sound Recording

Some call this the "master." It's the actual recording. The mastered track. Traditionally, labels (because they own the master) collect royalties for sound recordings. Sound recordings are not to be confused with compositions. Artists record sound recordings.

Composition

This is the song. Not the recording. Traditionally, publishing companies (because they own the composition and represent songwriters) collect royalties for compositions. Songwriters write compositions.

PRO

Performing Rights Organizations. In the United States, these are ASCAP, BMI and SESAC. In Canada this is SOCAN. Pretty much every country in the world has its own PRO and they work together to collect royalties from each other's territories. These organizations represent songwriters, not artists. These are organizations that collect performance royalties (not mechanical royalties—we'll get to those in a bit). PROs make money to pay their songwriters and publishers royalties by collecting money from thousands of venues and outlets (radio stations, TV stations, department stores, bars, live venues, etc.) that have been required to purchase "blanket licenses" giving these venues permission to play music in their establishment (or on the air). The PROs then pool all of this money and divide it among all of their songwriters and publishers based on the frequency and "weight" of each song's "public performance." The PROs then pay the publishing companies their 50% and the songwriters their 50%. PROs split "publishing" and "songwriter" royalties equally. 50/50. This is not a deal you negotiate. This is just how they do it for everyone from Taylor

Swift down to you and me. 50/50. Any songwriter in the U.S. can sign up for ASCAP or BMI without being invited or having to apply. ASCAP and BMI are both not-for-profit organizations. SESAC is for-profit and you must be accepted.

ASCAP

American Society of Composers, Authors and Publishers represents 560,000 members (songwriters and publishers) and over 10 million compositions. ASCAP is owned and run by its songwriter and publisher members, with a board elected by, and from, it's membership. They have paid out nearly $6 billion in the past seven years. They represent songwriters like Katy Perry, Dr. Dre, Marc Anthony, Chris Stapleton, Ne-Yo, Trisha Yearwood, Brandi Carlile, Lauryn Hill, Jimi Hendrix, Bill Withers, Carly Simon, Quincy Jones, Marvin Gaye, Stevie Wonder, Duke Ellington, annnnnd Ari Herstand.

BMI

Broadcast Music, Inc. represents over 700,000 members (songwriters and publishers) and over 10.5 million compositions. They represent songwriters like Taylor Swift, Lil Wayne, Mariah Carey, John Legend, Lady Gaga, Eminem, (members of) Maroon 5, Michael Jackson, Linkin Park, Sam Cooke, Willie Nelson, Loretta Lynn, Dolly Parton, Fats Domino, Rihanna, John Williams and Danny Elfman.

SESAC

SESAC is not an acronym. Really. It represents over 30,000 members (songwriters and publishers) and over 400,000 compositions. They represent songwriters like Bob Dylan, Neil Diamond, Rush, Zac Brown, Hillary Scott of Lady Antebellum, the Avett Brothers, Shirley Caesar, Paul Shaffer and one-half of Thompson Square.

You (as a songwriter) can only sign up for one PRO. You cannot be a member of ASCAP and BMI. You have to choose. Find out what the PROs are in your country and pick one and sign up.

The Bridge
How to Collect 100% of Your Performance Royalties

If you are signing with ASCAP and you are your own publisher, then in order for ASCAP to pay you both the writer's share and the publisher's share of your royalties, you need to register with ASCAP both as a songwriter and as a publisher. To register as a publisher, you have to provide the name of your publishing company. You can just make up a name and use it as a d/b/a (mine is Proud Honeybee Music). If you do that, make sure to tell ASCAP you are "doing business as" that name so they can write the checks appropriately. You can also sign up for direct deposit, which expedites this entire process. If you want to set up an actual company as your publishing company, you can set up an LLC or a corporation (speak to your accountant about which one makes sense for you) and set up a bank account for that company, and ASCAP will write your checks to that company or deposit your money directly to that bank account.

If you are an unaffiliated songwriter with BMI, you don't need to identify a publishing company. BMI will pay you 100% of the money.

However, if you sign up for an admin publishing company (like CD Baby Pro, Songtrust or TuneCore Publishing), they will collect your publishing money from ASCAP, BMI, SESAC or SOCAN, take their commission (10%–15%), and pay you out the rest. This is a far easier option.

I recommend you make sure all of your songs are registered with ASCAP or BMI (or SESAC, SOCAN) and that you work with an admin publishing company. If you distribute through CD Baby, use CD Baby Pro. If you don't, use Songtrust or TuneCore Publishing. If you haven't registered with a PRO yet, sign up for an admin publishing company first—they will then register your songs with a PRO (save some time and steps!).

Digital Distribution Company

Some people call them digital aggregators. These companies are how you get your music into iTunes, Spotify, Apple Music, Amazon, Google Play, Deezer, Tidal and 80+ other digital stores and streaming services around the world. We covered this a bit in Chapter 4.

HFA

Harry Fox Agency. HFA handles U.S. mechanical royalties. Mechanical royalties are another kind of songwriter royalty (full explanation at the end of this chapter). HFA is hired by companies like Spotify to calculate and pay out mechanical royalties to publishers. HFA represents 48,000 publishers.

HFA calculates, collects and pays mechanical royalties. They also issue "mechanical licenses." You can't sign up for HFA unless you are a publisher and have songs released by a third-party label (not self-released).

But you don't need to sign up with HFA to collect mechanical royalties. Admin publishing companies like Songtrust, CD Baby, TuneCore and Audiam will collect mechanical royalties for you if you sign up for their admin publishing programs. I wrote a comparison between CD Baby Pro and TuneCore Publishing on Ari's Take, which you can check out at http://bit.ly/pub-comparison.

Fun fact: HFA was recently bought by SESAC.

Admin Publishing Companies

"Admin" stands for "administration." All publishing companies have an admin department. They also have a synch licensing department, an A&R department and many other departments. Admin publishing companies have started popping up over the past few years to help unrepped song-writers (like you and me) collect all the royalties out there from around the world.

Again, companies like Songtrust, CD Baby, TuneCore and Audiam are some admin publishing companies who will do this. These companies will accept anyone and everyone. If you have a bit more clout, you should look into more exclusive companies like Kobalt, PEN, Riptide and Secret Road. These companies operate like normal publishers, but work on an admin (commission only) basis. They do not retain ownership—like traditional publishing companies. Fun fact: SOCAN recently acquired Audiam.

Synch Licensing

"Synch" stands for "synchronization." A synch license is needed to synch music to picture. TV shows, movies, commercials, video games, all need a synch license to legally put a song alongside their picture. Technically, so does YouTube (and you, when you make a cover video and upload it). Fun fact: Nearly every YouTube and Facebook video cover is illegal. A publisher (remember, publishers represent songwriters and compositions), could legally get YouTube and Facebook to remove your cover if they wanted. But a lot of publishers aren't really doing this anymore because they realize how great the promotion is. And, YouTube is now monetizing cover videos and getting the publishers (and songwriters) paid through ad revenue.

Some musicians have expressed to me their reluctance to put up covers on YouTube and Facebook for which they have not obtained the proper licenses. The honest folk of the world. Those who wouldn't dare fill up their free water cup at Chipotle with soda. I applaud your ethics. However, it's virtually impossible for an indie artist to obtain a synch license from a major publishing company. Believe me, I've tried. They don't make it easy. There's no streamlined way to do this. So if you are a law-abiding artist, unless you happen to have someone bankrolling you, you will just have to forgo YouTube, Facebook, Instagram and Vine covers. But there *is* a very easy (and legal) way to release cover songs without video, like on iTunes. We'll dig into this at the end of this chapter.

Licensing Company

Licensing companies work to get your music placed in TV shows, movies, trailers, commercials and video games. More on these in the next chapter

SoundExchange

A lot of people confuse SoundExchange with PROs because technically SoundExchange is a performing rights organization. But I'm not including them in the "PRO" classification out of clarity (and when most in the biz discuss PROs, they are just referring to the aforementioned ASCAP, BMI, SESAC, SOCAN). SoundExchange represents artists and labels whereas (the other) PROs represent songwriters and publishers.

Unlike the three PROs in America, SoundExchange is the only organization in America that collects performance royalties for "noninteractive" digital sound recordings (not compositions). "Noninteractive" means you can't choose your song. So, Pandora radio is noninteractive, whereas Apple Music and Spotify are "interactive." Beats 1 (within Apple Music) is digital radio (noninteractive). Spotify's radio service is also noninteractive, but more on that in a sec.

SoundExchange has agreements with twenty foreign collection agencies. When your music is played in their territory, they pay SoundExchange, and SoundExchange pays you.

Like the PROs, SoundExchange issues blanket licenses to digital radio (noninteractive) platforms (like Pandora and SiriusXM) which gives these outlets the ability to play any song they represent. Like the PROs, the outlets pay an annual fee for the blanket license.

But, SoundExchange collects only digital royalties. The PROs collect digital, terrestrial (AM and FM radio) and live royalties.

The way the copyright law is currently written, AM/FM radio has to pay only composition performance royalties and *not* sound-recording royalties. Makes no sense. The U.S. Copyright Office has recommended that this law be changed, but only Congress can do that, and the two times it has tried, the proposal was defeated, largely as the result of heavy lobbying by Big Radio.

So, again, SoundExchange = digital sound-recording royalties for noninteractive plays.

But, interestingly enough (I know this stuff is SOOO interesting), Pandora pays both digital sound-recording performance royalties (to SoundExchange) and digital composition performance royalties (to PROs). But, thanks to hundred-year-old consent decrees which limit the ability for ASCAP or BMI to work for higher royalty rates, Pandora pays about ten times more for sound-recording royalties (to SoundExchange) than for songwriter royalties (to the PROs). The Songwriter Equity Act (bipartisan) has been in Congress for years now to help fix this. But Congress moves slower than an Adele ballad (but involves about the same number of tears shed).

And to complicate matters even more, not all digital radio services work with SoundExchange (but 2,500 do). Some opt out (Spotify noninteractive radio has opted out) and they just negotiate rates directly with each label/distributor.

HOW TO SIGN UP FOR SOUNDEXCHANGE

Go to SoundExchange.com. If you are both the performer (artist) and the owner of the sound recording (meaning you don't have a record label), simply select "Both" on the second page of the registration when it asks you to select: Performer, Sound Recording Copyright Owner or Both. It's a long process and you have to submit a full catalog list. When I did this, I had to email in a complicated Excel doc with lots of info. Plan a weekend to do all of this. It's time-consuming, but worth it.

Fun fact: I encouraged Ari's Take reader and children's musician Andy Mason to sign up for SoundExchange, and the first check he got was for $14,000! Apparently, Pandora had his songs included on all the most popular children's music radio stations and he had no idea. Boom!

SoundExchange will hold your back royalties for three years, so register now if you haven't already. And if you have registered (maybe you did years ago), make sure you have also registered as the Sound Recording Copyright Owner (they previously called it "Rights Owner"). Because the "Both" option is very new, you may have missed it and are only receiving 45% of your total money. Why 45% and not 50%?

Session musicians can get some of this money too!

If you are a session musician, 5% of the total money earned for each song has been reserved for you. Contact the AFM (the musician's union) to grab this moola.

SoundExchange's breakdown for payment: 45% to featured artist, 50% to the sound recording owner (label—or you if you self-released), and 5% to session musicians or, as they put it, "nonfeatured artists." Whether you have session musicians or not on your record, SoundExchange withholds 5% of all royalties from everyone for them.

If you're a Canadian artist, you can sign up with Re:Sound (which is

Canada's version of SoundExchange). And, best thing, Re:Sound (unlike SoundExchange) will collect royalties from commercial, terrestrial radio (and other nondigital venues) for you!

So, just to clarify, here is a breakdown for the royalties artists and songwriters earn (and how to get them):

INDEPENDENT/UNSIGNED
MUSICIANS KEEP 95%

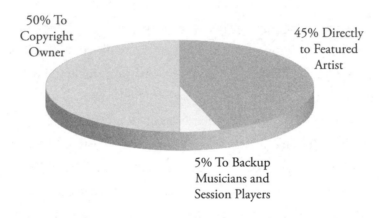

50% To Copyright Owner

45% Directly to Featured Artist

5% To Backup Musicians and Session Players

Breakdown of how SoundExchange royalties are split up.

ARTIST ROYALTIES

Recording Digital Performance Royalties

These come from noninteractive (you can't choose the song) digital platforms like internet and satellite radio.

How to Get Paid: Sound Exchange

Download Sales

These result from someone downloading your music on iTunes, Google Play, Amazon, etc.

How to Get Paid: Your distribution company

But, remember, if a fan downloads your music on Bandcamp, you get a check directly from Bandcamp because Bandcamp is a self-managed (as in you manage it yourself) store.

Interactive Streaming Revenue

There are lots of different kinds of streaming revenue. But interactive (meaning you choose the song) streaming revenue (like from Spotify, Apple Music, Deezer, Tidal) goes to the artist/label. When these services claim they pay out 70% of all revenue, the 70% is for both the artist/label revenue and the songwriter royalties (mechanicals). Streaming revenue to artists is way more than the mechanicals paid to songwriters.

How to Get Paid: Your distribution company

YouTube Sound Recording Revenue

Technically there are a bunch of "assets" (streams of revenue) for each YouTube video. To make it simple, we'll just get into how you can earn money. First, for the sound recording (we'll get into the composition in the next section). You can make money off of any video that uses your sound recording (whether you uploaded the video or not) if you allow YouTube to put ads on the video (they call it "monetize"). Either videos you upload or fan-made cat videos with your sound recordings can generate ad revenue that you can collect. YouTube splits the ad revenue 45%/55% in your favor.

How to Get Paid: Most digital distribution companies have this option via an opt-in check box. If your distributor doesn't handle this, you can sign up for independent YouTube revenue collection companies like Audiam, AdRev or InDMusic. But it's easiest if you keep everything under one roof.

Master Use License

Any TV show, movie, commercial, trailer or video game requires both a master use license (from the artist/label) for use of the sound recording and a synch license (from the songwriter/publisher) for use of the composition. These days, most music supervisors (the people who place the music), will just pay you (an indie artist) a bulk amount for both the master use license and the synch license (because most indie artists wrote and recorded the song).

But if you're repped by a label and a publisher, the supe (that's short for music supervisor) will go to your label and pay for a master use license and then to your publisher and pay for a synch license. Usually it's the same amount, but not always.

How to Get Paid: Directly from the TV studio, ad agency (for a commercial), production company (for a movie or trailer) or game company. It's best to work with a licensing company for this. More on this in the next chapter.

TV Royalties

If your music gets on a commercial, TV show, trailer or movie, you can also earn these royalties. And these definitely add up. I was in a Bud Light commercial (as an actor), and in SAG-AFTRA residuals, I got about $10,000 *a month* for the duration it was on the air. That was for hanging out at a (fake) barbecue holding a can of Lime-A-Rita and laughing on cue a lot. If one of your recordings gets into a commercial, you might make something like that, because you'll be treated as a voice-over actor. Many commercials run about six months, that could be $60,000 just in SAG-AFTRA residuals.

How to get paid: SAG-AFTRA

If, however, SAG-AFTRA doesn't have your mailing address, they won't know who to pay. You can check on the AFM & SAG-AFTRA Fund website (http://www.afmsagaftrafund.org/unclaimed-royalties_SR.php) to see if you have outstanding royalties. Or contact SAG-AFTRA directly and give them your info when you have a recording played on TV.

SONGWRITER ROYALTIES

Composition Performance Royalties

These come from plays on the radio (AM/FM or digital), interactive and noninteractive streaming services (Spotify, Apple Music, Tidal, Deezer), live at a concert (yes, even your own), in restaurants, bars, department stores, coffee shops, TV. Literally any public place that has music (live or recorded) needs a license from ASCAP, BMI and SESAC to be able to legally play music in their establishment. For some reason, American movie theaters are exempt from needing a public performance license for the music used in the films, and no one gets paid residuals when songs are played in the films. Music played in movie theater lobbies and bathrooms is different and can be licensed (and earned on). When a movie is played on TV, the songs in that movie earn royalties. When that same movie is played in a movie theater, those songs do not earn royalties. Makes no sense. It's just the way it is.

However, royalties are generated for foreign (outside the U.S.) movie theaters. And for an international smash, it could add up to be some serious cheddar. I've heard of amounts in the hundreds of thousands of dollars. Not yen. Dollars, baby!

Of course if a coffee shop has the AM/FM radio playing, and if you're with ASCAP, you (most likely) won't get paid when your song is played there, because ASCAP most likely won't be conducting a survey of that radio station at that exact moment, but if the shop has Pandora or SiriusXM on (or other piped-in Muzak services), this is tracked and you will (eventually) get paid on the plays. The system is currently being worked out and not everything is tracked yet, but eventually, say, in a few years, it will be. ASCAP uses a "sampling" method, where they employ an electronic monitoring system, MediaMonitors/MediaBase, for sample performance data from commercial, public, satellite and college radio. The sample data is then loaded into ASCAP's Audio Performance Management system where it is (mostly) electronically matched to the works in the ASCAP database. ASCAP states that they supplement this data with station logs and other technology vendors and methods that capture ads, promos and themes, and background music.

BMI also uses sampling. They say they use "performance monitoring data, continuously collected on a large percentage of all licensed commercial radio stations, to determine payable performances." They also use their "proprietary pattern-recognition technology." They call it a "census" and claim it's "statistically reliable and highly accurate."

My song was played as bridge music on NPR's *All Things Considered* (for 13 million people). I won't be getting paid for this (unless ASCAP happened to be running a sample of NPR at that exact moment).

TIP: ASCAP, BMI and SESAC have a program where you can import your setlist and venue information to secure payment of your live performance royalties (for performing your originals in a club, theater, grocery store, arena, wherever). They're called BMI Live, ASCAP OnStage and SESAC's Live Performance Notification System. Last I heard, most indie artists playing under 500-cap rooms were making about $10 a show. It ain't much, but it can add up—especially if you're a live act playing 200 dates a year. Who couldn't use an extra $2K? ASCAP also runs a separate survey of the 300 top-grossing tours of each year, according to Pollstar. This includes both headliners and openers' set lists.

How to Get Paid: Your PRO (ASCAP, BMI, SESAC, SOCAN)

Mechanical Royalties

Mechanical royalties are earned when a song is streamed, downloaded or purchased (like a CD or vinyl). In America, the rate is set by the U.S. government. It's currently 9.1 cents per download, and there's a very complicated formula involved in figuring out what you get per stream. But you can check out HFA's charts at (https://www.harryfox.com/find_out/rate_charts.html) to attempt to make sense of it. But it's around $.0007 per stream, but, of course, varies based on the streaming platform's user numbers, revenue, etc. Worldwide, it's about the same—about 8%–10% of the total sale/stream.

Worth noting, in the United States, mechanical royalties get passed on to the label/distributor from iTunes; however, nearly everywhere else in the world, mechanicals get collected by local collections agencies before the money gets to your distributor. That's why when you look at your statements, an iTunes download in the U.S. nets you $.69 (70% of $.99—Apple retains 30% from iTunes sales) whereas a download in England nets you around $.60. So if you don't have an admin publishing company, you won't get any of your international mechanical royalties from download sales. Like SoundExchange, these international collection agencies will hold on to this money (for about three years) until a publisher comes and claims it. You technically could try to do this by calling up collection agencies in every country, but I just recommend going with an admin pub company—they already have all the relationships built (and they only take about 10%–15%; it's worth it).

How to Get Paid: Admin publishing company

YouTube Performance Royalties

Because your music is being played on YouTube videos, it's technically a public performance. Any video on YouTube (by you or anyone else), cover, live performance, original recording lyric video, music video or cat video, with your compositions in it, earns a public performance royalty.

How to Get Paid: Your PRO

YouTube Composition Royalties

In addition to performance royalties, you can earn a percentage of the ad revenue generated from the video as composition royalties. Again, any video on YouTube that has your composition in it (uploaded by you or anyone else), can get an ad placed on it and start generating revenue. Your admin publishing company will handle this. I know you're wondering, but how will my admin publishing company know when Joe Schmo from Lincoln, Nebraska, uploads a cover of my song? Especially because my song title is "She Loves You" (and it's not the Beatles song). Yeah, you can see the difficulty. YouTube's Content ID program doesn't catch these (because covers and live recordings are different sound recordings than the original). Some admin publishing companies and YouTube collection companies are better at tracking this than others. Some do manual searches/listen. You can always ask your company how they do it.

How to Get Paid: Admin publishing company

Synch License

Like the master use license, any TV show, movie, commercial or video game requires a synchronization (synch for short) license to put the composition alongside their picture.

How to Get Paid: Directly from the TV studio, ad agency (for a commercial), production company (for a movie or trailer), or game company. It's best to work with a licensing company for this.

HOW TO RELEASE COVER SONGS (LEGALLY)

If you want to release a cover song (remember, song, not video), you have to get a mechanical license. The law states that once the song has been publicly released, anyone can cover it, without permission from the copyright owner as long as they get a compulsory mechanical license for the song. Sounds scary and complicated, but it's actually quite simple. Your digital distribution company may handle this for you. But if they don't, you have to get a license via HFA's Songfile, Easy Song Licensing or Loudr. These three services will ask you to estimate how many copies of your song you plan to sell. They then multiply this number by $.091 and that's the number you pay. It's worth mentioning that all three services ask you how many interactive streams you think you'll get. You'd think they mean from Spotify, Apple Music and the bunch. But most streaming services already cover these mechanical royalties and pay the publishers directly. The only reason that Songfile, Easy Song Licensing or Loudr ask you for this number is to cover the very few streaming services that do not have deals with the publishers yet, like SoundCloud (although by the time you're reading this, those streaming services probably will have made those deals). And all of these companies way overcharge for the interactive streaming rate. Remember, the government-set mechanical royalty rate is about $.0007 (yes, three zeros) a stream, but these services are charging you $.01 a stream. So, if you pay the penny a stream for plays on a service that is already paying these royalties directly, not only are you overpaying, the publisher is being paid twice (once from you and again from the streaming service).

RIGHT OF FIRST USE

A protection you have under U.S. copyright law prohibits anyone from releasing a song you wrote without your permission if it has not been publicly released. So, if you write a song, no one can release it before you do without your permission.

HOW TO COPYRIGHT YOUR MUSIC AND WHY YOU SHOULD

Remember when Marvin Gaye's kids sued Pharrell and Robin Thicke because "Blurred Lines" kind of sounded like "Got to Give It Up?" Utterly laughable. Except when they actually won and were awarded $7.4 million. Legal debates will rage on for years over the validity of this verdict, but regardless, one thing we can learn from this is to always copyright your songs. Had Marvin Gaye not registered the copyright of his song back in 1977, his kids would have never been able to even bring this suit nearly forty years later. So copyright your songs—you know, for your kids' retirement plan. It's actually not that tough to do, and the Library of Congress allows you to copyright all of your songs at once for $55. Just go to Copyright.gov and follow the prompts. Again, make sure you do this correctly. One tiny mistake could void your registration. It's always best to consult an attorney.

TRADEMARKING YOUR BAND NAME

Before you choose a band name, you want to make absolutely certain no one else is using that name. A simple Google and Facebook search will give you some indication, but it's always best to consult a trademark lawyer to be absolutely certain you can use the name you settle on. Once you land on a band name that no one else has, you should apply to register the trademark to be safe. Once you start using the name, you can use ™ on the name if you so choose, but to get a national registration and use the ®, you have to apply to the U.S. Patent and Trademark Office. To make sure you do this properly, as it's quite complicated, you should hire a trademark attorney to help you with this.

14.

HOW TO GET MUSIC PLACED IN FILM AND TELEVISION

American Authors, Snow Patrol, Imagine Dragons, Lumineers,
Ingrid Michaelson. The only reason you know these
bands is because they licensed their music.
—CATHY HELLER, CATCH THE MOON MUSIC

CREDIT ALEXANDRA PATSAVAS WITH WHAT SHE DID WITH THE O.C. BACK in 2003. She started the musical revolution in television by giving unknown indie artists featured placements on the show. *The O.C.* became known just as much for the soundtrack as for the girl-on-girl action. It paved the way for other music-heavy shows like Scrubs, Grey's Anatomy and One Tree Hill known for breaking artists in the early aughts.

Now shows, ad agencies and movie producers pride themselves on including the hottest undiscovered talent.

Alabama Shakes' song "Sound and Color" started charting on the Billboard Hot 100 the week Apple released a new commercial featuring the song (even though the song had been out for seven months).

The idea of "selling out" just doesn't exist anymore in the placement world. It's cool to get songs in ads. It's a career milestone. And it brings hot new artists into the homes of millions who may have otherwise never heard them. Many artists have in fact gotten their big breaks from being placed in commercials first.

But aside from "the big break," which is happening less and less these days, licensing has proven to be a serious revenue stream for unsigned, independent artists. As someone who has gotten over thirty songs placed in film and TV, I've seen firsthand what licensing pays (and does not pay). Some artists are so successful in the licensing world that they are able to support their family on just licensing income.

If pursuing licensing is your main focus, you need to plan this out long before you write your first song, let alone record it. The fact of the matter is, not every song or every genre works for licensing. If your chorus is all about Sarah, but the main character of the show is named Amy, they aren't going to use your song, no matter how perfect it may be musically. And because TV moves so quickly, they aren't going to ask you to go replace "Sarah" with "Amy." It either works or it doesn't. For the most part.

A good rule of thumb: *The more universal your songs are, the better chance you have at getting placements*. Lyrics are huge in the placement world. Sure, many times the spot will just use the instrumental version of the song, but often they want the option to use the full version, with vocals. If the lyrics don't work, the song doesn't work.

And production style is also huge.

I'm going to break down what each licensing category is looking for and what it pays. Just to clarify, this is for licensing of songs already recorded, not for composers creating scores specifically for the project. That's a completely different process for a completely different book.

MOVIE TRAILERS

Movie trailers call for a certain kind of production. They typically want epic. A song that has turning points. Because they only have about two and a half minutes to sell a two-hour film, they need to show how many dramatic twists and turns the film has. Similarly, the best movie trailer songs have dramatic twists and turns as well. Florence and the Machine got a major bump because her song "Dog Days Are Over" was used in a big movie trailer. This is a perfect example of a song that's epic and also contains multiple dramatic turning points.

Movie trailers for huge studio films pay upward of $100,000 (or more) for a single placement. I'll wait while you pick your jaw up from the floor.

COMMERCIALS

Commercials also demand a very specific production style. And also pay very, very well. Anywhere from $1,000 (for Internet only use) to $550,000 (or more, for a huge national campaign) for a single placement. No exaggeration. I've seen the briefs. The wonderful thing about commercials is that if the song works, it works. Whether you are a chart-topping superstar or a recently formed band and this is your first song, if your song gets selected, you get the money. Unlike TV and movie studios, ad agencies will pay top dollar for a song that works regardless of the party that reps the artist.

For a while, nearly every song in every commercial had whistles, handclaps and/or gang vocals yelling "Hey." And nearly every ad agency brief for a time called for songs that were either "edgy like the Black Keys or Fitz and the Tantrums" or sweet and sunshiney, like the Lumineers and Ingrid Michaelson.

Take, for instance, Imagine Dragons' "On Top of the World," the Lumineers' "Ho Hey," Mozella's "Life Is Endless," Kathryn Ostenberg's "Be Young," American Authors' "Best Day of My Life," Locksley's "The Whip," the Highfields' "I Like It," Fitz and the Tantrums' "The Walker," Edward Sharp and the Magnetic Zeros' "Home" and Philip Phillips's

"Home." All of these songs have been placed on commercials and/or TV shows (in some cases quite a few times). At first glance you wouldn't put these songs in the same category, but listen to them back-to-back and you'll see the common production themes. They all contain either hand-claps, whistles and/or gang vocals. Their lyrics are universal. And they fall into one of the two production camps.

And ad agencies will typically not use sad songs. They're trying to sell their product, not depress their audience. So if your album has only down-tempo ballads, kiss your chances for commercial placements good-bye. They mostly want fun, upbeat, high-energy, exciting, epic, happy songs.

Just as every song on top 40 radio sounds the same (thanks, Max Martin), most songs on commercials these days sound the same. There's a formula. And if you follow it, you can make a ton of moola.

Although the production styles ad agencies request evolve as contemporary music evolves, the lyrics used pretty much stay the same. Most ad briefs want lyrics that call for themes about "home," "together," "friendship," "freedom," "let's go," "sunshine," "feels great," "enjoying life," "new beginning," "things are gonna be great," "feels so good," "change," "tonight's the night," "light" and "time." Pay attention the next time you're watching commercials and note how many songs actually contain these lyrics.

To find the current production trends being used in commercials, just camp yourself out in front of network TV during prime time and crank up the commercials. Or, better yet, browse commercials and discover the songs used on splendAd.com, TuneFind.com and Whatisthatsong.net.

If you want to write songs for commercials, you need to master the current production standards and write songs with the most used lyrical themes. If you do, any licensing company on the planet will beg to work with you.

MOVIES

There's a bit more flexibility in the kind of music movies place because they are so narrative; however, using universal themes definitely helps. Movie placements for huge studio films pay very well. The sky is the limit. But $100,000 is not uncommon for an end title placement. Indie films, of course, pay much less because they're typically working on shoe-string budgets. Most will pay just a few thousand dollars, if anything. And if the movie hits television (or theaters outside the U.S.) you'll earn royalties from your PRO.

TV SHOWS

TV shows don't pay nearly as well as the rest of the bunch. They usually pay anywhere from nothing (for reality shows on MTV, VH1, Showtime) up to about $15,000 for a prime-time, network-TV-show, featured placement. These rates are for indie artists. Major labels and publishers demand much more. This is one main reason why TV shows actually prefer to place songs by independent artists. It's also a huge point of pride if they help break the artist off of the placement.

VIDEO GAMES

Like TV shows, video games don't typically pay nearly as much. Often-times they'll pay a "buyout" rate of $2,000 to $30,000 or so. But some-times they'll pay per game sale. Royalties are around 10 cents a sale.

IF IT WORKS, IT WORKS

The beauty of synch licensing is that the only thing that matters is if the song works with the spot. It doesn't matter what the band looks like, how many Facebook Likes they have, how many they can draw to their shows, or how many YouTube views they've gotten. If the song works, it works.

MUSIC SUPERVISORS

Music supervisors (or supes, as they're referred to) are the actual people who take the cues from the producers and director when the "picture is locked" and underscore the picture with songs.

How to Contact Music Supervisors

Well, I advise against contacting music supervisors directly, as most don't take music from people they don't know. They get too many pitches from too many people. Supes may get pitched hundreds of songs a week. They don't have time to listen to everything. And if they don't know you, your email will most likely go straight to the trash.

That being said, independent, unrepped artists have had success pitching supes on their own in the past (including me). To increase your chances, start with supes at new shows. They're going to be scrambling for music. If it's an established show, do your homework. Every show has a style of music they place. Many shows will have websites devoted to just the music. Some shows even have Spotify playlists of all songs placed. Above all, do not, I repeat, do not hit up a supe without knowing exactly what kind of music she is looking for.

So, if you're absolutely certain that your music will fit the project, you can try to cold-email.

1) **No Attachments** Do not clutter up their Inbox with attachments of mp3s. Only include links to where they can stream or listen to the song.

2) **Box.com Links** Most supes prefer Box.com for songs. This is not to be confused with Dropbox.com. Box.com links allow supes to stream or download the song. Most don't have time to download the song. So just send them the Box.com link and they will be able to stream the song. If they think it will work, they will download it and try it out.

3) **Tagged Mp3s** Many times, supes will have a bunch of songs they are trying out for a certain spot. Once they land on the song they want to use, they will need to "clear" it. That means to get the rights to use the song. But they will probably have forgotten where the song came from. But if you added your contact info to the metadata, they can find you easily. So, first, create a 320kbps mp3 from your original WAV file. You can do this in iTunes. In preferences, make sure you select "Custom" 320kbps. Then command click the song and select "Create MP3 Version." Then open the newly created mp3's info (Command i) in iTunes and type your info in the comments. Include contact email, phone number and "I own 200%" if you actually own all of the rights to your song.

4) **"I Own 200%"** In other words, you have the right to license both the song and the recording. Supes like placing music that is easy to clear. That's why they love working with licensing companies. They are one-stop shops for the music. Instead of having to go to a publisher and negotiate a synch license fee and then going to the label and negotiating a master use license, they'd like to just talk to one person and negotiate an "all-in" fee for the use (The sound-recording copyright and the musical composition copyright are actually totally separate copyrights, but "200%" is the term that supes like to hear). So, if you wrote and released the song yourself (or with your band), without a label, you own 200%. If you cowrote the song with someone else, you do not own 100% of the composition—unless your cowriter(s) signed off on these rights. But be careful, if your cowriter is signed to a publishing company, she may not know that she doesn't have the rights to clear the song. However, if you cowrote the song with an unrepped songwriter and you got permission from her to be able to place the song without her direct consent and you recorded the song with (or purchased Beats from) a producer who gave you full permission to place the song without further consent, then you're fine and you can say you "own 200%." It's good to get in writing from every collaborator that you have full permission to license your song.

5) **Subject Line: Sounds like** _____ **(artist you sound like).** Supes don't have time to open every email, let alone listen to every song. But, if they know what they're going to get when they open your email, you have a much better chance of getting a listen. So title your subject line who you sound like: "Sounds like Coldplay, Imagine Dragons." If they need a song that sounds like that, you'll definitely get a listen—even if they don't know you.

6) **Only Mastered Tracks** Do not send demos. They only want high-quality, mastered songs.

7) **You Must Have Instrumentals** Often they will want to use only a few lyrics of your song, or none at all. They will typically want the instrumental sent over in addition to the main master. So, before you give your mixing engineer the final check, make sure you get instrumentals for every song. It's also good to get stems (vocal only, drum only, etc.). These can be helpful for remixes as well.

8) **Work with a Licensing Company** This all being said, most supes prefer to work with people they know and trust. Find a licensing company to rep you.

LICENSING COMPANIES

Licensing companies typically only represent artists who are also the sole songwriters. Licensing companies are one-stop shops for music supervisors. They want to make it as easy as possible for the ad agency or TV show to use the song. Licensing companies can clear the songs immediately for the music supervisors.

So if you cowrite with anyone, first make sure they are not signed to a publishing company (if they are, it makes things very difficult and will almost certainly prevent a licensing company from working with you— or repping that song). And make sure you get in writing (email is fine), that you have full rights to the song to license without getting permission from your cowriters.

WORD TO THE WISE: Never pay a licensing company money up front to go pitch you. If they believe in your music, they will pitch you and work solely on commission. Commissions are typically between 30% and 50%

of the up-front fee. Some will take a commission of your backend PRO royalties and some will not.

14 OF THE BIGGEST AND MOST REPUTABLE LICENSING COMPANIES OUT THERE

Aperture
Bank Robber
Bleed 101
Blue Buddha
Catch The Moon
Crucial
dms.FM
Greater Goods
HyperExtension
Lip Sync
Platform
Secret Road
Terrorbird
ZYNC

However, there are literally hundreds more. You can purchase a music-licensing directory containing most licensing companies, publishing companies, music libraries and music supervisors from The Music Business Registry (musicregistry.com) for $100. The above licensing companies mostly won't take submissions directly from artists (they're too big). It's best to get someone they trust to refer you (like another artist on their roster, a manager or lawyer).

MUSIC LIBRARIES

Also, there are music library and licensing companies (like Triple Scoop Music, Audiosocket, Rumblefish, Shutterstock, Animoto and Musicbed) that specialize in issuing inexpensive synch licenses for wedding photographers, corporations (for in-house training videos) and indie filmmakers. This can help you bring in some extra dough. These kinds of companies are definitely worth looking into. They don't work to get you the $200,000 Verizon commercial spot; they're soliciting wedding photographers to pay $60 to license your song in their video. But these can add up. There are a bunch of these music library companies out there. Just Google around a bit: "music for wedding video" or "license music for indie film" or "license music library" and these companies will populate. Many are also listed in the Music Business Registry list. Most companies are quite selective about what songs they bring on (to keep their quality up). But they all take applications from unknowns. If the quality is there (and it fits their format—they're probably not going to take death metal or hard-core rap for a wedding video licensing business), you're golden. Most music libraries are non-exclusive, meaning you can work with a bunch of them.

Songtradr, which officially launched in March of 2016, is a new model for synch licensing. It's a hybrid of an instant-access music library and a hands-on licensing company. Like music libraries, buyers can search the database, but unlike other libraries, artists can set their songs at whatever price they'd like for each use. And like most music libraries, it's nonexclusive.

WHAT DO "NONEXCLUSIVE" AND "EXCLUSIVE" MEAN?

If a licensing company reps you nonexclusively, it means that you can also get pitched and repped by other licensing companies (or pitch yourself). Often, nonexclusive licensing companies will "retitle" your songs, meaning actually change the titles of your songs and reregister them with the PRO. So that they only get paid on the placements they actually secure.

It's worth noting that very few licensing companies are working on nonexclusive bases anymore because many ad agencies, music supervisors and TV networks refuse retitled songs. Many create cue sheets from sonic recognition software, and if conflicting rights holders come up, no one will know whom to pay. The nonexclusive practice primarily still exists only with music libraries.

If pursuing synch licensing is one of your top priorities, it's worth attending NARIP sessions and festivals like the Durango Songwriters Expo, the ASCAP "I Create Music" Expo and SXSW, where music supervisors and licensing companies regular speak on panels and review music.

There are also submission services like Music Xray, Taxi and Fluence, where you can submit your songs for review and possible placement.

15.

BUMP EVERYONE ELSE
OFF THE COVER

Watch The Weeknd survive a car crash in the
video for a new song, "The Hills."
—*PITCHFORK*

'VE TALKED A LOT ABOUT THE IMPORTANCE OF "YOUR STORY" IN THIS
book. You'll soon realize why it's so important for you to have a story.

Everyone wants press. It makes you feel important. Special. Validated. But does it really do much for your career? It can, but only if you approach it right.

Of course everyone wants a 5-star album review in *Rolling Stone* or an 8.7 in *Pitchfork*, but you have to be realistic about your press pursuits. If you have never received press, there is a very slim chance that you will get a review in a popular blog or nationally distributed magazine. Your best chance for media coverage is your hometown papers, magazines and blogs, or local publications in cities you're touring to.

The difference between *Rolling Stone*'s music editorial staff and the *La Crosse Tribune* music editorial "staff" (person) is that one of them has a backlog of tens of thousands of CDs waiting to be reviewed and the other is in constant need of material. Can you guess which is which?

The reason it's, dare I say, easy to get press when you're on tour is because local publications are always looking for material, especially the daily papers. Even blogs with a local focus need material. *Rolling Stone*, *Pitchfork*, *Pigeons & Planes*, *Consequence of Sound*, *Stereogum* and the bunch get inundated with more music than they have bandwidth for.

There is a different way to approach local, national, digital, trade and print outlets. You always want to keep in the back of your mind when reaching out to any outlet: "What can I do for them? Why does my story deserve coverage?"

Sometimes just being a touring band playing a reputable venue in their town is enough to get a few paragraphs. Other times you'll need an interesting story that sets you apart from every other band playing a show in town that night.

Don't expect album reviews. They are boring to read by the majority of the public. Very few publications even write them anymore. Yes, I know you'd like every publication to talk about how this new album of yours will be generation-defining, but the local newspaper is trying to bring the most interesting story to its readers. And right now it's that you are going to put on a great show in their town. Notes about your most recent album can be included in your press release—especially if you're on a tour supporting it—but they don't need to be more than a couple sentences.

Before you start this process, ask yourself why you want press. And what kind do you want?

THREE MAIN KINDS OF PRESS/MEDIA ATTENTION

1) Local
2) Trade
3) National

WHY YOU SHOULD GET LOCAL PRESS

Local press includes the local newspapers, magazines, news stations and radio stations. Even though most local outlets will have an online presence as well, with blogs and Facebook pages, the majority of their readership is local, so the majority of the things they discuss are local. So, when you pitch local media outlets, you must have a local focus. Are you a local band? OK, what are you promoting? A local show? A new album? A music video? Whatever you're pitching must be hyperlocal. Hometown press outlets take great pride in their city. So customize the press release to celebrate the local scene.

If you're a touring band approaching local media, it will most likely either be because you have a tour stop in town or because one of your members has some strong tie to the city.

Don't just seek press to get press. Make sure there's a coordinated effort to maximize your features around one important event: big show of some kind, new release (new means less than a month old) or career-defining moment like a record label signing, van crash, band breakup, viral song, tour announcement. It must be pressworthy. A local four-band bill on a Wednesday night is not pressworthy.

WHY YOU SHOULD GET TRADE PRESS

Trade press includes instrument, genre or craft-focused publications like *Guitar Player*, *Guitar World*, *Acoustic Guitar*, *Modern Drummer*, *Bass Player*, *American Songwriter*, *Billboard*, Digital Music News, *Pollstar*, *Hypebot*, *Music Connection Magazine*, *DownBeat*, *Electronic Musician*, *EQ*, *Live Sound International* and *Professional Sound*. They each have a specific focus. *DownBeat* primarily covers jazz. *Modern Drummer* obviously covers drums, drummers and everything drumming. If you want to get a feature in one of these publications you have to know the focus. You have to customize your pitch for the publication. If your drummer is doing something extremely innovative and is being recognized in the field for it, that's press-release-worthy for *Modern Drummer*. Just because your song has drums in it is not reason enough to contact *Modern Drummer*. Don't just send your music video to Digital Music News. DMN covers the business of music. DMN will not write about your innovative music video like *Pigeons & Planes* might. But if you had to sue your label to let them release your video, that is something that DMN would write about.

Know each publication's angle and focus.

HOW TO GET NATIONAL MEDIA AND WHY YOU SHOULD

National press includes national blogs (not run by a local newspaper/radio/TV station), NPR, CNN, *The Tonight Show*, *Ellen*, *SNL*, *Rolling Stone* and *Spin*. Obviously the national outlets like *Rolling Stone*, *Ellen* and *The Tonight Show* are very tough to crack if you have very little happening for you on a national scale. And NPR and CNN are only going to cover very interesting, unique stories that their audiences would appreciate. A cool music video won't cut it. A viral music video seen by 100 million people may.

National blogs are a different story though.

Like the trade publications, every blog has a focus. Some are specific to hip-hop and electronica. If you're a sensitive singer/songwriter, it's a waste of time to contact those blogs no matter how brilliant you are. They aren't going to write about you.

HOW TO FIND THE BLOGS TO CONTACT

Most of the top music blogs are included on the blog aggregator site Hype Machine (hypem.com).

If contacting blogs is part of your release campaign strategy, I highly recommend you spend some time getting to know Hype Machine. On the site, search for artists who are similar to you. You'll know if your style of music gets written about by the blogs they aggregate. For some reason, music bloggers love indie, experimental, electronic and hip-hop. They don't care very much for poppy singer/songwriters or right-down-the-center pop/rock bands. Knowing this going in will save you a lot of time and stress.

SubmitHub, created by Jason Grishkoff of Indie Shuffle, has over fifty blogs listed that you can submit to for a fee. Bloggers get paid to listen to your song and give you feedback (and/or write a review). Many blogs are only accepting submissions through services like this (or from publicists/managers/labels). However, I've heard mixed reviews about these platforms. Actually, vōx submitted to Indie Shuffle via SubmitHub and got rejected. But then a few days later a different writer at Indie Shuffle posted a review of that same (rejected) song that was submitted to her by vōx's publicist.

THE BLOG SHEETS

Make a shared Google spreadsheet of all the bloggers who have written about artists similar to you from Hype Machine, plus any other blogger you know of that writes about your kind of music. Invite your band members, fellow bands in your scene with similar sounds, and music taste-makers in your friend group who regularly read blogs to contribute to the Blog Sheets. Make eight columns: Blog, Website, Writers (include all the writers at the publication who cover your style of music), Location, Email, Twitter, Recent Article(s), Submission Requirements.

Once you have your list ready to go. You want to find one blog to premiere your song. Bloggers like writing about songs and music videos. Very few review full albums. So prioritize your list for premieres. Do your research and find a writer's email address at the blog. Try not to just submit through the general contact form. Send this person an email. Start it off with their name. A compliment about one of their most recent articles can't hurt either (shows you took the time to get to know them).

This is an actual email from vōx (Sarah Winters) to a writer at Nylon (before she had any kind of representation). It worked, and vōx got the premiere (and tens of thousands of SoundCloud plays because of it). Other bloggers followed Nylon's lead and wrote about the song.

Subject: FOR PREMIERE: vōx - Claws

Body: Hey Jasmine,

I'm looking to premiere the brand new vōx track "Claws."
The first three vōx singles lent comparisons to Rosie Lowe, BANKS, and Lorde and have been praised by The Wild Magazine, Konbini, Pigeons & Planes, Earmilk, and DIY Mag.

Produced by Josiah Kosier, "Claws" has an ethereal hip hop feel; harp plucks and soaring strings giving satisfying dichotomy to 808s and trap drums. Lyrically, it's the push and pull of this unstable relationship that draws you in. "There are wild things in me," vōx sings during the pre-chorus over eerie background noises. At one moment she's willing to be weak and the next telling her lover to bow down in worship.

Listen (and download) privately here: http://soundcloud.com/song . . .

Kristian Punturere promo photos: http://goo.gl/claws-photo . . .

Bio: http://itsmevox.com/bio

Thank you so much for your consideration!

Best,
Sarah

Make sure your SoundCloud profile is up to snuff, with images and branding that is consistent with your entire project. You don't need an endless list of accolades. Just enough to reel them in. Keep it succinct. To the point. Complimentary. Not desperate. Not needy. Let the music speak for itself. Unlike nearly every other pursuit in this industry, for bloggers (and supes) it really is all about the music. You can also include a link to your bio (if you don't have a Wikipedia entry), so they can easily get more info about you. It should be a page on your website, so once they land on it they can easily browse your site with a couple clicks. And if you don't get a response, make sure to follow up!

Once you get someone to agree to the premiere, it's an exclusive to them for about a day.

They'll let you know when they will post it. Out of respect for the blog that chose to premiere your song, hit up all other blogs on your list the day after the premiere with a similar email, except this time you're not asking for a premiere, just a write-up. Tell them which blog premiered it (with the link).

It may be worthwhile to hire a publicist if you have the funds and believe you're ready for one. Go reread the section on publicists in Chapter 2.

HOW TO OBTAIN LOCAL AND TRADE PRESS

The traditional media world operates very differently from the indie music blog world. Many times they will respond better to someone not in the band than to the band itself. It may be worth breaking out your alias for this kind of press pursuit.

They will want and appreciate a press release.

HOW TO WRITE A PRESS RELEASE
AND WHY YOU SHOULD

The beauty of the digital age is that most publications rarely ask for hard press kits anymore. Some music editors (especially the older ones) do ask for you to mail your CD to them, but many are OK with a Bandcamp, SoundCloud or YouTube link. Regardless of how they listen to your music, they all want a press release.

A press release is a one-page, objective (more or less) fact sheet illuminating the who, what, where, why and when of your event.

Contact Information

Make sure it is very clear who the reviewer should contact. Include your phone number just in case they're on deadline.

Title

Every press release should have a title. Put the title in the subject line of your initial email. Titles should be to the point, but exciting enough for a reviewer to look deeper. "Touring Band to Play Birmingham" is boring. "Red Pills Bring Their Fire/Rock Show to Birmingham" is better. "This Band Lights Stuff on Fire on a Birmingham Stage" will definitely get a read. Like "Watch The Weeknd survive a car crash in this video for a new song."

Old-school publicists may disagree with the sensationalist approach of the title, but we've entered into a new era of press. Upworthy and BuzzFeed are masters at click baiting and are trumping nearly every traditional news outlet's digital traffic.

Reprinting Word for Word

Many times a publication will reprint your press release word for word. So make it readable and enticing. I'd say about 20% of my local press coverage has been a publication (online or in print) literally reprinting my press release about my visit to town. These sometimes will get added to the digital edition's calendar or "Upcoming Events" or "What to Do This Weekend" section. Oftentimes, the music reviewer runs out of time and needs to fill content. So your press release gets reprinted.

It Must Be an Event

There's no use sending a press release to let a reviewer know that you have a three-month-old album out. And, uh, how about a review? No. The only way you're going to get press is if you're pitching an event. A show. A release. The birth of your baby (if you're a celebrity). A charity event. A dance-off. The release of a music video. Something newsworthy.

First Paragraph

Who, what, where, why, when, how much. The facts. This needs to be first so the reviewer (or reader) can easily find this information and immediately know what this event is.

Second Paragraph

This is where you list the background of your band, your interesting story (the hook) and accolades. What makes your band unique? Include only the background info that's most interesting—one or two sentences. Include your most impressive accolades: who you have toured with, opened for;

TV shows/movies your songs have been placed in; quotes from celebrities about your band; awards/contests you've won; festivals you've played. Be careful not to make it seem too braggy. If this press release is sent by you, the reviewer will know you wrote it. Keep it objective(ish).

You can use adjectives, but no superlatives.

Third Paragraph

Information about the event. Why should they cover this event? What makes it special? If this is a general tour press release, you can discuss the tour here (50-date U.S. tour with stops at local children's hospitals in 20 cities).

Last Sentences

Other interesting information. This is your final effort to showcase to the reviewer why she should cover your event or band and to the reader why he should come out to your show, watch your music video, listen to your album.

These are loose paragraph guidelines, but this is the order.

Never Attach It to an Email

When you contact a reviewer via email, the subject line should be your title. You should write a brief personalized introductory paragraph, link to the album on Bandcamp or SoundCloud, a YouTube video, Facebook Page and your website, and explain that you've included the press release and link to promo photo below.

It can be something like this:

> Hi, Kim, Minneapolis-based, The Red Pills, are stopping through Denver on October 3rd as part of our 50 date US tour. Our new song, "I Hope I Never Know," was just featured on How To Get Away With Murder on

ABC last week. Let me know if you'd like to set up an interview with the band for a piece in the Denver Post. I've included a link to our album, new music video and the press release below. If you like, I can put our vinyl record and/or CD in the mail for your consideration.

Thanks!

New Album: http://linktobandcamp.com
Music Video: http://linktoyoutubevideo.com
Facebook: http://linktofacebook.com
Website: http://linktowebsite.com
Promo Photo: http://LinkToHighResPromoPhotos.com

—Ari Herstand (The Red Pills manager/guitarist)

<PRESS RELEASE GOES HERE>

Directly below your signature should be the press release, beginning with the title.

No Response Does Not Mean No Coverage

I can't tell you how many times I have reached out to press outlets with an email very similar to the one above when I have never received a response, but I got either a full preview of my show in the paper/blog or they copy/pasted my press release.

Always check the publication in print and online when you tour through the city. Sometimes their print edition will list show previews which do not make the digital version, and vice versa.

"For Immediate Release"

You see this statement in many press releases sent out by companies announcing things like a new iPhone or whatnot. However, when you're contacting music reviewers weeks before your show, you don't want them to print a show preview in the weekly newspaper a month before your show. So list at the top of the release when you'd like it printed/posted:

"For release the week of October 2nd."

Lead Time

For local press, contact them about four weeks before your show. Many times the music reviewers will have stuff cued up a couple weeks in advance of printing, but sometimes they are scrambling looking for content for this week. Sometimes (depending on how organized they are) they'll ask you to get back to them a few days before they go to print (or post the blog). If you're too early (two months), they'll ignore it because it's not pressing, but if you're too late (less than a week), you may have missed your window and that edition may be already set. If the reviewer only reviews physical CDs (some still do), you need enough time to get it in the mail to her.

If you don't get a response, follow up a week later. Giving yourself a four-week window allows for follow-ups. Giving yourself one week does not.

Publication Research

Before contacting the reviewer, make sure you do a bit of research on the publication. Make sure they actually cover arts and entertainment. Find out how often (weekly, daily, monthly). And, of course, make sure you get the contact email and name of the music or community events reviewer.

Don't Be Afraid of the Phone

If you can't find an email on the website, most likely they'll have a contact phone number listed. Pick up the phone and call and ask. You'll most likely reach the receptionist. All you need to do is then say "Hi, I'm looking for Kim Smith's email." Yes, learn the name of the music reviewer before calling. This is not tough to find. The receptionist will have this information and gladly give it to you. And if you haven't gotten an email response from the reviewer, give her a call, ask if she got your press release and if she needs any more info from you. Sometimes all it takes is a phone call to sift your email out of the pile.

THE CRITICS

Critics have been giving me a hard time since day one. Critics
say I can't sing. I croak. Sound like a frog. Why don't critics say
that same thing about Tom Waits? Critics say my voice is shot.
That I have no voice. Why don't they say those things about
Leonard Cohen? Why do I get special treatment? Critics say
I can't carry a tune and I talk my way through a song.
Really? I've never heard that said about Lou Reed.
Why does he get to go scot-free?
—BOB DYLAN

You know you're doing something right when you get criticized. The only thing worse than bad publicity is no publicity. I was once trashed three times in the span of five months by the same publication. Did it hurt? You're damn right it did. But, you know what? Hearing Dylan talk about his critics kind of gives me solace. As it should you. If you do your job right, you will be criticized. Wear it as a badge of honor.

16.
OUTRO

CONGRATULATIONS! YOU MADE IT THROUGH. IF YOU REALLY made it to the end and read every word, then you must be actually serious enough to pursue a full-time, professional, money-making music career. I applaud you. Yeah, it's tough. Yeah, it's hard. But is anything in life that's worth pursuing easy? I truly hope this book has brought you a few steps closer to becoming a full-time musician. And if you already are a full-time musician, I hope this brings you ten steps closer to world domination.

I wrote this book because I don't want to see any more talented bands break up or any more talented musicians quit what they love because they can't support themselves doing it. If you work hard enough, you can and will have a very successful career doing what you love. Don't let anyone tell you that music is not a viable career path. Hand them this book and tell them to shut the . . . front door.

Hopefully we will get to meet out there on the road someday, share a bill or two, jam together, cowrite, or just high-five. I'm into it all. We're all in this together. You and me. Us and them.

Let's define what this new music industry can look like.

And, so far, it's looking pretty darn amazing.

Much love,
Ari

MUSIC PUBLICATIONS YOU SHOULD BE READING

(in alphabetical order)

Ari's Take (aristake.com)

ASCAP Daily Brief (sign up at ascap.com/email)

Billboard (billboard.com)

CD Baby's DIY Musician (diymusician.cdbaby.com)

The Daily Digest (sign up at motiveunknown.com)

Digital Music News (digitalmusicnews.com)

Hypebot (hypebot.com)

Indie on the Move (indieonthemove.com/blog)

Lefsetz Letter (lefsetz.com)

Music 3.0 (Music3point0.com)

Music Business Worldwide (musicbusinessworldwide.com)

ReverbNation Blog (blog.reverbnation.com)

SonicBids Blog (blog.sonicbids.com)

TuneCore Blog (tunecore.com/blog)

MY CURRENT RANT ABOUT THE MUSIC INDUSTRY

Apple, Spotify, Google All Miss the Point—This Is the Future of Recorded Music

A few nights ago I was listening to the Daft Punk album Random Access Memories on Spotify. I never gave it a proper listen when it came out. Yeah, "Get Lucky" was funky, but I didn't realize the depth of this. And the musicianship! Anyway, I was funking out and I couldn't get over the rhythm section. So tight. The drummer's pocket was locked down. Such an interesting, almost mechanical (yet still human) groove. I needed to know who this was! And that funky guitar! Gahhh.

But how do I do this? Impossible on Spotify. Impossible even if I downloaded it on iTunes. Impossible in Apple Music, Deezer, YouTube, Google, Tidal or anywhere else.

So I went to one of the only places where this information clearly exists. No, not Wikipedia. AllMusic.com. But, for some sadistic reason, AllMusic.com on Safari on my iPhone takes over audio control from Spotify and shuts off the funk!

Tidal includes the most track info for (major-label) artists, but still has major holes. I just tried finding this info in Tidal on my phone and it included Producer, Lyricist, Composer and Featured Artist information for the Daft Punk album. But no players!

AllMusic.com has this info. How difficult is it to integrate all of the information from AllMusic.com to Spotify? To Apple Music. To Tidal. To iTunes . . .

And what about lyrics?

The services didn't include lyrics for the first few years of their existence—and many still don't! So what are we supposed to do? Head on over to Google and search for them, which inevitably brings up an ad-laden, "illegal" lyric-hosting site. Which isn't mobile friendly, so I have to manually pinch in.

What a horrible experience. All around.

Doesn't anybody understand it's not JUST about the music?

There needs to be a platform that is the destination for true music fandom. A beautiful, all-encompassing music-listening experience. Why is listening to vinyl so enjoyable? In part, it's the ritual of taking the record out of the package, placing it on the turntable, but also exploring the liner notes, lyrics and artwork.

iTunes has completely neglected this experience for the past ten years, but because there was no competitive alternative, it got lazy and forgot what a true music experience could be. It's not just about the transaction! Or the audio quality.

The destination for music should be an identically pleasurable experience on mobile, tablet, desktop and . . . wait for it . . . television.

Yes, with everyone owning a smart TV, we should be able to fully immerse ourselves in the music on the TV. Show me HD album artwork, credits, lyrics, music videos, photos, bio, everything with a couple clicks of the remote.

On mobile, play the song, swipe right for lyrics, swipe right again for full credits (include the ability to click featured artists, songwriters and producers to then see their credits—in app), swipe right for bio info, album artwork, swipe again for tour dates, ticket info, merch options, crowdfunding campaigns.

How to do this? Link up with AllMusic.com. Link up with Song-Meanings.com (one of the few legal lyric sites out there). Merge with PledgeMusic to have the crowdfunding live within this app. Ongoing. Stop making the users hop around the Internet, apps, phones, platforms. What is going to be the hub to kill off everyone else?

And what about jazz and classical? No service, download or streaming, has gotten this right. How do I search for all albums with Herbie Hancock? No, not just his albums, but the records on which he's a sideman for Miles Davis, Freddie Hubbard, Wayne Shorter, and the list goes on. Impossible! And what about Olga Kern's version of the Rachmaninoff Piano Concerto No. 3? Good luck finding that.

Yes, exclusives are important. And the 2013 Nielsen study revealed that music fans would pay up to $2.6 billion more if they were offered behind-the-scenes, VIP access, exclusives and experiences. But the superstars are so out of touch they don't know what exclusives fans actually crave. The Tidal exclusives are laughable. A video? Come on! It's thrown up on YouTube minutes after it hits Tidal.

Want to know exclusives people would pay for?

Live-streaming hangouts and home concerts in the app, interacting with the fans commenting in real time. That can't be replicated. Early access to tickets. The ability to buy backstage, preshow hangouts. Forums, message boards and fan collaborations where they know the artist will peek in once in a while to ask "What's up?"

Why isn't anyone thinking like this? And if they are, what's the damn holdup?!

Complaining about streaming royalty amounts dilutes the true issue at stake. The user experience is abysmal. Let's get people to fall in love with the experience of listening to music again. Yes, audio quality is important. But so is everything else.

The app world has it right. Get the user hooked on the free version, then get them to make their purchases in app. The free version of these streaming services could include just the music with ads. The paid version would unlock a music-listening experience so great that fans wouldn't think twice about upgrading. And with their credit cards on file, they'll buy tickets, support crowd funding campaigns, buy merch and tip their favorite artists.

Want to win the future of recorded music? Don't play catch-up. Innovate!

SOME WORDS OF CAUTION (AND OTHER STUFF YOU REALLY NEED TO READ)

The advice I give in this book is based on my experience. As I said up front, "results may vary." I can't promise you that if you do what I've done in any particular situation, you'll get the same results that I did. For example, my product recommendations come from my own experience or from artists I trust. But you should always do your own research.

As I also said at the beginning, I'm not a lawyer, and I can't give legal advice. In parts of the book, I describe or suggest doing things that seem simple but can cause legal problems if not done right. A lawsuit can kill you financially even if you end up winning, and saving money by doing without legal advice up front is almost never a good idea. I've tried to point out situations where you need an attorney throughout the book, but here is a short list of the kinds of things that should scream "ask a lawyer":

■ *Anything in writing that puts you on the hook to someone else or puts someone else on the hook to you.* Whether or not it's a formal contract, if it obligates you or someone else to pay money or perform services, it should be written or reviewed by an experienced lawyer. The same goes for any agreement that gives you rights in something, whether it's a share of revenue or a copyright. Some examples are agreements about rights and responsibilities of band members; the details of a gig; an arrangement with a publicist, photographer, band manager or tour manager; use of a song or recording on TV; the formation of a corporation or partnership; sponsorship or investment deals; and even the terms and conditions of online services.

■ *Anything relating to ownership of copyright in a song or in anything else that someone creates for you.* Just paying someone for something—a logo, a poster—does not mean you own it.

■ *Copyright registration.* I've mentioned a few times in the book that you can register several songs for copyright at once, for one fee, instead of paying separately for each song. There are different ways to do this, but it's trickier than it looks, and doing it wrong can cause you problems later on. Talk to a copyright lawyer or follow the Copyright Office's guidelines very, very carefully.

- *Licenses and permissions to use other people's content.* Don't pull stuff off the Internet, whether it's a photo, a graphic or a few bars of a recording. Get a permission agreement that specifically covers what you want to do, and make sure it comes from the person or company that owns or controls the rights.

- *Choosing and registering a band/artist name (trademark).* You can get sued for using someone else's band name or something very close to it. A trademark attorney can help you find out if the name you want is available (it's rarely enough just to do a Google and Facebook search, or even to search the U.S. Trademark Office database) and can guide you through the process if you want to apply for a federal trademark registration in the U.S. Trademark Office.

- *Forming a company.* There are different kinds of companies. An LLC is not the same as a corporation, and neither of those may be right for your financial or tax situation. Also, if you are forming a company with someone else, you'll probably want your operating or shareholders' agreement to include an exit strategy, among other protections for you, so that you don't end up spending thousands of dollars later trying to arrive at a fair split. There is no one-size-fits-all form for these agreements, despite the websites that offer them.

- *Raising money.* Any time you are going to raise money that will have to be paid back someday, talk to a securities lawyer or a music lawyer who is experienced in this kind of deal and knows federal and state securities laws. You really don't want problems in this area.

- *Collecting email addresses and other personal information on your site.* In the privacy world that we all read about every day, names, email addresses, credit cards and other kinds of information about your fans are "personally identifying information." If you collect any of that kind of information on your site, you'll need a privacy policy that tells users what you do with the info and who has access to it. Here, too, one size does not fit all (and you can't rely on your eblast provider's policy). Your best bet is a lawyer that specializes in this kind of thing.

■ *Sending out eblasts.* Emails that promote your upcoming gigs or sell merch to U.S. recipients are subject to federal law and have to meet certain legal requirements. In Canada, you can't send this kind of email at all unless the recipient has "opted in" to receive it from you.

■ *Running sweepstakes, contests and other promotions.* Contests, sweepstakes and other kinds of promotions have to comply with very specific rules and requirements that vary from state to state. Plus, Facebook, Twitter and other social media sites have their own rules about running promotions. Talk to a lawyer who knows this area of the law to be that sure you're covered and that your promotion is not technically a lottery, which is illegal in all fifty states.

This is not a 100% complete list of every legal issue that may come up in the course of your music career. In an ideal world, you should have a lawyer—or a stable of different kinds of lawyers—peering over your shoulder all the time to make sure you don't get yourself in trouble. But if you can't have that—and most of us can't afford it—you have some idea of what to look for as you go along.

GLOSSARY

∎

3 OF 5   A discount given to colleges at NACA and APCA conferences if 3 schools within a close geographic location book an act within 5 days.

360 DEAL   Labels take a percentage of nearly every aspect of an artist's income including merch, touring, sponsorships and sales.

5 OF 7   A discount given to colleges at NACA and APCA conferences if 5 schools within a close geographic location book an act to give performances at the schools within 7 days.

THE 50/50 SPLIT   You should spend half of your time and money on the music (the art) and half of your time and money on the business.

ADVANCE (VERB)   Getting in touch with the show's point person in advance of the show to go over details.

ADVANCE (NOUN)   A lump sum a record label or publisher pays a new signee up front which is recouped (paid back) from royalties earned.

AGENT   Also referred to as booking agent. This is the person that books your shows and tours.

ALBUM   A collection of songs released at the same time. Traditionally albums were packaged on vinyl records (LPs), cassettes or CDs, contained at least 6 songs and were approximately 35 to 70 minutes long. "Album" and "record" are sometimes used interchangeably.

AMAZON PRIME MUSIC   A subscriber-based, music-streaming service.

APCA   Association for the Promotion of Campus Activities. The second-largest college entertainment conference.

APPLE MUSIC   One of the world's largest subscriber-based music-streaming services.

A&R   Artist and Repertoire. Typically the scouts at a record label or publishing company. The artist's point person at the company. Helps guide the production process.

ASCAP   American Society of Composers, Authors and Publishers. An American not-for-profit performing rights organization (PRO) representing songwriters, composers and publishers.

ARI'S TAKE   The most important music business advice blog on the planet.

ARTIST   Sometimes referred to as recording artist. This is the person or act that records the songs and performs the shows. Sometimes the artist is also the songwriter, but the terms mean different things legally (and for purposes of royalty payments).

BANDCAMP   Artist-managed download store, merch store and subscription service.

BANTER   The talking an artist does in the mic, on stage, in between songs.

BANDZOOGLE   Recommended website building platform.

BFM   Best Friend Manager.

THE BIG 3   The three parent companies of all major labels in the world: Sony, Warner Music Group (WMG) and Universal Music Group (UMG). All major labels fall under one of The Big 3.

BMI   Broadcast Music, Inc. An American not-for-profit performing rights organization (PRO) representing songwriters, composers and publishers.

BOOKER   The person who books music at a venue. Sometimes "booker" and "talent buyer" are used interchangeably.

BRASSROOTS DISTRICT   The greatest band in the world.

BUSKING   Street performing.

CAB   Campus Activities Board. The group that books entertainment for their college.

CONSOLE   A mixing board that can be used in live settings or in the studio. Every input is run through the console before the signal reaches the speakers or the DAW (or tape). "Console" and "board" can be used interchangeably.

COMPOSITION   The music and lyrics. "Composition" and "song" are sometimes used interchangeably. Songwriters write compositions.

COVER   A song performed or recorded by an artist that was previously released (and made popular) by a different artist.

CROWDFUNDING   Raising a bulk amount of funds from your fans for a singular project (like an album). Kickstarter, Indiegogo, PledgeMusic and GoFundMe are the most popular music crowdfunding services.

CROWDFUNDING 2.0   The new fan club. Having fans contribute funds on an ongoing basis. A subscription or patronage service. Patreon and Bandcamp are leading this front.

DISTRIBUTION COMPANIES   The companies that send releases from labels (and artists) to stores and streaming services.

DUPLICATION   The process of burning a CD. A duplicator extracts data (music) from a master disc and writes it to a blank CD. The CDs that result from this process are less professional discs and sometimes won't play in every CD player.

DAW   Digital audio workstation is a recording program like Pro Tools, Logic, Cubase, FL Studio, Reason and Ableton Live.

DAY SHEET   The sheet that outlines all details about the day while on tour (travel, lodging, venue, times).

DEEZER   A subscriber-based music-streaming service.

DIY   Do It Yourself. Musicians who are unsigned and run their careers without the help of a manager, agent, label or publicist.

DP   Director of photography. Camera person.

ENGINEER   Also referred to as the recording engineer. This is the person that operates the DAW (like Logic or Pro Tools), sets up all mics and knows how everything in the studio works. There are also mixing and mastering engineers.

THE ELEVATOR PITCH   The one-sentence description of your sound as compared to other artists. You should be able to say this aloud at any moment without stumbling.

EP   Stands for extended play and originated from an extended-play single. It's a compilation of 4 to 6 songs released at the same time on any format (vinyl, CD, cassette or digital download/stream).

FACEBOOK   The social network your grandma is on.

FM   Family Manager.

FOH   Front of house engineer. Sound guy. The person who mixes the live performance.

THE FOLLOW BACK   A method most often used on Twitter and Instagram where you follow all of the followers of an artist similar to you with the hopes they will follow you back.

GATEKEEPER   The person in charge of the decisions that aid artists' success. These can be bookers, radio DJs, bloggers, playlisters and music editors.

GOOGLE PLAY MUSIC   A subscriber-based music streaming and locker service.

HEADLINER   The main act most people at the concert came to see. Typically the headliner is listed at the top of the bill and plays last.

HFA   Harry Fox Agency. A mechanical rights and royalties organization. (See "mechanical royalty.")

HIRED GUN   Freelance musician for the stage or studio typically hired by singer/songwriters, band leaders and music directors.

INSTAGRAM   The social network your best friend is on.

INTERACTIVE   You can choose the song you'd like to listen to. Interactive streaming services include Apple Music and Spotify.

ITUNES The world's largest music store.

LICENSING COMPANY A company that works to get songs placed on TV shows, commercials, trailers, video games and films. Also referred to as synch licensing companies. Sometimes referred to as "song plugger."

LOAD-IN The time designated at the venue for the band to bring their gear inside.

LOCKER Cloud-based storage of owned data (like song downloads).

LOGIC Apple-made digital audio workstation (DAW). One of the most popular DAWs used by recording studios worldwide.

LP Stands for long play. It's a 33⅓ vinyl record which holds about 22 minutes per side. Sometimes "albums," "records" and "LPs" are used interchangeably.

MANAGER This is the person in charge of your career. The manager helps craft the vision and direction of your career, and the manager is the buffer between you and everyone else.

MASTER (NOUN) The final recording. Sometimes the word "master" is used to differentiate between the song (composition) and the sound recording. "Master" and "sound recording" are sometimes used interchangeably.

MASTER (VERB) The process of putting the finishing touches on a fully mixed recording. This is the final step of the recording process. Mastering makes the highs glisten and the lows thump. Mastering also makes sure the volume of every track is at about the same level and places the amount of space between songs (also called sequencing).

MASTERING ENGINEER The person who puts the finishing touches on a record. This person "masters" the record.

MECHANICAL ROYALTY Songwriter royalty generated from sales of CDs, downloads on digital music retail sites, and interactive streams.

MERCH Short for merchandise. Any branded item an artist sells, typically at concerts or online.

MD Music director. The person who is hired to lead the band during rehearsals. The MD is typically in the band as well.

MIX (NOUN) The unfinished version of a recording.

MIX (VERB) The act of making all of the tracks in a recording (or live performance) sound good.

MIXING ENGINEER The person who mixes the recording.

MUSIC SUPERVISOR The person who places music on TV, film and commercials. The music supervisor also clears all of the rights for the song.

NACA National Association of Campus Activities. The largest college entertainment conference in America.

NONINTERACTIVE You cannot choose the song you'd like to listen to. Noninteractive services include Pandora and Satellite radio.

NSAI Nashville Songwriters Association International.

ONE-OFF One show, not during a tour.

OPENER Sometimes referred to as the opening act. This artist plays before the headliner at a concert.

P.A. The sound system.

PANDORA The largest American digital radio service.

PATREON Crowdfunding 2.0 patronage site.

PAY-TO-PLAY When a promoter or venue charges a band to perform. Or when a promoter or venue requires bands to purchase tickets in advance of a show to resell.

PER DIEM (PD) Literally means "per day." The amount of money given to members on tour for food and other daily expenses.

THE PERFECT 30 The test every gig should pass before being accepted. Compensation = 10, Career Building = 10, Enjoyment = 10. Don't take gigs that equal less than 15.

PERFORMANCE ROYALTY Songwriter royalty generated from any public performance of a composition.

PERISCOPE Live-streaming app started by Twitter.

PINTEREST The social network your girlfriend is on.

PRO Performing rights organization. Organizations of this kind represent songwriters and publishers. In America, these are ASCAP, BMI and SESAC. In Canada, this is SOCAN. Nearly every country in the world has their own PROs.

PRODUCER The person who helps create your record. Typically this person crafts the sound, vision and overall vibe of the record.

PROMOTER The person who is the liaison between the venue and the booking agent. The promoter works out deals with the venue and pays the artist or agent.

PRO TOOLS The industry standard, Avid-made digital audio workstation (DAW). The DAW used by most recording studios worldwide.

PUBLISHING COMPANY Also called a publisher. An organization that represents songwriters and compositions.

RECORD (NOUN) Can mean a single recording (like the Grammy classification) or more commonly it is another term for album.

RECORD (VERB) The process of capturing music for a recording. "Record" and "track" are sometimes used interchangeably.

RECORD LABEL Sometimes just referred to as a label. An organization that represents artists and sound recordings.

REPLICATION Creating CDs by injection mold. The data (music) is added during the creation process of the disc, and this is how most professional CDs are made.

THE RULE OF 7 Fans need to be hit at least 7 times before they will take action.

SAG-AFTRA Screen Actors Guild and American Federation of Television and Radio Artists. The union that represents screen actors.

SETTLE UP To count and collect the money from the point person at the venue (or the promoter) at the end of the night.

SEQUENCING Done during the mastering process. The act of placing the amount of space between tracks on an album.

SESAC An American for-profit performing rights organization (PRO) representing songwriters, composers and publishers.

SINGLE One song released outside of (or as part of) an album (typically in advance of the album release). Traditionally, this was the song promoted to radio a couple months before the album was released.

SOCAN Society of Composers, Authors and Music Publishers of Canada. A not-for-profit performing rights organization (PRO) representing songwriters, composers and publishers.

SOUND CHECK The time on stage at a venue the band and live sound engineers and stage crew spend testing all of the gear to make sure everything works and to get a feel for the venue. This typically happens before the doors open to the public.

SNAPCHAT The social network that won't come back to bite you in the a** from future employers.

SONY MUSIC One of the Big 3 major labels. Many major labels fall under Sony's umbrella.

SONGWRITER This is the person that writes the words and music for the artist to record and perform. Sometimes the songwriter is also the artist, but these terms are differentiated for legal clarity (and royalty payments).

SOUNDCLOUD Artist-managed music-streaming platform and social network heavily favored by DJs, hip-hop and electronic artists.

SOUNDEXCHANGE Sound-recording performing rights organization. Collects royalties for artists and labels from digital, noninteractive streaming services.

SOUND RECORDING The actual audio recording (not to be confused with the composition). "Sound recording" and "master" are sometimes used interchangeably.

SPOTIFY One of the world's largest interactive, subscriber-based music-streaming services.

SQUARESPACE Recommended website building platform.

STREET TEAM Fans that help promote artists' music and concerts. Typically, they put posters up and pass flyers out around town in advance of the show.

SYNCH LICENSING "Synch" stands for synchronization. The process of getting music placed in TV shows, commercials, video games, trailers and films.

SUPE Short for music supervisor.

TALENT BUYER The person who books talent at a venue or festival. Sometimes "talent buyer" and "booker" are used interchangeably.

TIDAL An artist-owned, subscriber-based, music-streaming service founded by Jay Z.

TM Tour manager. The person who goes on tour with the band and handles all of the business on the road like advancing shows, settling up, managing meet and greets, training the merch seller, etc. The TM is the liaison between the band and everyone else while on the road.

TRACK (NOUN) Can refer to a single recording on an album or a single recording element in the mix. Every mix is made up of multiple tracks.

TRACK (VERB) To record. "Record" (verb) and "track" are sometimes used interchangeably.

TWITTER The social network your dad is on.

UGC User-generated content. This is content uploaded by average users (who do not own the rights to the content). This is how "unauthorized" content gets uploaded to YouTube and SoundCloud.

UMG Universal Music Group. One of the Big 3 major labels. Many major labels fall under UMG's umbrella.

VENUE Any establishment that hosts music.

VINE The social network that King Bach (and others) are on.

VINER An entertainer whose primary audience has been built on Vine.

WCM Well-Connected Manager. See pages 44–45 for full description.

WINDOW (VERB) To withhold a release from streaming services to maximize sales.

WMG Warner Music Group. One of the Big 3 major labels. Many major labels fall under WMG's umbrella.

YOUNOW Live-streaming platform.

YOU PICK TWO Fast, good, cheap. You can only have two of these.

YOUTUBE The social network where you can find the shaky, iPhone-shot video of your concert from five years ago with the drunk dude yelling "Free Bird" incessantly.

YOUTUBER An entertainer whose primary audience has been built on YouTube.

ACKNOWLEDGMENTS

■

If you had told me five years ago that I would be an author of a book, I would have called you crazy. "I'm a musician, not an author," I'd protest. But here we are. And I couldn't have completed this thing without the love and support of some incredible people.

First off, Amy Draheim. She has been with me every step of the way from playing empty bars to packed arenas. She has kept me grounded when I flew a bit too high and propped me up when I dropped a hint too low. She has edited nearly every Ari's Take and Digital Music News article and has basically managed my entire life for the better part of nine years. Without her, I wouldn't be where I am today. Period. I can't express enough thanks to her in mere words. But maybe my songs can.

Philip Marino, you're a rock-star editor. Thank you for believing in this thing and being my cheerleader.

David Dunton, I never knew agents could be so real. No offense to my other agents out here in Hollyweird. The sweater you wore on that cold New York November day when we met sealed the deal. Never toss that thing.

Thank you, Andrew Leib, for emailing me out of the blue saying that because we're both music people from Wisconsin living in L.A. we had to meet. You have been a great friend, supporter and advisor. This book wouldn't be what it is without you.

Micah Herstand, my brother. My friend. The smarter son. Your constant support has truly been so encouraging and meaningful. When the world ignored a song I put out, just hearing your heartfelt praise was enough to keep me going. Thank you for using your web genius to create my websites and for accepting hearty hugs and cheap whiskey as payment.

Gadi Rouache, my brother from another mother. I'll never forget looking out at the festival in Rochester, Minnesota over a thousand bobbing heads to see you singing along in the back. Since we were twelve, you have been there for me. Thank you for pulling an all-nighter designing Ari's Take and for accepting high-fives and beer for payment. You're one of the most talented people I've ever met, and I'm honored to call you my close friend.

Thank you, Paul Resnikoff, for allowing me to spout my radical ideas on your site.

Thank you, Marc Behar and Jeff Sbisa, for allowing me to stay in your beautiful guesthouse in New Orleans as my respite from the craziness of L.A. to focus on this book. What a magical city.

Thank you to the District Donuts in New Orleans for allowing me to write this book ten hours a day for a month straight in your inspiring establishment. Your staff couldn't have been more welcoming and your extra-hot chais couldn't have been tastier.

Derek Sivers, thank you for inspiring me for so many years through your teachings. You are my guru. I am humbled and honored that you responded to my request to write my foreword with an all caps "F*&K YEAH!" You were my one and only choice.

Thank you, Mom and Dad, for raising me right. You taught me to care about people other than myself. And that's really why I started Ari's Take in the first place. And why I wrote this book.

These people and groups have given me tremendous support and guidance over the years and I wouldn't be where I am without you. Thank you (in alphabetical order):

Jerome Behar
Gabriel Douglas
Lisa Felix
Susan Goldberg
The Hotel Cafe
Will Hutchinson
Los Angeles music community
Jesse MacLeod
Paul Marino
Roster McCabe
McNally Smith College of Music
Minneapolis music community
My Patreon supporters
David Olson
Odin Ozdil
Julia Price
Saurabh Saluja
David Steffen
Scott Talarico and everyone at Neon
Varsity Theater
Marilyn Victor
Dan Wilson
Sarah Winters

And these tremendous people were incredible references for this book's research. Thank you!

Ken Abdo
Sarah Abelson
Andrea and Mark from Makar
Baby G
Rob Bondurant
Kevin Breuner
Jack Conte
Dave Cool
Chris Crawford
Gaetano DiNardi
Katie Ferrara
Bruce Flohr
Jessica Friedman
Champian Fulton
Steve Gordon
Andy Grammer
Devin Gray
Robin Greenstein
Lynn Grossman
Jeb Hart
Cathy Heller
Peter Hollens
Danika Holmes
Bruce Houghton
Philip Kaplan
Zack Lodmer
Gabriel Mann
Yael Meyer
Arnold Pinkhasov
Ron Pope

DJ Axis Powers

Jeff Price

Benji Rogers

Etan Rosenbloom

A. Sarr

Dane Schmidt

all the members in Shinobi Ninja

Kid Shreddi

Duke Sims

Ali Spagnola

Liam Sullivan

Terminator Dave

Madonna Wade-Reed

Adam Weiner

Fred Wiemer

Sarah Winters

Lindsay Wolfington

INDEX

ABOUT THE AUTHOR

ARI HERSTAND is a DIY musician who has played over six hundred shows around the country; has opened for or toured with Ben Folds, Cake, Matt Nathanson, The Milk Carton Kids and Ron Pope; has performed on *The Ellen DeGeneres Show*; and has had his music featured in countless TV shows, commercials and films. He currently fronts the funk band Brassroots District and is a member of the acoustic trio Young Canyon. In 2012, Herstand launched the music business advice blog Ari's Take [aristake.com], which was nominated by *L.A. Weekly* as one of the best music blogs of Los Angeles.

Herstand has written for many of the top musician trade magazines and websites including *Music Connection*, Digital Music News, *American Songwriter*, *Playback*, CD Baby, Tunecore, ReverbNation, Roland, Discmakers, ASCAP, Hypebot and others. He has been a featured speaker at SXSW, ASCAP Music Expo, SF MusicTech, CD Baby's DIY Musician Conference and in music business classrooms worldwide.

As an actor, he has been featured in TV shows including *Transparent*, *Aquarius*, *Mad Men*, *2 Broke Girls*, *The Fosters*, *Sam & Cat* and *Touch*.